W9-CKM-161

THE
BASKETBALL
ALMANAC

RED-LETTER PRESS, INC.
Saddle River, NJ 07458

"BASKETBALL EMBODIES EVERYTHING OUR CULTURE NOW CRAVES: EXCITEMENT, SPEED, DYNAMIC PERSONALITIES, UP-CLOSE RELATIONSHIPS WITH STARS, THE EXCITING PHYSICAL NATURE OF THE CONTEST, AND, OF COURSE, THE INCREDIBLE SUSPENSE THAT IS POSSIBLE WITH EACH GAME."

—Bill Walton

THE BASKETBALL ALMANAC
Copyright © 2007 Red-Letter Press, Inc.
ISBN-10: 0-940462-59-1
ISBN-13: 978-0-940462-59-5
All rights reserved
Printed in the United States of America

RED-LETTER PRESS, INC.
P.O. Box 393
Saddle River, NJ 07458
www.Red-LetterPress.com
info@Red-LetterPress.com

THE BASKETBALL ALMANAC

BY:
Jeff Kreismer

EDITED BY:
Steve Heldt

CONTRIBUTORS:
Jack Kreismer
David Reyneke
Eddie Charshafian
Jimmy Charshafian

ACKNOWLEDGMENTS:
Cover design: Behum Graphics
Typography: Christina Chybinski

THE
BASKETBALL
ALMANAC

A Daily Celebration

TODAY'S THOUGHT:

 ut Coach, we only made four baskets." –USC guard *Dan Anderson*, responding to coach Bob Boyd, who remarked during halftime of a 47-13 thumping by UCLA that the Trojans had just two first-half assists

HISTORY:

On this date in 1974 the Buffalo Braves' Ernie DiGregorio established a new rookie record, handing out 25 assists in a 120-119 win over the Trail Blazers. The Sonics' Nate McMillan tied the mark in 1987.

BIRTHDAYS:

Jimmy Jones, 1945; Mike Mitchell, 1956

TRIVIA:

Despite averaging just 5.6 assists per game during his nine ABA seasons, the Kentucky Colonels' Louie Dampier holds the league's all-time assist mark with 4,044. The total is nearly 1,000 higher than Mack Calvin, who ranks second on the list.

QUIZ:

Three men have led the NBA in assists for a single season at least six times. Name them.

ANSWER: *Bob Cousy, Oscar Robertson, and John Stockton*

TODAY'S THOUGHT:

During the scrimmage, Tarkanian paced the sideline with his hands in his pockets while biting his nails." *—Associated Press*

HISTORY:

On this date in 1985 coach Jerry Tarkanian led UNLV to a 142-140 victory over Utah State. The Runnin' Rebels scored 93 points after halftime in this triple overtime thriller, and the 282 combined points set a new scoring mark for a Division I men's basketball game.

BIRTHDAYS:

Bob Feerick, 1920; Gerald Govan, 1942; Ed Manning, 1944; Mike Newlin, 1949; Kirk Hinrich, 1981

TRIVIA:

The record-breaking game also marked the 600th career coaching victory for Tarkanian. He reached the milestone in just his 720th game, the second fewest in NCAA history, behind only Kentucky's Adolf Rupp.

QUIZ:

What NBA team did Jerry Tarkanian briefly coach during the 1992-'93 season?

ANSWER: *Tarkanian compiled a 9-11 record with the San Antonio Spurs.*

TODAY'S THOUGHT:

"**A**re you any relation to your brother Marv?" *–Leon Wood*, to announcer Steve Albert

HISTORY:

On this date in 1993 Johnny Most, the voice of the Boston Celtics for 37 years, died at the age of 70. After his retirement in 1990, Most was honored with the permanent installation of his microphone to the facade at Boston Garden where his radio booth sat "high above court-side."

BIRTHDAYS:

Paul Mokeski, 1957; Buck Johnson, 1964; Cedric Simmons, 1986

TRIVIA:

Most was a self-proclaimed homer who was known for ridiculing opposing teams and their players. He would criticize the rival Pistons when Boston played at Detroit by commenting, "Oh, the yellow, gutless way they do things here!" He also referred to Isiah Thomas as "Little Lord Fauntleroy."

QUIZ:

Who is the all-time leading scorer in Celtics history?

ANSWER: *John Havlicek, with 26,395 points*

TODAY'S THOUGHT:

"I hate to do it, but I have to give Steve Smith some credit for his defense. Steve did a nice job of yelling for help every time Cliff got the ball." *–David Robinson*, after the Pistons' Cliff Robinson shot 1 for 5 against the Spurs

HISTORY:

On this date in 1986 Navy center David Robinson set an NCAA record for blocked shots when he recorded 14 rejections in a 76-61 win over NC-Wilmington. That year, Robinson would also set the record for the most blocks in a season, with 207.

BIRTHDAYS:

Sidney Green, 1961; Cliff Levingston, 1961; Joe Kleine, 1962; Corie Blount, 1969; Al Jefferson, 1985

TRIVIA:

The Navy excused Robinson from three of the normal five years of his military service because his height made it impossible for him to take on certain roles, like aviation or the submarine corps. Despite the nickname "The Admiral", Robinson's actual rank when his commitment expired was Lieutenant Junior Grade.

QUIZ:

When David Robinson put up 71 points in the last game of the 1993-'94 season, he edged out what player to win the league scoring title?

ANSWER: *Shaquille O'Neal - Robinson finished with 29.8 ppg, while Shaq had 29.3.*

TODAY'S THOUGHT:

 ou talk of Jerry West or Oscar Robertson or any of those great ones who scored and passed so well. Maravich is better. He's a show." *–Lou Carnesecca*, St. John's coach, on Pete Maravich

HISTORY:

On this date in 1988 Hall of Famer "Pistol" Pete Maravich died suddenly at the age of 40 after suffering a heart attack during a pickup basketball game in California. Maravich remains the NCAA's all-time leading scorer, with 3,667 points in three years at LSU.

BIRTHDAY:

Lou Carnesseca, 1925; Alex English, 1954

TRIVIA:

Maravich was forced to retire in 1980 after just ten seasons in the pros due to a leg injury. Because his career was so short, in 1987 he became the youngest player to be inducted into the Basketball Hall of Fame at 39 years of age.

QUIZ:

Name the first college basketball player to win the Sullivan Award as the nation's top amateur athlete.

ANSWER: *Bill Bradley of Princeton, in 1965*

TODAY'S THOUGHT:

"**B**asketball is like war in that offensive weapons are developed first, and it always takes a while for the defense to catch up."
–*Red Auerbach*

HISTORY:

On this date in 1995 Atlanta's Lenny Wilkens became the NBA's all-time winningest coach, passing Red Auerbach, with a 112-90 Hawks victory over the Washington Bullets. For Wilkens, it was win number 939.

BIRTHDAYS:

Duane Klueh, 1926; Tom Marshall, 1931; Pearl Washington, 1964; Gilbert Arenas, 1982; Denham Brown, 1983

TRIVIA:

Basketball history was also made on this day in 1951 when the Indianapolis Olympians and Rochester Royals battled through six over-times before Indianapolis prevailed, 75-73, in what remains the longest game in NBA history.

QUIZ:

What future coaching legend and Rochester guard set a record by playing in 76 of the 78 total minutes in the defeat to Indianapolis?

ANSWER: *Red Holzman, who led the Knicks to two NBA Championships in 1970 and 1973*

TODAY'S THOUGHT:

"**I** don't cover losers." *–Mal Florence*, Lakers beat writer, when asked by L.A. coach Bill Sharman why he was leaving the team hotel after the Lakers' 33-game win streak was snapped

HISTORY:

On this date in 1972 the L.A. Lakers defeated the Atlanta Hawks, 134-90, to extend their winning streak to 33 games, the longest in major professional sports. Their run would come to an end two nights later with a 120-104 loss to Kareem Abdul-Jabbar and the Bucks.

BIRTHDAY:

Marquis Daniels, 1981

TRIVIA:

The Lakers finished the '72 season with a record of 69-13, the best mark in NBA history at the time. That year, they met the New York Knicks in the Finals, defeating them in five games to win their first title since moving from Minneapolis to Los Angeles in 1960.

QUIZ:

Who owned the Lakers until Dr. Jerry Buss bought the team in 1979?

ANSWER: *Jack Kent Cooke*

TODAY'S THOUGHT:

"Winning is overemphasized. The only time it is really important is in surgery and war."** *–Al McGuire*

HISTORY:

On this date in 1955 Adolph Rupp's Kentucky Wildcats had their home winning streak snapped by Georgia Tech. Some of the fans in attendance that night hadn't been born when the 'Cats basketball team began its 129-game run twelve years earlier.

BIRTHDAYS:

Bill Closs, 1922; Cedrick Hordges, 1957; Calvin Natt, 1957; Willie Anderson, 1967; Todd Lichti, 1967

TRIVIA:

Adolph Rupp was nicknamed the "Baron of the Bluegrass" due to his success in developing local talent. He got more than 80 percent of his players from Kentucky.

QUIZ:

What two coaches led the Kentucky Wildcats to NCAA titles in the 1990's?

ANSWER: *Rick Pitino, over Syracuse in 1996, and Tubby Smith, over Utah in 1998*

TODAY'S THOUGHT:

"I think the whole game hinged on one call- the one I made last April scheduling the game." –Maine women's basketball coach *Peter Gavett*, after losing 115-53 to Virginia

HISTORY:

On this date in 1958 Cincinnati's Oscar Robertson made college basketball history when he single-handedly defeated Seton Hall by scoring 56 points. That was two more than the entire Pirates squad, who were blown out, 118-54, by the Bearcats.

BIRTHDAYS:

M.L. Carr, 1951; Muggsy Bogues, 1965

TRIVIA:

Robertson and Jerry West co-captained the 1960 U.S. Olympic basketball team that won gold in Rome. Arguably the best amateur basketball team ever assembled, ten of the twelve college players on the undefeated squad went on to play in the NBA.

QUIZ:

Robertson and West were chosen first and second in the 1960 NBA Draft, by the Royals and Lakers. What other Hall of Famer was chosen in the top ten that year?

ANSWER: *Lenny Wilkens, taken with the sixth pick by the St. Louis Hawks.*

TODAY'S THOUGHT:

"**T**he way to stop Kareem Abdul-Jabbar is to get real close to him and breathe on his goggles." *–John Kerr*

HISTORY:

On this date in 1986 the Lakers' Kareem Abdul-Jabbar scored his 34,000th career point in an L.A. win over the Indiana Pacers, making him the first player in NBA history to reach that milestone.

BIRTHDAYS:

George Carter, 1944; Glenn Robinson, 1973

TRIVIA:

Only four players in NBA history have scored over 30,000 career points. Abdul-Jabbar is the all-time leader with 38,387. Karl Malone's 36,928 is second, followed by Michael Jordan's 32,292 and Wilt Chamberlain's 31,419 points.

QUIZ:

Four players have led the NBA in both rebounding and blocked shots in the same season. Kareem Abdul-Jabbar is one. Name the other three. (Remember, blocks weren't recorded until the 1970's.)

ANSWER: *Bill Walton, Hakeem Olajuwon and Ben Wallace*

TODAY'S THOUGHT:

I hate it. It looks like a stickup at a 7-Eleven. Five guys standing there with their hands in the air." *–Norm Sloan*, on zone defense

HISTORY:

On this date in 1947 the NBA, in just its third month in existence, decided to outlaw the use of zone defenses. League officials felt the zone, originally taken from the college rules, was slowing down the game. However, in 2001 the league reinstated the zone in an attempt to create more pass-oriented offenses.

BIRTHDAYS:

Chris Ford, 1949; Darryl Dawkins, 1957; Damien Wilkins, 1980; Tony Allen, 1982

TRIVIA:

Until 1937, after a team scored a basket, rather than simply awarding the other team possession, a jump ball was held at center court. Because the clock continued to run during the stoppage, the actual playing time of the game was significantly reduced.

QUIZ:

Playing by the Rules: Shaq taps a jump ball and grabs it after it hits the floor without being touched by another player. OK or not OK?

ANSWER: OK - He cannot, however, grab the ball before it hits the ground.

TODAY'S THOUGHT:

"**W**hen I die my tombstone will say, 'He was underrated. Now he's underground.'" *—Terry Porter*, on his career

HISTORY:

On this date in 2000 Hornets guard Bobby Phills died in an automobile accident outside the Charlotte Coliseum following a team shoot-around. He was 30 years old. The Hornets game that night against the Bulls was postponed.

BIRTHDAYS:

Arthur Becker, 1942; Campy Russell, 1952; Dominique Wilkins, 1960; Scott Burrell, 1971

TRIVIA:

Just four months after Phills' death, the Timberwolves' Malik Sealy was killed in a car accident when driving home from a birthday party for teammate Kevin Garnett. He was also 30.

QUIZ:

The Hornets retired Bobby Phills' number 13 in February of 2000. What other player has the franchise honored by hanging his number from the rafters?

ANSWER: Pete Maravich - The Hornets retired his number 7 during their first game in New Orleans to honor his college days at LSU and his NBA career with the New Orleans Jazz.

TODAY'S THOUGHT:

 He's one of the best power forwards of all-time. I take my hands off to him." *–Scottie Pippen*, on Tim Duncan

HISTORY:

On this date in 1999, just before the lockout-shortened season was set to begin, Michael Jordan announced his second retirement from the NBA. After Scottie Pippen and Phil Jackson followed Jordan out the door, the Bulls would finish last in their division five of the next six seasons.

BIRTHDAYS:

Tom Gola, 1933; James Posey, 1977; Ronny Turiaf, 1983

TRIVIA:

The San Antonio Spurs hold the mark for the worst full season, one-year turnaround in NBA history. After going 59-23 in 1996, they lost David Robinson to injury the next year and went 20-62, a 39-game difference. However, thanks to their poor season, the Spurs landed Tim Duncan with the number one pick in the 1997 draft.

QUIZ:

Who replaced Phil Jackson as the head coach of the Bulls in 1999?

ANSWER: *Tim Floyd, who would resign in 2001 after compiling a 49-190 record with the team*

TODAY'S THOUGHT:

I learned a long time ago that minor surgery is when they do the operation on someone else, not you." *–Bill Walton*

HISTORY:

On this date in 1993 the Portland Trailblazers retired uniform number 77 to recognize their 1977 championship season and honor former coach Jack Ramsay. Ramsay became the sixth member of the organization's Walk of Fame in Memorial Coliseum.

BIRTHDAYS:

Kenny Sailors, 1922; Wayne Hightower, 1940; Swen Nater, 1950; Ron Behagen, 1951; John Lambert, 1953

TRIVIA:

Portland's only championship came in 1977, Ramsay's first year with the team. In 1978, the Blazers were 50-10 after 60 games, but when center Bill Walton missed several games, the team finished the season 8-14 and lost in the playoffs to Seattle.

QUIZ:

True or false? The Trail Blazers made the playoffs 27 straight years from 1977 to 2003.

ANSWER: False - *They missed the playoffs only once, in 1982, despite going 42-40 that year.*

TODAY'S THOUGHT:

 **"W**hen he comes through the door, they now strike up the band and play 'Inhale to the Chief.'" *–Kevin McHale*, ribbing former Celtics teammate Robert Parish for his arrest on marijuana charges

HISTORY:

On this date in 1965 the San Francisco Warriors, in the middle of a 17-game losing streak, traded Wilt Chamberlain to the Philadelphia 76ers for Connie Dierking, Lee Shaffer and Paul Neumann. The Warriors would finish the year 17-63, while the 76ers would be NBA champions in two seasons.

BIRTHDAYS:

Bob Davies, 1920; Joe Graboski, 1930; Dan Kojis, 1939; Al Smith, 1947; Ricky Sobers, 1953

TRIVIA:

Perhaps an even worse move made by the Warriors was in 1980, when they dealt Robert Parish and the number three pick in the draft, Kevin McHale, to the Celtics. Golden State received the number one pick, Joe Barry Carroll, and the thirteenth choice, Rickey Brown.

QUIZ:

Kevin McHale is one of five members of the 1985-86 Celtics championship team to serve as an NBA head coach. Can you name the other four?

ANSWER: *Larry Bird, Danny Ainge, Dennis Johnson and Rick Carlisle*

TODAY'S THOUGHT:

I t's like hopping out of the shower without a towel, running into a meat freezer and staying there for about 10-15 minutes, and running back out. It's chilling." *–Kevin Garnett*, on what it's like being an NBA All-Star

HISTORY:

On this date in 1962 Bob Pettit of the St. Louis Hawks set an NBA All-Star record by grabbing 27 rebounds. He topped Wilt Chamberlain, who set an All-Star record with 42 points, for MVP honors, as the West beat the East, 150-130.

BIRTHDAYS:

Gerald Henderson, 1956; Don MacLean, 1970; Marc Jackson, 1975; Jeff Foster, 1977; Justin Reed, 1982

TRIVIA:

Bob Pettit, named as one of the 50 Greatest Players in NBA History, was the first player to score 20,000 career points.

QUIZ:

Who was the MVP of the first NBA All-Star Game, played in 1951?

ANSWER: *Ed Macauley of the Boston Celtics, who helped lead the East to a 111-94 victory*

TODAY'S THOUGHT:

"**D**o NBA players think that Dennis Rodman's latest suspension- deliberately hitting Milwaukee's Joe Wolf in the groin- will teach him a lesson? Well, let's just say they're keeping their legs crossed." *–Bob Lacey* of the *Half Moon Bay* (CA) *Review*

HISTORY:

On this date in 1997 NBA bad boy Dennis Rodman of the Chicago Bulls was fined $25,000 and suspended eleven games for kicking Eugene Amos, a courtside photographer, in the groin at a game in Minnesota.

BIRTHDAY:

Dwyane Wade, 1982

TRIVIA:

Rodman had a costly habit of head-butting throughout his career. In 1993 and '94, Rodman was fined a total of $12,500 for knocking heads with the Bulls' Stacey King and Utah's John Stockton. In 1996, Rodman's next incident involved a referee, costing him a six game suspension and a loss of $228,000.

QUIZ:

What player was called for a record 41 technical fouls in the 2000-'01 NBA season?

ANSWER: *The Portland Trailblazers' Rasheed Wallace - He broke his own record of 38, set the year before.*

TODAY'S THOUGHT:

"**N**ot only is there more to life than basketball, there's a lot more to basketball than basketball." *–Phil Jackson*

HISTORY:

On this date in 1967 Reece Tatum died at the age of 45. Nicknamed "Goose" because of his 84-inch wingspan, Tatum is considered to be the original "Clown Prince" of the Harlem Globetrotters. He is one of only four players to have his number retired by the team.

BIRTHDAYS:

Bud Stallworth, 1950; Larry Smith, 1958; Bob Hansen, 1961

TRIVIA:

This date also marked the death of Alex Hannum, the first coach to win championships in both the ABA and NBA. Hannum died in 2002 at the age of 78.

QUIZ:

What was the first former ABA team to win an NBA championship?

ANSWER: *The 1999 San Antonio Spurs, who defeated the New York Knicks*

TODAY'S THOUGHT:

 "**W**in or lose, I eat my ass off." *–Rick Majerus*, on his post-game eating habits

HISTORY:

On this date in 1974 the UCLA Bruins' historic streak of 88 consecutive wins over three years ended when they were defeated by Notre Dame, 71-70. UCLA blew an 11-point lead in the last three minutes of the game in the loss.

BIRTHDAYS:

Jeff Van Gundy, 1962; Michael Adams, 1963; Luc Longley, 1969

TRIVIA:

Playing the Fighting Irish in South Bend was all too familiar for UCLA. A loss at Notre Dame was the Bruins' last before their streak began in 1971, and it was the Irish again when the Bruins passed San Francisco in the record book with their 61st consecutive win.

QUIZ:

I was the man who played center at UCLA immediately after Kareem and right before Bill Walton. My teams won three NCAA titles. Who am I?

TODAY'S THOUGHT:

The invention of basketball was no accident…Those boys simply would not play Drop the Handkerchief." *–Dr. James Naismith*, inventor of basketball

HISTORY:

On this date in 1892 the first official basketball game took place at the YMCA gymnasium in Springfield, Massachusetts. Two teams of nine players each played with a soccer ball and two peach baskets nailed ten feet above the floor.

BIRTHDAYS:

Bailey Howell, 1937; Bill Robinzine, 1953; Ron Harper, 1964; Chris Morris, 1966; Nick Anderson, 1968; Ira Newble, 1975; Jason Richardson, 1981

TRIVIA:

In the first nationally televised college basketball game on January 20, 1968, the University of Houston ended UCLA's 47-game winning streak, 71-69. Houston extended their own winning streak to 18 games.

QUIZ:

True or false? When James Naismith invented basketball he was not a citizen of the United States.

ANSWER: *True - Naismith was born in Ontario, Canada, and did not become a U.S. citizen until the 1920's.*

TODAY'S THOUGHT:

 "Don't you ever pass?"** *–Bob Cousy*, after teammate Bill Sharman's length-of-the-court pass attempt to him went in the basket during the 1957 NBA All-Star Game

HISTORY:

On this date in 1954 and 1958 two All-Star Game firsts occurred. In 1954, Bob Cousy scored 10 points in the first-ever overtime in an All-Star Game to earn the MVP Award. Four years later, the West's Bob Pettit became the first player from the losing team to win All-Star MVP honors.

BIRTHDAYS:

John Chaney, 1932; Clifford Ray, 1949; Hakeem Olajuwon, 1963; Detlef Schrempf, 1963

TRIVIA:

The first, and only, pair of teammates to be named co-MVP's of an All-Star Game were Utah's John Stockton and Karl Malone. The two led the West to a 135-132 overtime victory at the 1993 All-Star Game, held fittingly in Salt Lake City.

QUIZ:

Who holds the NBA record for the most All-Star Game appearances?

ANSWER: *Kareem Abdul-Jabbar, 18 - He was selected 19 times, but did not play in 1973.*

TODAY'S THOUGHT:

"**T**hese young guys are playing checkers. I'm out there playing chess." *–Kobe Bryant*, on his youthful Lakers team

HISTORY:

On this date in 2006 Kobe Bryant scored a career-high 81 points in a Lakers' win over the Raptors. Bryant hit 28 of 46 field goal attempts in the game, scoring 55 points in the second half. Only he and Wilt Chamberlain have ever scored 80 points in an NBA game.

BIRTHDAYS:

Quintin Dailey, 1961; Mike Iuzzolino, 1968; Leon Powe, 1984

TRIVIA:

Kobe Bryant's season-low for the 2005-06 season was 11 points. The Lakers' opponent that night...the Toronto Raptors.

QUIZ:

Who is the shortest player in NBA history to win a league scoring title?

ANSWER: *Allen Iverson - In the 1999 lockout-shortened season, the six foot guard averaged 26.8 points per game.*

TODAY'S THOUGHT:

"**I**n my prime I could have handled Michael Jordan. Of course, he would be only 12 years old." *–Jerry Sloan*, Utah Jazz coach

HISTORY:

On this date in 1998 Michael Jordan scored in double figures for the 800th consecutive game as the Bulls defeated the Nets, 100-98, in overtime. Jordan would add 66 more games to his record streak before it would come to an end in December of 2001, as a member of the Wizards.

BIRTHDAYS:

Lonnie Wright, 1944; Haywoode Workman, 1966; Larry Hughes, 1979

TRIVIA:

In 1997, the Bulls signed Jordan to the richest one-year contract in NBA history, paying him $33.14 million. Due to the format of the current cap system, the amount a player can make is restricted, meaning that what Jordan received that year is not likely to be surpassed.

QUIZ:

Who was Michael Jordan's first coach when he entered the NBA?

ANSWER: *Kevin Loughery - Chicago would replace him with Stan Albeck the following season.*

TODAY'S THOUGHT:

 aybe I need to write a book and say I was misquoted, or punch somebody in Milwaukee." *–Michael Jordan,* after being informed that he trailed Charles Barkley in NBA All-Star voting

HISTORY:

On this date in 1956 Bob Pettit won the first of his record four All-Star Game MVP Awards. The St. Louis Hawk led the West with 20 points and 24 rebounds as his squad defeated the East, 108-94, in the sixth annual All-Star Game.

BIRTHDAY:

Mark Eaton, 1957

TRIVIA:

In 1997, Michael Jordan became the first player in All-Star Game history to record a triple-double when he scored 14 points, grabbed 11 rebounds, and dished out 11 assists.

QUIZ:

What player set two All-Star records in one game by scoring 20 points in a quarter and 24 points in one half?

ANSWER: *Glen Rice, in 1997, who was named MVP for the East which won, 132-120*

TODAY'S THOUGHT:

"**N**o, I clean giraffe ears." –NBA great *Elvin Hayes*, when asked if he played basketball

HISTORY:

On this date in 1960 Wilt Chamberlain set a rookie record by scoring 58 points in a Warriors' 127-117 win over Detroit. Chamberlain would tie his own record less than a month later against the Knicks. His 37.6 points per game in the 1959-60 season remains the highest average for a first-year NBA player.

BIRTHDAYS:

Dick McGuire, 1926; Byron Beck, 1945; Walt Wesley, 1945; Chris Mills, 1970

TRIVIA:

In 1969, first-year man Elvin Hayes of the Rockets led the NBA in scoring average, minutes played, and field goals. Still, he lost out in Rookie of the Year voting to the Bullets' Wes Unseld, who was also named the NBA's MVP.

QUIZ:

Hayes and Unseld were teammates on the 1977-78 Bullets squad that won the last NBA title for the Washington/Baltimore franchise. What team did they defeat?

ANSWER: *The Bullets defeated the Seattle Supersonics in seven games to win the championship, despite finishing the regular season with a mark of 44-38.*

TODAY'S THOUGHT:

 hat was some of the worst fun I ever had." *–Bob Betz,*
Longmont (CO) High School basketball coach, after a bad loss

HISTORY:

On this date in 1960 Danny Heater of Burnsville, WV scored 135 points in a 32-minute high school basketball game. With Heater also pulling down 32 rebounds, Burnsville "edged" Widen High, 173-43.

BIRTHDAYS:

Tom Henderson, 1952; Sly Williams, 1958; Vince Carter, 1977; Gerald Green, 1986

TRIVIA:

In 2006, Epiphanny Prince of Murry Bergtraum HS in New York scored 113 points in a game against Brandeis HS. Prince broke the girls' national prep record previously held by Cheryl Miller, who dropped in 105 points.

QUIZ:

What former NBA player scored exactly 100 points for Camden (NJ) High School in a 157-67 win over Gloucester Tech (NJ) in 2001?

ANSWER: *Dajuan Wagner, who was drafted by Cleveland the following year*

TODAY'S THOUGHT:

 "**T**he more Final Fours you go to, the more cousins you find you have who need tickets." *—Mike Krzyzewski*

HISTORY:

On this date in 2001 tragedy struck Oklahoma State University. Ten people, including basketball players Nate Fleming and Dan Lawson and several team staffers and broadcasters, were killed when their plane crashed in a snowstorm in Colorado.

BIRTHDAYS:

Todd MacCulloch, 1976; Jiri Welsch, 1980

TRIVIA:

Former Cowboys coach Eddie Sutton was the first man to lead four different schools (Creighton, Arkansas, Kentucky, and Oklahoma State) to the NCAA Tournament. Two of them, Arkansas and Oklahoma State, went to the Final Four.

QUIZ:

Name the last college basketball team to have a perfect season.

ANSWER: *Indiana University, which went 32-0 in 1976*

TODAY'S THOUGHT:

I don't think he's going to have a lot of fun over the next 31 games... But it could be worse. He could be going to the Clippers." *—Bill Fitch*, on interim Timberwolves coach Kevin McHale

HISTORY:

On this date in 1980 and 1985 two NBA coaches reached a milestone. In 1980, New York Knicks coach Red Holzman won his 600th game. Five years later to the day, Houston Rockets coach Bill Fitch became the sixth coach in NBA history to post 600 career wins.

BIRTHDAYS:

Greg Smith, 1947; Greg Popovich, 1949; Michael Cage, 1962; Tony Delk, 1974; Mark Madsen, 1976; Andre Iguodala, 1984

TRIVIA:

Regarded as one of the top coaches in the NBA, Bill Fitch compiled a record of just 944-1106 in his 25 seasons as a head coach. While Fitch had three consecutive 60-win seasons with Boston, he also lost at least 65 games four times in his coaching career.

QUIZ:

True or false? As the head coach of the Boston Celtics from 1950-66, Red Auerbach did not have a single losing season.

ANSWER: *True - His club did, however, go .500 in 1955, with a 36-36 record.*

TODAY'S THOUGHT:

"**W**hen I dunk, I put something on it. I want the ball to hit the floor before I do." *–Darryl Dawkins*

HISTORY:

On this date in 1984 the NBA's first All-Star Saturday took place in Denver. The inaugural Schick Legends Classic, featuring retired players, was won by the West. The Nestle Crunch Slam Dunk Contest winner was the Suns' Larry Nance.

BIRTHDAYS:

George Ballard, 1955; Eddie Jordan, 1955

TRIVIA:

The first dunk contest in 1976 was a creation of the old American Basketball Association. The rules back then made each player attempt certain mandatory dunks, including one ten feet from the basket. Julius Erving took it a step further when he launched himself from the 15-foot foul line to win the contest.

QUIZ:

With what ABA team did Julius Erving begin his career?

ANSWER: *The Virginia Squires, in 1971*

TODAY'S THOUGHT:

"They said playing basketball would kill me. Well, not playing basketball was killing me."** *—Earvin "Magic" Johnson*

HISTORY:

On this date in 1996 Magic Johnson made his return to the NBA, scoring 19 points in a win over the Warriors in L.A. It was Johnson's first regular season game since 1991, when he announced his retirement because of the AIDS virus.

BIRTHDAYS:

Paul Seymour, 1928; Paul Neumann, 1938; Tom Izzo, 1955; Mychal Thompson, 1955; Rick Robey, 1956; Otis Smith, 1964; Jalen Rose, 1973; Sharone Wright, 1973; Jonathan Bender, 1981; DeSagana Diop, 1982

TRIVIA:

Before his comeback as a player, Johnson coached the Lakers for the remaining sixteen games of the 1993-94 season, replacing Randy Pfund. He managed only a 5-11 record in those games, as L.A. missed the playoffs.

QUIZ:

In 1979, the Lakers had two first-round draft choices. Magic was their first pick, and I was the second. Who am I?

ANSWER: *Brad Holland of UCLA*

TODAY'S THOUGHT:

This year we plan to run and shoot. Next season we hope to run and score." *–Billy Tubbs*, Oklahoma coach

HISTORY:

On this date in 1989 defense hid in the locker room as Loyola Marymount defeated U.S. International, 181-150. Loyola's score and the 331 combined points set college basketball single-game scoring records.

BIRTHDAYS:

Len Chappell, 1941; Rod Higgins, 1960; Othella Harrington, 1974

TRIVIA:

The first five-player men's intercollegiate basketball game was played in January of 1896 in Iowa City. It didn't quite match the excitement of today's game, as the University of Chicago defeated the University of Iowa, 15-12, before a crowd of about 400 people.

QUIZ:

Who is the only player to lead the NCAA, NBA and ABA in scoring?

ANSWER: *Rick Barry, with the University of Miami (1965), the NBA's San Francisco Warriors ('67), and the ABA's Oakland Oaks ('69).*

TODAY'S THOUGHT:

 he reality is that all TV ratings for shows across the board are down, unless you're getting the opportunity to marry a millionaire, become a millionaire, or watch millionaires wrestle."
–NBA Commissioner *David Stern*, on declining TV ratings

HISTORY:

On this date in 1984 David Stern became the NBA's fourth commissioner, replacing Larry O'Brien, who had served for nine years. Stern had previously served in an executive capacity for the league.

BIRTHDAYS:

Dick Snyder, 1944; George Irvine, 1948; Malik Sealy, 1970; Walter McCarty, 1974; Robert Traylor, 1977; Kevin Martin, 1983

TRIVIA:

The NBA Championship Trophy, created in 1978, was renamed for Larry O'Brien in 1984. Unlike awards such as the Stanley Cup, a new Larry O'Brien Trophy is made every year for the winning team to keep permanently.

QUIZ:

Who was the first Commissioner of the NBA?

ANSWER: *Maurice Podoloff, who was in office from 1946 to 1963*

The Basketball Almanac

TODAY'S THOUGHT:

We were the quintessence of athletic atrocity." *–Mike Newlin*, Houston Rockets guard, after a loss to the New York Nets

HISTORY:

On this date in 1967 the American Basketball Association was born. The league would compete with the NBA for nine years before folding because of financial difficulties. Four of the strongest ABA teams- the Nets, Nuggets, Pacers, and Spurs, were voted entry into the NBA.

BIRTHDAYS:

Sean Elliott, 1968; Dan Gadzuric, 1978

TRIVIA:

The Indiana Pacers and Kentucky Colonels are the only two franchises to survive all nine seasons in the league's history without changing their team names or locations.

QUIZ:

What former NBA great became the inaugural Commissioner of the ABA?

ANSWER: *George Mikan - He was responsible for introducing both the three-point line and the league's red, white and blue basketball.*

TODAY'S THOUGHT:

It's a simple game to understand. Players race up and down a fairly small area indoors and stuff a ball into a ring with Madonna's dress hanging on it." *–Dan Jenkins*, writer, on basketball

HISTORY:

On this date in 1876 Albert Spalding, whose namesake remains on the NBA game ball, used $800 to start his sporting goods company, which manufactured, among other items, the first official basketball.

BIRTHDAYS:

Darnell Valentine, 1959; Vlade Divac, 1968; Robert Pack, 1969

TRIVIA:

The NBA introduced a new official game ball for the 2006-07 season that allows for a better grip. The change, the first in over thirty-five years, features Spalding's Cross Traxxion™ technology and a design of two interlocking, cross-shaped panels.

QUIZ:

Eight teams from the original NBA, created in 1949, are still in action. How many do you know?

ANSWER: Boston Celtics, New York Knickerbockers, Golden State Warriors (originally Philadelphia), Philadelphia 76ers (formerly the Syracuse Nationals), Atlanta Hawks (Tri-Cities Blackhawks), Detroit Pistons (Ft. Wayne Zollner Pistons), L.A. Lakers (Minneapolis Lakers), and Sacramento Kings (Rochester Royals)

TODAY'S THOUGHT:

"**I**t's so bad that the players are giving each other high fives when they hit the rim." *–Ron Shumate*, Southeastern Missouri coach, on his team's poor shooting

HISTORY:

On this date in 1987 the Sacramento Kings scored a shot clock-era record-low four points in the first quarter of a blowout loss to the L.A. Lakers. The Kings missed every shot they took in the quarter, trailing, 29-0, before four foul shots made the score 40-4 at the buzzer.

BIRTHDAYS:

Neil Johnston, 1929; Jim Loscutoff, 1930; Lee Winfield, 1947; Vern Fleming, 1962; Jason Kapono, 1981; Dajuan Wagner, 1983

TRIVIA:

In 1999, the Chicago Bulls set an NBA record for the fewest points scored in a single game since the introduction of the shot clock in 1954. They failed to break the half-century mark, losing, 82-49, to the Miami Heat.

QUIZ:

In the 1981-82 season, what NBA team set a record for the highest points-per-game average?

ANSWER: *The Denver Nuggets, at 126.5 - Amazingly, they scored and gave up at least 100 points in every game they played that season.*

TODAY'S THOUGHT:

They say that nobody is perfect. Then they tell you practice makes perfect. I wish they'd make up their minds."
—Wilt Chamberlain

HISTORY:

On this date in 1960 Boston's Bill Russell broke his own record of 49 rebounds in a game, grabbing 51 in a win over Syracuse. The following season, Wilt Chamberlain wiped the glass, and the record off the books, with 55 boards against Russell and the Celtics.

BIRTHDAYS:

John Beasley, 1944; Kris Humphries, 1985; Maciej Lampe, 1985

TRIVIA:

In his thirteen-year NBA career, Bill Russell never scored more than 50 points in a game. In fact, his career low in *rebounds* per game, 18.6 in 1968, is just below his career high in *points* per game, 18.9 in 1962.

QUIZ:

Apart from Wilt Chamberlain and Bill Russell, only two NBA players have grabbed 40 or more rebounds in a game. Can you name either man?

ANSWER: *Jerry Lucas, with 40, and Nate Thurmond, with 42*

TODAY'S THOUGHT:

 "**T**hey should have focused more on me." *–Sebastian Telfair*, giving his opinion on the documentary *Through the Fire*, the story of...Sebastian Telfair

HISTORY:

On this date in 1925 basketball's longest winning streak came to an end, and it wasn't the Lakers or UCLA. Passaic (NJ) High School won 159 straight games over five years before being tripped by Hackensack, 39-35.

BIRTHDAYS:

Eric Money, 1955; Carlos Rogers, 1971; Antoine Wright, 1984

TRIVIA:

Before his NBA career, the Boston Celtics' Sebastian Telfair made history when he led Lincoln High School to three New York City titles and one state championship. He also became New York State's all-time leading scorer, surpassing Kenny Anderson.

QUIZ:

What high school did NBA phenom LeBron James attend?

ANSWER: *St. Vincent–St. Mary High School in Akron, Ohio*

TODAY'S THOUGHT:

"**T**here's something odd about going up to Michael Jordan and slipping him $16 a day." *–Terry Francona*, Jordan's minor league baseball manager, on giving Jordan his daily meal money

HISTORY:

On this date in 1994 Michael Jordan signed a minor league contract to play for the Double-A Birmingham Barons, a farm club of the Chicago White Sox. Jordan would hit a measly .202, and finish the season with 51 RBIs and 30 stolen bases.

BIRTHDAYS:

Mike O'Koren, 1958; Juwan Howard, 1973; Steve Nash, 1974; Mickael Pietrus, 1982

TRIVIA:

Tongue-wagging Michael Jordan acquired this odd habit as a child from his father, James, who always worked on his car with his tongue sticking out between his teeth.

QUIZ:

Before joining the Boston Celtics, what Major League Baseball team did Danny Ainge play for?

ANSWER: *The Toronto Blue Jays, as a utility infielder from 1979 to 1981*

TODAY'S THOUGHT:

"**I**t was a weekend of brilliant and short people. I was brilliant, the rest of them were short." *—Larry Bird*, recalling his All-Star experience in Dallas

HISTORY:

On this date in 1986 five-foot-seven-inch Spud Webb recorded two perfect scores of 50 to top fellow Atlanta Hawk Dominique Wilkins in the Slam Dunk Contest in Dallas. The inaugural Three-Point Shootout was won by Larry Bird.

BIRTHDAYS:

Donnie Butcher, 1936; Stephen Chubin, 1944; Marques Johnson, 1956; Alonzo Mourning, 1970; Alexander Johnson, 1983

TRIVIA:

In 2006, the Knicks' five-foot-nine Nate Robinson became the second-shortest player to win the dunk contest, thanks in part to Webb. Robinson earned a perfect score for a stunt in which he took a bounce pass from the former Hawk and leapt over him to dunk the ball.

QUIZ:

In 1987 and '88 Michael Jordan became the first person to win consecutive slam dunk titles. Only one other person has done it since then. Name him.

ANSWER: *Jason Richardson, in 2002 and 2003*

TODAY'S THOUGHT:

 agic Johnson, former basketball player, may run for mayor of L.A. in the next election. Remember the good ol' days when only qualified people ran for office like actors and professional wrestlers?" *–Jay Leno*

HISTORY:

On this date in 1992 Magic Johnson returned to take part in the NBA All-Star Game, three months after announcing his retirement because of the AIDS virus. Magic scored 25 points and added 9 assists to win the MVP Award in a 153-113 Western Conference win.

BIRTHDAYS:

Phil Ford, 1956; Jameer Nelson, 1982; Maurice Ager, 1984

TRIVIA:

The Magic Hour, a talk show hosted by Earvin "Magic" Johnson, made its debut in June of 1998 on syndicated television. The talk show was immediately criticized and cancelled after just eight weeks on the air.

QUIZ:

What former Milwaukee Bucks All-Star had small roles in basketball films such as *White Men Can't Jump* and *Blue Chips*?

ANSWER: *Marques Johnson*

TODAY'S THOUGHT:

 He's instant offense, on both ends of the floor, I might add." —*Charles Barkley*, on Rockets' teammate Cuttino Mobley

HISTORY:

On this date in 1949 Joe Fulks of the Philadelphia Warriors scored 63 points in a 108-87 win over the Indianapolis Jets. Fulks' single-game point total is the record for an NBA player before the shot clock was introduced in 1954.

BIRTHDAYS:

Abdul Jeelani, 1954; Tom LaGarde, 1955; John Calipari, 1959; Tina Thompson, 1975; Jumaine Jones, 1979; Zaza Pachulia, 1984; Paul Millsap, 1985

TRIVIA:

Elgin Baylor, who in 1959 broke Fulks' record by scoring 64 in a game, was the first person to surpass the 70-point mark, putting up 71 against the Knicks the following season.

QUIZ:

Who was the first player to score 20-plus points in 50 consecutive NBA playoff games?

ANSWER: *Kareem Abdul-Jabbar - He scored 20 or more in each of his first 57 NBA playoff games.*

TODAY'S THOUGHT:

inning." *–Shaquille O'Neal*, on what he missed most about not coming back to Vancouver since the Grizzlies left for Memphis

HISTORY:

On this date in 1973 the Philadelphia 76ers lost their 20th straight game, a 108-90 defeat to the Lakers, dropping their record to 4 wins and 58 losses. The team would only win 5 more games that year, finishing at 9-73, the worst mark in NBA history.

BIRTHDAYS:

James Silas, 1949; Jacque Vaughn, 1975; Tony Battie, 1976

TRIVIA:

The record for the most consecutive losses in one season is shared by the 1997-98 Nuggets and the 1995-96 expansion Grizzlies, with 23. Cleveland lost 24 straight, but that streak spanned the 1981-82 and 1982-83 seasons.

QUIZ:

The Boston Celtics lost only one game at home in the 1985-86 season. Name the only team to defeat them.

ANSWER: *The Portland Trail Blazers, 121-103, on December 6, 1985*

TODAY'S THOUGHT:

 e're so young, we've decided to dress only seven players on the road. We're pretty confident the other five can dress themselves." *–Charlie Just*, women's basketball coach at Bellarmine College, on his team's inexperience

HISTORY:

On this date in 1994 the NBA held its inaugural Schick Rookie Game at All-Star Weekend. The Phenoms, led by Golden State's Chris Webber, defeated the Sensations, 74-68. Orlando's Anfernee Hardaway was named MVP, despite being on the losing team.

BIRTHDAYS:

Al Cervi, 1917; Bill Russell, 1934; Larry Nance, 1959; Scot Pollard, 1975

TRIVIA:

When the fans voted Kobe Bryant to the Western Conference team for the first time in 1998, he became the youngest starter in the history of the All-Star Game, at 19 years and 169 days old.

QUIZ:

Who is the youngest player to win the NBA's All-Star Game MVP?

ANSWER: *21-year old LeBron James, who scored 29 points in the 2006 All-Star Game in Houston*

TODAY'S THOUGHT:

"At that juncture in history, where he met that fork in the road, Bevo was the greatest shooter in the history of basketball." *–William Nack*, former *Sports Illustrated* writer, on Bevo Francis

HISTORY:

On this date in 1954 Furman's Frank Selvy scored 100 points in a 149-95 win against Newberry. The game was the first televised sporting event in the state of South Carolina. Selvy entertained the viewers by hitting 41 of his 66 shots, including a last-second 40-footer to reach the milestone.

BIRTHDAYS:

Mike Krzyzewski, 1947; Luke Ridnour, 1981

TRIVIA:

Earlier that year, Bevo Francis of Rio Grande set a small-school record by scoring 113 points in a 134-91 win over Hillside. Three weeks before that Francis pumped in 116 points against Ashland, but went unrecognized in the record book because he did it against a two-year school.

QUIZ:

At what college were NBA big men Charles Oakley and Ben Wallace small-school standouts?

ANSWER: *Virginia Union*

TODAY'S THOUGHT:

 " **M** ichael is just getting too old for the game. In fact, Nike just introduced its latest line of shoes, the 'I Need Some Air Jordans.'" *–Jim Barach*, on Michael Jordan

HISTORY:

On this date in 1975 the San Diego Conquistadors defeated the New York Nets, 176-166, in four overtimes, the highest-scoring game in ABA history. The Nets' Julius Erving scored a career-high 63 points.

BIRTHDAYS:

Wali Jones, 1942; Fred Carter, 1945; Reggie King, 1957; Gheorghe Muresan, 1971; Tyus Edney, 1973; Richard Hamilton, 1978; Darius Songaila, 1978

TRIVIA:

Julius Erving was the first basketball player to endorse an athletic shoe. His Pro Leather Converse sneaker, which would become known simply as "The Dr. J," was released in 1976. The shoe's motto: "Limousines for the Feet."

QUIZ:

What was the original name of the Anaheim franchise during the 1967-68 season of the American Basketball Association?

ANSWER: Amigos - *They would become the Los Angeles Stars the following season and later move to Utah.*

TODAY'S THOUGHT:

"**I**t was like Elvis and the Beatles put together. Traveling with the Dream Team was like traveling with 12 rock stars. That's all I can compare it to." *–Chuck Daly*

HISTORY:

On this date in 1991 the U.S. Men's Olympic basketball team began to take shape. Pistons coach Chuck Daly was selected to lead a squad of NBA players in the following year's Summer Games, the first time professionals would be allowed to compete.

BIRTHDAY:

Mark Price, 1964

TRIVIA:

While the gold-medal winning Dream Team included the best basketball talent in the world, half of the players on the roster never won an NBA title in their careers: Charles Barkley, Patrick Ewing, Christian Laettner, Karl Malone, Chris Mullin and John Stockton.

QUIZ:

Only one player was a member of the USA Olympic Men's basketball teams in Seoul (1988), Barcelona ('92), and Atlanta ('96). Name him.

ANSWER: *David Robinson*

TODAY'S THOUGHT:

"**I** see that Wilt Chamberlain's Philly schoolboy career scoring mark was broken by Maurice Davis. Upon surpassing Wilt's 2,206 points, Davis was mobbed by teammates, students, and 20,001 women." *—Peter Vecsey* of the *New York Post*

HISTORY:

On this date in 1972 the Lakers' Wilt Chamberlain, in his 13th season in the league, became the first player in NBA history to score 30,000 career points in a 110-109 loss to the Phoenix Suns.

BIRTHDAYS:

Pep Saul, 1924; Larry Finch, 1951; Herb Williams, 1958; Kelly Tripucka, 1959; Qyntel Woods, 1981; Shawne Williams, 1986

TRIVIA:

During the 1971-72 season, Chamberlain and teammate Happy Hairston each accumulated over 1,000 rebounds, an extremely rare feat. Hairston recorded 1,045 boards, while "The Big Dipper" grabbed 1,572.

QUIZ:

What three players had at least 60 double-doubles during the 2005-06 NBA season?

ANSWER: *Kevin Garnett (62), Shawn Marion (60) and Dwight Howard (60)*

TODAY'S THOUGHT:

"**B**e strong in body, clean in mind, lofty in ideals."
–*Dr. James Naismith*, the father of basketball

HISTORY:

On this date in 1968 The Naismith Memorial Basketball Hall of Fame opened its doors to the public. After seventeen years on the campus of Springfield College (MA), the Hall was moved to a bigger downtown location in 1985, and then to its current home in 2002.

BIRTHDAYS:

Rick Majerus, 1948; Michael Jordan, 1963; Al Harrington, 1980

TRIVIA:

Even without a place to honor them, the Basketball Hall of Fame inducted its first class in 1959. Among the inaugural members were basketball's founder, Dr. James Naismith, and legendary big man George Mikan of the Minneapolis Lakers.

QUIZ:

Playing by the Rules: The Nets have submitted their starting lineup to the official scorer. Can head coach Lawrence Frank make a change before the start of the game?

ANSWER: *Yes*

TODAY'S THOUGHT:

 "**H**ouston Rockets forward Scottie Pippen was arrested on suspicion of drunk driving a few hours after a loss to Dallas. His mistake was to tell the officers that he just had a 'triple-double.'" –Comedian *Jerry Perisho*

HISTORY:

On this date in 1986 San Antonio Spurs guard Alvin Robertson recorded just the second quadruple-double (Nate Thurmond was first) in NBA history. Robertson's stat line: 20 points, 11 rebounds, 10 assists, and 10 steals in a win over the Suns.

BIRTHDAYS:

Bill Turner, 1944; Randy Denton, 1949; Maurice Lucas, 1952; Andrei Kirilenko, 1981

TRIVIA:

That same year, Robertson became the first winner of the NBA's Most Improved Player Award, as his scoring average jumped from nine to seventeen points per game. He also won the Defensive Player of the Year Award, leading the league in steals.

QUIZ:

On February 17, 1994, what player recorded the fourth quadruple-double in league history?

ANSWER: David Robinson, with 34 points, 10 rebounds, 10 assists, and 10 blocks for the Spurs in a win against the Pistons

TODAY'S THOUGHT:

"**I** remember sitting down with the Rockets and saying, 'Yeah. I'm going to retire.' They said, 'Well, we'll give you $9 million.' And I said, 'You got a pen on you?'" *–Charles Barkley*, thinking about retirement

HISTORY:

On this date in 1995 and '96 two NBA legends recorded their 10,000th career rebounds. In 1995, it was Houston's Hakeem Olajuwon, who grabbed nine boards in a Rockets' loss at New York. Exactly one year later, the Suns' Charles Barkley reached the milestone in a win over the Grizzlies.

BIRTHDAYS:

Chico Vaughn, 1940; Jahidi White, 1976; Mike Miller, 1980

TRIVIA:

Hakeem was born Akeem Abdul Olajuwon. "Abdul" was dropped prior to his entering the NBA, and in 1991, he decided to change his first name to the proper Arabic spelling.

QUIZ:

Who's the only player in basketball history to average over fourteen rebounds per game for his career (ABA or NBA), and not be elected to the Basketball Hall of Fame?

ANSWER: *Mel Daniels, with 14.9 boards per game*

TODAY'S THOUGHT:

 "**Y**eah, I got a way to defend it. Bring a bat to the game and kill one of them." *–Nick Van Exel*, on defending the Stockton-Malone pick-and-roll

HISTORY:

On this date in 1996 John Stockton became the NBA's all-time leader in steals with 2,311, passing previous leader Maurice Cheeks in a 112-98 win over the Boston Celtics. He would finish his career with an astounding 3,265 steals.

BIRTHDAYS:

Charles Barkley, 1963; Stephon Marbury, 1977

TRIVIA:

In his entire 19-year NBA career, Stockton missed a total of 22 regular season games, playing in 1,504 of a possible 1,526 contests. Four came in his first 13 seasons, with the remaining 18 coming at the start of the 1997-98 season following off-season knee surgery.

QUIZ:

What veteran point guard did John Stockton play behind when he entered the league in 1985?

ANSWER: *Rickey Green*

TODAY'S THOUGHT:

"If the NBA were on channel 5 and a bunch of frogs making love was on channel 4, I'd watch the frogs even if they were coming in fuzzy." *–Bobby Knight*

HISTORY:

On this date in 1952 the Boston Celtics and Fort Wayne Pistons tipped off at midnight in a "Milkman's Special" following an Ice Follies performance at Boston Garden. Bob Cousy led the way with 24 points and the Celtics did their best to keep the 2,368 fans awake with an 88-67 win.

BIRTHDAYS:

Jack Ramsay, 1925; Steve Francis, 1977; Andre Barrett, 1982

TRIVIA:

In 1982, the Boston Celtics selected Indiana's Landon Turner, who had recently been paralyzed in a car crash, in the tenth round of the NBA Draft. GM Red Auerbach did it as a favor to Hoosiers coach Bobby Knight.

QUIZ:

Two players from the University of Indiana have been number one NBA Draft picks, in 1961 and 1977. Can you name either?

ANSWER: *Walt Bellamy, by the Chicago Packers in 1961, and Kent Benson, by the Milwaukee Bucks in 1977*

TODAY'S THOUGHT:

 "**P**aying full price for a Clippers ticket- that is March Madness."
—Comic *Jenny Church*

HISTORY:

On this date in 1988 Bradley senior Hersey Hawkins scored a school-record 63 points in the Braves' 122-107 victory over the University of Detroit. Hawkins' point total was also a record for the Missouri Valley Conference.

BIRTHDAYS:

Chet Walker, 1940; Dick and Tom Van Arsdale, 1943; Goose Ligon, 1944; Julius Erving, 1950; Lewis Lloyd, 1959; Chris Dudley, 1965; Jayson Williams, 1968; Lee Nailon, 1975; Rajon Rondo, 1986

TRIVIA:

Hersey Hawkins and Kansas' Danny Manning, the 1988 Naismith Award winner, were both drafted by the Clippers that year. Manning was taken first overall. Hawkins, selected sixth, was traded to the Philadelphia 76ers before the season started.

QUIZ:

The Los Angeles Clippers franchise began play in the NBA under what name?

ANSWER: *The Buffalo Braves*

TODAY'S THOUGHT:

"**I** hope when I die, they bury me upside down, so all my critics can kiss my ass." *–Bobby Knight*

HISTORY:

On this date in 1985 during a game against Purdue, Indiana coach Bobby Knight, protesting a technical foul call, hurled a chair across the court, narrowly missing Purdue's Steve Reid on the foul line. Knight was ejected and Purdue won, 72-63.

BIRTHDAYS:

Lee Shaffer, 1939; Larry Lentz, 1945; Flip Saunders, 1955

TRIVIA:

Steve Reid, a 95 percent foul shooter, was apparently shaken up by the incident. He hit just three of his six attempts, including the technical foul shots. To add salt to the wound, he was then scolded by his own coach, Gene Keady, about the missed shots.

QUIZ:

Can you name the coach whose first and only NCAA title came in his last career game in 1977?

ANSWER: *Al McGuire of Marquette*

The Basketball Almanac

TODAY'S THOUGHT:

"It gives you a nice warm feeling to know you're the highest-paid guy in the huddle." *–Rick Pitino*, on the difference between coaching in the pros and in college

HISTORY:

On this date in 2004 New Jersey Nets head coach Lawrence Frank won his 13th straight game, setting a mark for the most consecutive wins to begin an NBA head-coaching career. His streak would end the following game against the Timberwolves.

BIRTHDAYS:

Al Tucker, 1943; Mike Fratello, 1947; Tom Burleson, 1952; Eddie Johnson, 1955

TRIVIA:

Frank never played professional, college, or even high school hoops. Instead, he gained valuable experience at Indiana, where he spent four seasons as a manager for the Hoosiers basketball team under Bobby Knight.

QUIZ:

Name the four colleges where Rick Pitino has coached.

ANSWER: *Boston University, Providence, Kentucky and Louisville*

TODAY'S THOUGHT:

"**I** don't need the ball to score." *–Anthony Mason*, former NBA player

HISTORY:

On this date in 1977 New Orleans' Pete Maravich set a new record for guards, scoring a career-high 68 points in a 124-107 Jazz victory over the New York Knicks. Pistol Pete led the league in scoring that year with 31.1 ppg.

BIRTHDAYS:

Cincinattus Powell, 1942; Samaki Walker, 1976

TRIVIA:

At LSU, Maravich scored 69 points against Alabama in 1970 to set an NCAA record. He would be surpassed in 1991 by U.S. International's Kevin Bradshaw, who tallied 72 points against Loyola Marymount.

QUIZ:

Who's the only New York Knick to win a scoring title in the NBA?

ANSWER: *Bernard King, in 1984-85, with an average of 32.9 ppg*

The Basketball Almanac

TODAY'S THOUGHT:

 "Players sometimes benefit from a change in scenery. Well, good players can benefit from a change of scenery. Bad players are bad players wherever they are." *–Doug Moe*

HISTORY:

On this date in 2002 13-year journeyman Chucky Brown set a league record by taking the floor with his twelfth NBA team, the Sacramento Kings. Tony Massenburg and Jim Jackson would later match Brown's travels.

BIRTHDAYS:

Bingo Smith, 1946; Rolando Blackman, 1959; Sasha Danilovic, 1970; Tim Thomas, 1977; Steve Blake, 1980

TRIVIA:

The NBA regular season is 82 games, but in 1992, Thurl Bailey played in 84. He started out the season with the Jazz, where he played in 13 games. After being traded to Minnesota, who had played fewer scheduled games than Utah at that point, he was able to participate in 71 more.

QUIZ:

Journeyman Sam Cassell has been on seven NBA teams in his career. How many can you name?

ANSWER: *In order: Rockets, Suns, Mavericks, Nets, Bucks, Timberwolves and Clippers*

TODAY'S THOUGHT:

"**I**n the NBA, nothing recedes like success." *—Bob Cousy*

HISTORY:

On this date in 1959 the Boston Celtics defeated the Minneapolis Lakers, 173-139, in a shootout at the Boston Garden. Bob Cousy dished out 28 assists, including 19 in one half, to go along with his 31 points.

BIRTHDAYS:

Wil Jones, 1947; Mike Montgomery, 1947; Dwight Jones, 1952; James Worthy, 1961; Loy Vaught, 1968; Devin Harris, 1983; David Noel, 1984; James Augustine, 1984; Daniel Gibson, 1986

TRIVIA:

In 1970, as head coach of the Cincinnati Royals, the 42-year old Cousy suited up for seven games in an attempt to generate fan interest. He teamed up with Oscar Robertson to make up a future Hall of Fame backcourt.

QUIZ:

Pete Maravich finished his NBA career with the Boston Celtics. Do you know what team made him their number one draft choice in 1970?

ANSWER: *Pistol Pete was selected third overall by the Atlanta Hawks.*

TODAY'S THOUGHT:

"**N**obody roots for Goliath." *—Wilt Chamberlain*

HISTORY:

On this date in 1967 Wilt Chamberlain finally missed a shot, eleven days after making the first of 35 straight field goals, a new NBA record. Exactly 14 years later, Houston's Calvin Murphy made the last of his 78 consecutive free throws.

BIRTHDAYS:

Dean Smith, 1931; Ticky Burden, 1953; Adrian Dantley, 1956; Vincent Askew, 1966; Francisco Elson, 1976; Jamaal Tinsley, 1978; Tayshaun Prince, 1980

TRIVIA:

Wilt's 72.7% field goal percentage for the 1972-73 season is well ahead of the second best performance in NBA history - the 68.3% Chamberlain shot in the 1966-67 season.

QUIZ:

What player holds the current record for the most consecutive free throws made?

ANSWER: *Micheal Williams of the Timberwolves, who hit 97 straight from March 24 to November 9, 1993*

TODAY'S THOUGHT:

 e need books with all pictures in them... We have enough trouble learning the offense right now. We don't need these guys thinking deep inner thoughts." *–Will Perdue*, on coach Phil Jackson handing out books to a young Bulls team

HISTORY:

On this date in 1964 Jerry Lucas and Oscar Robertson of the Cincinnati Royals formed their own 40-40 club. Lucas, who would go on to win Rookie of the Year, grabbed 40 rebounds, and Robertson, the season's MVP, scored 43 points as the Royals defeated the 76ers, 117-114.

BIRTHDAY:

Vonteego Cummings, 1976

TRIVIA:

In the 1970's, the multi-talented Jerry Lucas appeared on TV, amazing audiences with his ability to memorize the first 500 pages of the Manhattan phone directory. Lucas is the co-author of *The Memory Book*, a how-to best seller that sold over two million copies.

QUIZ:

What Basketball Hall of Famer who coached the Baltimore Bullets from 1952 to 1954 authored the *Chip Hilton* series of sports books?

ANSWER: *Clair Bee*

TODAY'S THOUGHT:

"**D**on't get caught looking at the apple in case someone takes the ladder away." *–Lenny Wilkens*, coach, on the possibility of winning a division title

HISTORY:

On this date in 1996 Atlanta's Lenny Wilkens reached yet another coaching milestone, becoming the first in NBA history to reach 1,000 career wins when the Hawks beat the Cleveland Cavaliers, 74-68.

BIRTHDAYS:

Frank Scolari, 1922; Willie Long, 1950; Brian Winters, 1952; Yolanda Griffith, 1970; Chris Webber, 1973; Travis Diener, 1982

TRIVIA:

Wilkens was the last player-coach in NBA history. In his final year as a player, he coached Portland to a 38-44 record. Wilkens didn't make the playoffs as a head coach until his sixth season, when Seattle made it to the conference finals.

QUIZ:

Who is the only coach in NBA history to win three straight titles three different times?

ANSWER: Phil Jackson - He led the Bulls to three championships from 1991 to '93 and then again from '96-'98. When he joined the Lakers, he won three more from 2000 to 2002.

TODAY'S THOUGHT:

"**A**s time goes by, I feel more and more a part of that 100-point game. It has become my handle, and I've come to realize just what I did." –*Wilt Chamberlain*, more than 30 years after his historic record

HISTORY:

On this date in 1962 Wilt Chamberlain made 36 field goals and 28 free throws to become the only pro to score 100 points in a game. The Philadelphia Warriors outgunned the New York Knicks, 169-147, before only 4,124 fans in Hershey, Pennsylvania.

BIRTHDAY:

Mike McCarron, 1922

TRIVIA:

The man credited with the assist on the basket that gave Chamberlain the record was Joe Ruklick, who found Wilt for a short shot with forty-six seconds left in the game.

QUIZ:

True or false? Wilt Chamberlain was on the court for every single minute of the 1961-62 season.

ANSWER: *False- Chamberlain missed eight minutes of action during the season.*

TODAY'S THOUGHT:

"After all the traveling I have done, I demand to be called an international disgrace." *–John Chaney*, Temple coach, after Howard Cosell called him a national disgrace

HISTORY:

On this date in 1951 the Temple Owls' Bill Mlkvy outscored the entire Wilkes College team in a 99-69 win. Mlkvy erupted for 73 points in the game, shooting 32 for 69 from the floor. He surpassed a mark set just two weeks earlier, when Washington & Lee's Jay Handlan scored 66.

BIRTHDAYS:

Willie Wise, 1947; Johnny Moore, 1958

TRIVIA:

Mlkvy was remembered for the unique nickname he earned in college, "The Owl Without a Vowel." Despite being drafted fourth overall in 1952 by the Warriors, Mlkvy lasted only 31 games as a pro.

QUIZ:

In 1994, John Chaney nearly assaulted what opposing coach at a post-game news conference?

ANSWER: *University of Massachusetts coach John Calipari - Chaney accused Calipari of intimidating the referees in a one-point Temple loss.*

TODAY'S THOUGHT:

"**T**here has never been a great athlete who died not knowing what pain is." *–Bill Bradley*

HISTORY:

On this date in 1990 college star Hank Gathers of Loyola Marymount collapsed on his home court during the first half of a game against Portland. After scoring on an alley-oop dunk, Gathers fell to the floor and began convulsing. He was pronounced dead on arrival at a nearby hospital.

BIRTHDAYS:

Kevin Johnson, 1966; Trenton Hassell, 1979; Guillermo Diaz, 1985

TRIVIA:

In 1989, Gathers became the only player to lead the nation in scoring in a season he shot better than sixty percent from the floor. Gathers averaged 32.7 points per game while shooting 60.8 percent.

QUIZ:

Kurt Thomas, the last player to lead the NCAA in scoring and rebounding the same year, attended what college?

ANSWER: *Texas Christian University*

TODAY'S THOUGHT:

"**I** have three-point shooters. I just wish I had three-point scorers."
–Dallas Mavericks coach *Dick Motta*

HISTORY:

On this date in 1996 the Dallas Mavericks set an NBA record for three-point field goal attempts when they shot 49 during a win over the Nets. They went on to set single-season records for three-point shots made (735) and attempted (2,039).

BIRTHDAYS:

Denny Crum, 1937; Scott Skiles, 1964; Reggie Williams, 1964; Mike Brown, 1970; Brian Grant, 1972; Sarunas Jasikevicius, 1976; Wally Szczerbiak, 1977

TRIVIA:

In 1989, Gathers became just the second man to lead all NCAA Division I players in scoring and rebounding in the same season, averaging 32.7 points and 13.7 rebounds per game. Wichita State's Xavier McDaniel (in 1985) was the first.

QUIZ:

In 1997, what player set a rookie record for three-point field goals made in a season, with 158?

ANSWER: *Kerry Kittles, as a member of the New Jersey Nets*

TODAY'S THOUGHT:

 e was just so saucy." *–Gary Payton*, on why George Gervin was his favorite player growing up

HISTORY:

On this date in 1982 the San Antonio Spurs defeated the Milwaukee Bucks, 171-166, in triple-overtime. George Gervin led the way with 50 points for the Spurs, and the 337 combined points were at the time an NBA record.

BIRTHDAYS:

Sleepy Floyd, 1960; Darrick Martin, 1971; Shaquille O'Neal, 1972; Michael Finley, 1973; Greg Ostertag, 1973

TRIVIA:

In 1978, in the closest scoring race in NBA history, Gervin edged Denver's David Thompson by seven hundredths of a point (27.22 to 27.15). In the final game of the year, Thompson scored 73 points, but Gervin maintained his lead by putting up 63.

QUIZ:

Who was the last NBA player to win back-to-back league scoring titles?

ANSWER: *Tracy McGrady, in 2003 (32.1 ppg) and 2004 (28.0 ppg)*

TODAY'S THOUGHT:

 "**T**he secret is to have eight great players and four others who will cheer like crazy." *–Jerry Tarkanian*, on succeeding in college basketball

HISTORY:

On this date in 1970 Notre Dame guard Austin Carr scored 61 points in a 112-82 NCAA Tournament win over Ohio University. Carr's effort broke the tourney's single-game scoring record of 58 set five years earlier by Princeton's Bill Bradley.

BIRTHDAYS:

Andy Phillip, 1922; Oliver Taylor, 1947

TRIVIA:

Of the top ten NCAA Tournament single-game scoring performances, Austin Carr is responsible for four of them. In that 1970 tourney, Carr averaged 52.7 points per contest in the three games Notre Dame played.

QUIZ:

What player holds the record for most points in a single NCAA Tournament with 184?

ANSWER: *Michigan's Glen Rice, in their 1989 championship season*

TODAY'S THOUGHT:

"If you went to my school with two ears, it was obvious you were a transfer student." *–George Raveling*, college basketball coach, recalling his youth in urban Washington, D.C.

HISTORY:

On this date in 1954 the Milwaukee Hawks and Baltimore Bullets played in the NBA's first two-team doubleheader. Both games (shortened to 40 minutes) were won by the Hawks, 64-54, and 65-54.

BIRTHDAYS:

Buck Williams, 1960; Kenny Smith, 1965; Sasha Vujacic, 1984

TRIVIA:

Washington was persuaded to change its name in 1997 to "Wizards" because "Bullets" suggested violence. The name "Dragons" was rejected because of Ku Klux Klan overtones, but ironically, "Wizards" was not.

QUIZ:

What was the original name of the Washington Wizards?

ANSWER: *They were known as the Chicago Packers when they began play in the NBA in 1961.*

The Basketball Almanac

TODAY'S THOUGHT:

"**T**o say a good defensive center is more important than a high-scoring forward is like saying that the intestinal tract is more vital than the circulatory system." *–Tetford Taylor*

HISTORY:

On this date in 1958 Detroit forward George Yardley became the first NBA player to score 2,000 points in a season, finishing the year with 2,001. That total broke the single-season scoring record of 1,932 points held by the Lakers' George Mikan.

BIRTHDAYS:

Jeff Wilkins, 1955; Darrell Walker, 1961; Mahmoud Abdul-Rauf, 1969; Adonal Foyle, 1975; Matt Barnes, 1980

TRIVIA:

If it's a matter of seconds, Karl Malone comes in first. He finished runner-up in the NBA scoring race a record five times in his career, all thanks to Michael Jordan. The Mailman finished behind M.J. four straight times from 1989-92, and again in 1997.

QUIZ:

Who is the all-time leading scorer in the history of the Minneapolis/Los Angeles Lakers?

ANSWER: *Jerry West, with 25,192 points in his 14 years with the club*

TODAY'S THOUGHT:

"**L**oose ball foul on whatever the hell his name is."
–Referee *Joey Crawford*, calling a foul on Stojko Vrankovic

HISTORY:

On this date in 1987 Kareem Abdul-Jabbar became the NBA's all-time leader in personal fouls committed. Abdul-Jabbar's 4,194th career foul, a charge on Denver's Danny Schayes, moved him past Elvin Hayes. He would end his career with 4,657, a record that still stands.

BIRTHDAYS:

Leroy Ellis, 1940; Jim Valvano, 1946; Austin Carr, 1948; Tim McCormick, 1962; Kwame Brown, 1982; Jackie Butler, 1985; Chris Taft, 1985

TRIVIA:

George Mikan is the only player in NBA history to lead the league in both fouls and scoring in the same season. Mikan, in fact, did it twice, in the 1949-50 and 1950-51 campaigns.

QUIZ:

Playing by the Rules: An unsportsmanlike foul is assessed against Texas Tech coach Bobby Knight. Is this a team foul?

ANSWER: *No*

TODAY'S THOUGHT:

 or a college basketball player or coach, to reach the Final Four is la-la land. You've achieved, you've got your stamp of approval." *–Mike Krzyzewski*

HISTORY:

On this date in 1979 March Madness held form in the NCAA East Regional. Number ten-seed St. John's shocked number two Duke, 80-78, and number nine Penn took out number one-seed North Carolina, 72-71. Penn eventually advanced to the Final Four, beating St. John's, 64-62, to get there.

BIRTHDAYS:

Shellie McMillon, 1936; Jackie Moreland, 1938; Jim McMillian, 1948; Becky Hammon, 1977; Elton Brand, 1979; Fred Jones, 1979

TRIVIA:

Only twice since the seeding of tournament teams began in 1979 have no number one-seeds made it to the Final Four. The years were 1980 (#2 Louisville, #5 Iowa, #6 Purdue and #8 UCLA) and 2006 (#2 UCLA, #3 Florida, #4 LSU and #11 George Mason).

QUIZ:

Name the only school to win the NIT and the NCAA tournaments in the same year.

ANSWER: *City College of New York won both tournaments in 1950.*

TODAY'S THOUGHT:

" **C** hemistry is a class you take in high school or college, where you figure out two plus two is 10, or something."
–Dennis Rodman, on team chemistry

HISTORY:

On this date in 1956 Syracuse's Dick Farley got his 15 minutes of fame. Make that five. That's how long it took him to foul out of a game against St. Louis. 41 years later, however, Dallas' Bubba Wells fouled out in three minutes against the Bulls, breaking the NBA mark for the fastest disqualification.

BIRTHDAYS:

Bob Houbregs, 1932; Eddie Sutton, 1936; Erwin Mueller, 1944; Grant Long, 1966; Isaiah Rider, 1971; Charlie Bell, 1979

TRIVIA:

Wells was out so quickly because Dallas coach Don Nelson instructed him to keep fouling Dennis Rodman, a poor foul shooter. The tactic inspired the "Hack-a-Shaq," used on Shaquille O'Neal, another bad free throw shooter.

QUIZ:

Until 1896, how many points was a player awarded for a free throw?

ANSWER: Three - *The foul line used to be twenty feet from the basket, rather than the current fifteen.*

TODAY'S THOUGHT:

"**T**he only difference between a good shot and a bad shot is if it goes in or not." *–Charles Barkley*

HISTORY:

On this date in 1999 the Rockets' Charles Barkley recorded his 4,000th career assist in a 100-89 win over Cleveland. He became only the third player in NBA history to record 20,000 points, 10,000 rebounds and 4,000 assists, joining Kareem Abdul-Jabbar and Wilt Chamberlain in that elite group.

BIRTHDAYS:

Fatty Taylor, 1946; Cliff Robinson, 1960; Bobby Jackson, 1973; Troy Hudson, 1976; Caron Butler, 1980

TRIVIA:

Speaking of the Big Dipper, exactly 37 years before Barkley's milestone, Wilt Chamberlain ended the 1962 season as the first player to exceed 4,000 points (4,029) and over 50 points per game (50.4) in a single season.

QUIZ:

Wilt Chamberlain shares the record for the most free throws made in a game, 28, with what other player?

ANSWER: *Adrian Dantley of the Utah Jazz*

TODAY'S THOUGHT:

"**D**on't measure yourself by what you have accomplished, but by what you should have accomplished with your ability."
—John Wooden

HISTORY:

On this date in 1991 the Richmond Spiders became the first fifteen-seed to knock off a number two, stunning the nation's seventh-ranked Syracuse Orangemen, 73-69, in the first round of the NCAA Tournament.

BIRTHDAYS:

Chuck Share, 1927; Don Haskins, 1930; Ira Harge, 1941; Clyde Lee, 1944; Wes Unseld, 1946; Larry Johnson, 1969

TRIVIA:

Richmond had pulled another upset three years earlier when they knocked out the defending national champion Indiana Hoosiers, 72-69, as a thirteen-seed. The Spiders lost to number one-seed Temple in the Sweet 16.

QUIZ:

True or false? Since the NCAA Tournament began in 1939, no number sixteen-seed has ever beaten a number one-seed.

ANSWER: *True*

TODAY'S THOUGHT:

 ell, you can certainly teach free-throwing. And you can teach the boys to pass at angles and run in curves."
—*Phog Allen*, when told by James Naismith that basketball couldn't be coached

HISTORY:

On this date in 1997 North Carolina beat Colorado, 73-56, in the NCAA Tournament, making Dean Smith the all-time leader in wins in college basketball. Smith vaulted past Adolph Rupp with his 877th victory.

BIRTHDAYS:

Connie Simmons, 1925; Terry Cummings, 1961

TRIVIA:

Smith was a member of the Kansas Jayhawks squad that won the national championship in 1952. He was coached by the legendary Forrest "Phog" Allen, who, in turn, was coached at Kansas in the early 1900's by basketball's inventor, James Naismith.

QUIZ:

Who succeeded the legendary Adolph Rupp as coach at the University of Kentucky?

ANSWER: *Joe B. Hall*

TODAY'S THOUGHT:

"The guy in front of us is wearing a T-shirt that says, "Good coaches win, great coaches cover." *–T.J. Simers* of *The Los Angeles Times*, on betting in Las Vegas for the NCAA Tournament

HISTORY:

On this date in 1938 the Temple Owls beat the Colorado Buffaloes, 60-36, to win the first National Invitational Tournament, and the collegiate basketball championship, at Madison Square Garden in New York. The NCAA would begin its own tournament the following year.

BIRTHDAY:

Bob Harris, 1927

TRIVIA:

The 1939 NCAA Tournament involved just eight schools, playing in single-elimination games. The first champion was Oregon, who defeated Ohio State, 46-33.

QUIZ:

From 1964 to 1973 UCLA won nine of ten NCAA basketball titles. Who was the only other champ in that span?

ANSWER: *Texas Western, now known as Texas-El Paso, won the title in 1966, defeating Kentucky, 72-65.*

TODAY'S THOUGHT:

 "**W**hen you can get a discount at Denny's, it's time to retire." *–Charles Barkley*, on the retirement of 41-year old Karl Malone

HISTORY:

On this date in 1963 and 1984 the NBA paid tribute to two of its future Hall of Famers. In '63, the Boston Garden faithful bid a tearful farewell to The Houdini of the Hardwood on Bob Cousy Day. Twenty one years later, the Rockets retired Calvin Murphy's number 23, making him the second player, after Rudy Tomjanovich, to be honored.

BIRTHDAYS:

Danny Ainge, 1959; Sam Bowie, 1961; Kyle Korver, 1981

TRIVIA:

Wendell Ladner is the only non-NBA player to have his number retired by an NBA team. Ladner played just two years with the New Jersey Nets in the ABA, and was admired for his personality rather than his basketball talent. His number 4 was retired by the Nets shortly after he died in a plane crash in 1975.

QUIZ:

The New York Knicks have retired the same number, 15, twice. What players did they honor?

ANSWER: *Guards Earl Monroe and Dick McGuire*

TODAY'S THOUGHT:

"**I** 've missed more than 9,000 shots in my career. I've lost almost 300 games. Twenty-six times, I've been trusted to take the game winning shot and missed. I've failed over and over and over again in my life. And that is why I succeed." *–Michael Jordan*

HISTORY:

On this date in 1995 Michael Jordan announced his return to the NBA through a two-word press release: "I'm back." He would play 24 hours later against the Indiana Pacers at Market Square Arena, scoring 19 points in an overtime loss.

BIRTHDAYS:

Jeff Mullins, 1942; Fred Foster, 1946; Mike Lewis, 1946; Brian Scalabrine, 1978

TRIVIA:

Michael Jordan participated in the 1990 Three-Point Shootout at the All-Star Game and set a record - for the worst score ever posted in a round, five points.

QUIZ:

What three uniform numbers has Michael Jordan donned in his NBA career?

ANSWER: *23, 45, and 12 (Jordan wore number 12 for a Bulls-Magic game after his jersey had been stolen.)*

TODAY'S THOUGHT:

"**I**t was perhaps the most socially significant win in the history of sports. Every coach out there owes (Don Haskins) a debt of gratitude." *–Rick Majerus*, on the 1966 champion Texas Western team

HISTORY:

On this date in 1966 Texas Western coach Don Haskins started the first all-black lineup in NCAA championship history. The Miners, led by Bobby Joe Hill, stunned top-ranked and all-white Kentucky, 72-65, to win the national title.

BIRTHDAYS:

Scott May, 1954; Tyrone Hill, 1968; Antonio Daniels, 1975; Andre Miller, 1976; Hedo Turkoglu, 1979

TRIVIA:

The movie *Glory Road*, released in 2006, chronicles Texas Western's inspirational story. Wheaties celebrated the 40th anniversary of the team's title with a "Breakfast of Champions" cereal box featuring images from the '66 season.

QUIZ:

In the 1963-64 season, the Celtics were the first NBA team to start five black players. Can you name them all?

ANSWER: *Bill Russell, K.C. Jones, Tom Sanders, Willie Naulls and Sam Jones*

TODAY'S THOUGHT:

If you don't know the answer to an NBA trivia question, just say 'Oscar Robertson' -you'll probably be right." *–Wilt Chamberlain*

HISTORY:

On this date in 1968 Philadelphia 76ers big man Wilt Chamberlain ended the regular season by becoming the first center in NBA history to lead the league in assists. His 702 season total was good for an average of 8.6 per game.

BIRTHDAYS:

Belus Smawley, 1918; John Barnhill, 1938; Pat Riley, 1945; Derrek Dickey, 1951; Mookie Blaylock, 1967; Jamal Crawford, 1980; Ronnie Brewer, 1985

TRIVIA:

Oscar Robertson had a record 181 career triple-doubles. But that's nothing compared to what he did during the 1961-62 season. He *averaged* a triple-double for the entire year. His numbers: 30.8 points, 11.4 assists and 12.5 rebounds per game.

QUIZ:

Who was the first player to lead the NBA in scoring and assists in the same season?

ANSWER: Nate Archibald scored 34 points per game and handed out 11.4 assists for the Kansas City Kings in the 1972-73 season.

TODAY'S THOUGHT:

"**L**osing wasn't a disaster. Getting home after a game and finding no scotch in the liquor cabinet- that was a disaster."
–Red Holzman, on his days in the NBA

HISTORY:

On this date in 1953 Boston outlasted Syracuse, 111-105, in quadruple overtime, to clinch Game 2 of the Eastern Division Semifinals. Bob Cousy carried the Celtics, becoming the first player to score 50 points in a playoff game.

BIRTHDAYS:

Mike Dunleavy, 1954; Vitaly Potapenko, 1975

TRIVIA:

The New York Knicks were the first team to lose three consecutive NBA Finals. Defeated by the Royals in 1951, the Knicks were beaten by the Lakers in '52 and '53. The Lakers would match New York in 1970, losing their third straight NBA Finals to…the Knicks.

QUIZ:

How many times have the Lakers and Celtics met in the NBA Finals?
a. 8 b. 10 c. 12

ANSWER: *b. 10*

TODAY'S THOUGHT:

 "**G**oing into a game against Lew Alcindor [later Kareem Abdul-Jabbar] is like going into a knife fight and finding there's no blade in your handle." *–Bill Fitch*

HISTORY:

On this date in 1969 UCLA legend Lew Alcindor ended his college career by leading the Bruins to their third straight championship, a 92-72 win over Purdue. Alcindor scored 37 points and grabbed 22 rebounds to become the first man to win three Final Four Most Outstanding Player Awards.

BIRTHDAYS:

Ed Macauley, 1928; Don Chaney, 1946; Sonny Parker, 1955; Brian Shaw, 1966; Shawn Bradley, 1972; Marcus Camby, 1974

TRIVIA:

Lew Alcindor declined to participate in the 1968 Olympics in Mexico City in support of the threatened black boycott of the Games.

QUIZ:

Milwaukee won a coin toss in the 1969 NBA Draft for the right to select Kareem Abdul-Jabbar with the first pick. Which team lost the toss?

ANSWER: *The Phoenix Suns, who settled for Neal Walk*

TODAY'S THOUGHT:

"**I** consider playing basketball…the most shallow thing in the world." *–Bill Russell*

HISTORY:

On this date in 1956 Bill Russell scored 26 points and pulled down 27 rebounds as San Francisco defeated Iowa, 83-71, for their second straight NCAA title. The victory, the team's 55th in a row over two seasons, made them the first undefeated team to win the title.

BIRTHDAYS:

Rich Kelley, 1953; Moses Malone, 1955; Jason Kidd, 1973

TRIVIA:

Hall of Famer Bill Russell was the second player chosen in the 1956 NBA Draft. The Rochester Royals, armed with the first pick, gazed into their crystal ball, passed on Russell, and chose Si Green of Duquesne instead.

QUIZ:

On March 23, 1957, North Carolina won the NCAA championship, but it took them two straight triple-overtime games to do it. Who were their opponents in the semifinal and final games?

ANSWER: *The Tarheels beat Michigan State, 74-70, in the semis, and then defeated Kansas, 54-53, to win the title.*

TODAY'S THOUGHT:

 e're not eating, we're not sleeping. We're like Gandhi." *–Pete Gillen*, Xavier University basketball coach, before a game with rival Cincinnati

HISTORY:

On this date in 1962 Cincinnati beat Ohio State in the National Championship Game for the second straight year, as the Bearcats' Paul Hogue outplayed the Buckeyes' injured Jerry Lucas in the 71-59 win. In 1961, Cincinnati beat Ohio State, 70-65, in overtime in the title game.

BIRTHDAYS:

Steve Fisher, 1945; Mike Woodson, 1958; T.J. Ford, 1983; Chris Bosh, 1984

TRIVIA:

In 1944, Arkansas was forced to decline a tournament bid when two of its players each suffered a broken leg when they were struck by a passing car while trying to change a tire. The team that replaced the Razorbacks, Utah, won the national championship.

QUIZ:

Who was known as "The Wizard of Westwood?"

ANSWER: *UCLA coach John Wooden*

TODAY'S THOUGHT:

 hen I coached at Marquette, I told the players we go first class. We don't take the towels from the hotel rooms. We take the television sets." *–Al McGuire*

HISTORY:

On this date in 1974 North Carolina State, led by David Thompson, defeated Marquette, 76-64, to win the NCAA title. The Wolfpack, who defeated UCLA in double-overtime in the semifinals, ended the Bruins' run of seven straight championships.

BIRTHDAYS:

Avery Johnson, 1965; Dale Davis, 1969; Sheryl Swoopes, 1971; Bob Sura, 1973; Kyle Lowry, 1986

TRIVIA:

Thompson was nicknamed "Skywalker" because of his incredible vertical leap. He and teammate Monte Towe are credited with popularizing the alley-oop pass. At that time, dunking in college games wasn't allowed, so Towe would toss the ball high up over the rim for Thompson to lay in the basket.

QUIZ:

Name the Division I college basketball team that holds the record for the most consecutive winning seasons: a.UCLA b.Louisville c.North Carolina d.Indiana

ANSWER: b. *Louisville - From 1944-45 until 1989-90 they strung together 46 straight winning seasons. In 1990-91 the Cardinals slipped to 14-16.*

TODAY'S THOUGHT:

"**W**e had a special team. We played together, played to win, and everyone knew their roles... Everyone knew I was going to take all the shots." *–Larry Bird*, on his Indiana State team

HISTORY:

On this date in 1979 in one of the most-watched college games ever, Magic Johnson's 24 points led the Michigan State Spartans over Larry Bird and the undefeated Indiana State Sycamores, 75-64, for the school's first NCAA championship.

BIRTHDAYS:

Al Bianchi, 1932; Wayne Embry, 1937; John Stockton, 1962; Daniel Ewing, 1983

TRIVIA:

In 2005, Eric James Torpy was sentenced to 30 years in prison after being convicted of robbery. A fan of Larry Bird, Torpy requested that his prison term be increased to 33 years to match his hero's jersey number. His wish was granted.

QUIZ:

Can you name the two Michigan State hoops coaches who have won NCAA titles?

ANSWER: *Jud Heathcote in 1979 and Tom Izzo in 2000*

The Basketball Almanac

TODAY'S THOUGHT:

"**L**et's play at the Inglewood YMCA or someplace where we can have a sellout." *–Tom Tolbert*, L.A. Clippers, on the team playing at the Forum because of structural damage to the Clippers' home court

HISTORY:

On this day in 1998 a new NBA single-game attendance mark was set when 62,046 fans flocked to the Georgia Dome to see the Atlanta Hawks take on the Chicago Bulls in what was supposed to be Michael Jordan's final game in the city. Chicago won, 89-74.

BIRTHDAY:

Danny Fortson, 1976

TRIVIA:

In 1969, the ABA's Houston Mavericks set an attendance low for a profes-sional basketball game when 89 people showed up at the Sam Houston Coliseum to see the Mavs in their final home game of the year. Houston had drawn an average of 355 fans per game the previous two months.

QUIZ:

What was the original home court of the Dallas Mavericks?

ANSWER: *Reunion Arena*

TODAY'S THOUGHT:

"**W**e both went to great academic institutions. One of us went to class, one of us didn't. That's where the similarities end." *–Charles Barkley*, Auburn alumnus, on Christian Laettner

HISTORY:

On this date in 1992 Duke's Christian Laettner hit a turnaround jumper that beat the buzzer and propelled Duke to a 104-103 overtime win over Kentucky in the East Regional Final. Laettner finished with 31 points, leading Duke to its fifth straight Final Four.

BIRTHDAYS:

Kevin Loughery, 1940; Jerry Sloan, 1942; Rick Barry, 1944; Sam Lacey, 1948; Len Elmore, 1952; Byron Scott, 1961; Wesley Person, 1971; Luke Walton, 1980

TRIVIA:

Lost in the drama of that final shot was Laettner's performance throughout the game. He didn't miss a shot, going 10 for 10 from the field and 10 for 10 from the foul line.

QUIZ:

Name the last team to reach the NCAA National Championship game in three consecutive seasons.

ANSWER: Kentucky Wildcats - *They beat Syracuse in 1996, were defeated by Arizona in '97, and then defeated Utah in '98.*

TODAY'S THOUGHT:

"**I** probably couldn't play for me. I wouldn't like my attitude."
–John Thompson, former Georgetown coach

HISTORY:

On this date in 1982 freshman Michael Jordan's jumper with 16 seconds left lifted North Carolina past Patrick Ewing and Georgetown, 63-62, in the NCAA title game. For Tarheels coach Dean Smith, it was the first championship of his career.

BIRTHDAYS:

Walt Frazier, 1945; Walt Ratleff, 1950

TRIVIA:

Before coaching at Georgetown, John Thompson played two years in the NBA for the Boston Celtics from 1964 to 1966. A center, Thompson backed up Bill Russell, earning the nickname "The Caddy" for his role on the team.

QUIZ:

What's the only school to win both the men's and women's NCAA Tournament in the same season?

ANSWER: *The University of Connecticut, in 2004*

TODAY'S THOUGHT:

"**I** looked down the floor and saw Dale Brown and I knew we had a chance." *–Bobby Knight*, whose Hoosiers beat LSU in a game they trailed by 12 with 12 minutes left

HISTORY:

On this date in 1987 the Indiana Hoosiers won their fifth NCAA championship. Baton Rouge native Keith Smart hit a baseline jumper with four seconds left to give Indiana a 74-73 victory over Syracuse at the Louisiana Superdome.

BIRTHDAY:

Jerry Lucas, 1940

TRIVIA:

When Indiana defeated North Carolina in 1981 for their fourth title, the school became the first to win an NCAA Championship in four different decades. The previous titles were in 1940, 1953, and 1976.

QUIZ:

What Syracuse player tied Indiana's Steve Alford by scoring a total of 138 points in the 1987 tourney?

ANSWER: *Rony Seikaly*

TODAY'S THOUGHT:

 "**S**tacy was a little disturbed at the salary cap when he came here. They don't have one at UNLV." *—Bob Weiss*, Atlanta Hawks coach, on Stacy Augmon

HISTORY:

On this date in 1991 Duke shocked a heavily favored UNLV squad, 79-77, in the NCAA semifinals. Two free throws by Christian Laettner proved to be the difference in the win that snapped the Runnin' Rebels' 45-game winning streak. Duke went on to beat Kansas for the title.

BIRTHDAYS:

Don Barksdale, 1923; J.R. Reid, 1968; Steve Smith, 1969

TRIVIA:

Three players from that UNLV team were selected among the top fifteen picks in the 1991 NBA Draft. Larry Johnson went first overall to the Hornets, Stacey Augmon was picked ninth by the Hawks, and Greg Anthony went at number twelve to the Knicks.

QUIZ:

What former Duke basketball standout was drafted in the sixth round of the 1994 Amateur Baseball Draft by the San Diego Padres?

ANSWER: *Trajan Langdon*

TODAY'S THOUGHT:

 e already won the non-Catholic championship of the nation." –Memphis State coach *Dana Kirk*, on joining Georgetown, St. John's and Villanova (all Catholic institutions) in the 1985 Final Four

HISTORY:

On this date in 1985 eighth-seeded Villanova shot a tournament-record 78.6% from the field to upset number-one Georgetown, 66-64, in a championship game for the ages. The Wildcats hit 11 of 14 free throws over the final two minutes to become the lowest seed ever to win a national title.

BIRTHDAYS:

Norm Van Lier, 1947; Tim Bassett, 1951; Kevin Duckworth, 1964; Mark Jackson, 1965; Etan Thomas, 1978

TRIVIA:

Georgetown, located in the District of Columbia, is the only school to win the NCAA men's basketball championship that is not located in any of the fifty states. The Hoyas' lone title came in 1984, an 84-75 win over Houston.

QUIZ:

What NBA team did colorful college basketball commentator Dick Vitale coach?

ANSWER: *Vitale coached the Detroit Pistons from 1978-79 and compiled a 34-60 record.*

TODAY'S THOUGHT:

 "Even though he lived on the beach in college, he didn't have a tan. Now that's a serious player!"* –Bill Fitch*, on rookie Conner Henry

HISTORY:

On this date in 1990 UNLV, led by 29 points from Anderson Hunt, crushed Duke, 103-73, for the school's first NCAA basketball title. The 30-point margin of victory was the largest ever for a final game.

BIRTHDAYS:

Jim McDaniels, 1948; Larry Drew, 1958; Andris Biedrins, 1986

TRIVIA:

Eleven-seed Loyola Marymount, playing for fallen teammate Hank Gathers, made an improbable run in the 1990 Tournament, advancing to the Elite Eight before being eliminated by UNLV. Bo Kimble, Gathers' best friend and teammate, shot his first free throw of each game left-handed in his memory.

QUIZ:

Two college basketball players have led the nation in scoring three consecutive years. Name them.

ANSWER: *Cincinnati's Oscar Robertson from 1958-60 and LSU's Pete Maravich from 1968-70*

TODAY'S THOUGHT:

"e was a high school All-American, but there weren't a hell of a lot of Americans in those days." *–George Raveling*, on Ralph Miller, who played basketball at Kansas in the early 1940's

HISTORY:

On this date in 1989 Michigan defeated Seton Hall, 80-79, in overtime to win the NCAA championship. Rumeal Robinson sank two free throws with three seconds left to give the Wolverines the win. It was the first title game to go into overtime in 26 years.

BIRTHDAYS:

Earl Lloyd, 1928; McCoy McLemore,1942; Pervis Ellison, 1967; Michael Olowakandi, 1975; DeShawn Stevenson, 1981

TRIVIA:

Only once has a National Championship Game gone past the first overtime. In 1957, North Carolina defeated Kansas, 54-53, in triple OT. The Jayhawks' Wilt Chamberlain was named the tournament's Most Outstanding Player with 55 points and 25 rebounds in the Final Four.

QUIZ:

Since 1987, what song has CBS traditionally played at the end of the tournament's championship game?

ANSWER: *One Shining Moment*

TODAY'S THOUGHT:

 "My sister's going to have a baby and I don't know if I'm going to be an uncle or an aunt." –player *Chuck Nevitt*, to North Carolina State coach Jim Valvano

HISTORY:

On this date in 1983 North Carolina State became the first team with 10 losses to win the national championship, stunning the Houston Cougars, 54-52. Lorenzo Charles rebounded Dereck Whittenburg's 30-foot desperation shot and threw down a dunk as time expired.

BIRTHDAYS:

Bill Bridges, 1939; Larry Miller, 1946; Stanislav Medvedenko, 1979; Ben Gordon, 1983; Sean May, 1984

TRIVIA:

In 1993, cancer-stricken Jim Valvano was given the inaugural Arthur Ashe Courage and Humanitarian Award at the first ESPY Awards. In his emotional acceptance speech, he announced the creation of the "V Foundation" for cancer research, and the foundation's motto: "Don't give up. Don't ever give up."

QUIZ:

Besides Dean Smith, who is the only man to play on, and later coach, a basketball team to the NCAA title?

ANSWER: *Bobby Knight, who played with Ohio State and coached Indiana*

TODAY'S THOUGHT:

"If you make every game a life-and-death thing, you're going to have problems. You'll be dead a lot." *–Dean Smith*

HISTORY:

On this date in 1993, North Carolina beat Michigan 77-71 to win the NCAA championship. A technical foul on the Wolverines' Chris Webber for calling a timeout the team didn't have, secured the game for the Tarheels with eleven seconds to play.

BIRTHDAYS:

Skip Thoren, 1943; Stephen Jackson, 1978; Matt Bonner, 1980

TRIVIA:

At North Carolina, Dean Smith always started all his seniors on "Senior Day," the last home game of the season. One year, when the team included six seniors, Smith opted to put all of them on the floor for the opening tip and willingly took a technical foul, refusing to leave one out of the starting lineup.

QUIZ:

Chris Webber was one member of Michigan's "Fab Five." Can you name the other four?

ANSWER: *Juwan Howard, Jalen Rose, Jimmy King and Ray Jackson*

TODAY'S THOUGHT:

 "Our consistency has been up and down all season."
–Robert Parish

HISTORY:

On this date in 1970 Hall of Famer Maurice Stokes died at age 36 of a heart attack. A paralyzing head injury during his third season shortened his promising career, but Stokes still left his mark by playing on three All-Star teams with the Royals and averaging over 17 rebounds a game.

BIRTHDAYS:

John Shumate, 1952; Bison Dele, 1969; Oliver Miller, 1970

TRIVIA:

Jack Twyman, a former teammate of Stokes and a fellow Hall of Famer, became Stokes' legal guardian after his injury to help pay the medical bills. Twyman also organized the Maurice Stokes Memorial basketball game to raise money for needy former players.

QUIZ:

On April 6, 1999, Robert Parish passed what Hall of Famer to become the NBA's all-time leader in games played?

ANSWER: *Parish passed Kareem Abdul-Jabbar's mark of 1,560. He would finish his career with 1,611 games played.*

TODAY'S THOUGHT:

" **I** like all sports, and I like to play them all - except ice hockey."
–Shaquille O'Neal

HISTORY:

On this date in 1975 the New York Nets' Julius Erving and the Indiana Pacers' George McGinnis were voted co-MVP's of the ABA- the first, and only time this occurred in basketball history. McGinnis led the league in scoring, with Erving in second place.

BIRTHDAYS:

Ji Fox, 1943; Zaid Abdul-Aziz, 1946; Bo Lamar, 1951; Thurl Bailey, 1961

TRIVIA:

In 1972, as a member of the ABA's Squires, Julius Erving's attempt to sign with Atlanta of the NBA was denied by the league. The following year he was dealt to the Nets, upsetting Hawks owner Tom Cousins. To placate him, the Nets' Roy Boe, who also owned the NHL's Islanders, agreed to send defenseman Pat Ribble to the Flames, an NHL team owned by Cousins.

QUIZ:

Who is the only player to have won back-to-back regular season MVP Awards while playing for different teams?

ANSWER: *Moses Malone, with Houston in 1982 and Philadelphia in '83*

TODAY'S THOUGHT:

 "Good. Bad. OK. Terrible. OK. Bad. And Good.**"** –Chicago Bulls coach *Phil Jackson*, assessing the team's seven-game road trip

HISTORY:

On this date in 1996 the Chicago Bulls had their NBA-record 44-game home winning streak snapped by the Charlotte Hornets, losing 98-97. A week later, the Bulls would set another mark by winning their 70th game of the year.

BIRTHDAYS:

John Havlicek, 1940; Jimmy Walker, 1944; Terry Porter, 1963

TRIVIA:

Before moving into Chicago Stadium in 1967, the Bulls played one year in the International Amphitheater. The indoor arena, which sat 9,000, hosted several Democratic and Republican National Conventions in the 1950s and '60s.

QUIZ:

What two Chicago Bulls have won the NBA's Sixth Man of the Year Award?

ANSWER: *Toni Kukoc in 1996 and Ben Gordon in 2005*

TODAY'S THOUGHT:

"If we played Boston four on four, without Russell, we probably would have won every series...He's the one who prevented us from achieving true greatness." *–Hot Rod Hundley*, former Laker, on Bill Russell

HISTORY:

On this date in 1959 the Boston Celtics defeated the Minneapolis Lakers, 118-113, to capture the NBA crown in four straight games. This was the first-ever sweep in championship play and the first of a record eight consecutive NBA titles for the Celtics.

BIRTHDAYS:

Jack Nichols, 1926; Paul Arizin, 1928; Zeljko Rebraca, 1972; Wayne Simien, 1983

TRIVIA:

Exactly one year later, the Celtics would win their second straight championship, defeating the St. Louis Hawks, 122-103, in Game 7. Boston would beat just three teams in their eight-year title run: the Lakers five times, the Hawks twice, and the Warriors once.

QUIZ:

Who was the head coach of the Celtics in 1986, the last time the franchise won an NBA crown?

ANSWER: K.C. Jones

TODAY'S THOUGHT:

 "**T**here is no such thing as coulda, shoulda, woulda. If you shoulda and coulda, you woulda." *–Pat Riley*

HISTORY:

On this date in 1953 the Minneapolis Lakers defeated the New York Knicks, 91-84, in Game 5 of the NBA Finals. It was the fourth title in five years for the Lakers, and they would go on to "three-peat" the following season, beating the Syracuse Nationals.

BIRTHDAY:

Terry Teagle, 1960

TRIVIA:

The L.A. Lakers entered the 1988-89 season in search of their third consecutive title. Coach Pat Riley copyrighted the term "three-peat," but claimed it was Laker guard Byron Scott who coined the phrase in reference to the team's goal. The Pistons, however, would sweep the Lakers in the Finals that season.

QUIZ:

What team did the Lakers lose to in their lone NBA Finals appearance in the 1990's?

ANSWER: *In 1991, the Chicago Bulls beat L.A. four games to one.*

TODAY'S THOUGHT:

"**U**nstoppable, baby!" –Warriors rookie *Marc Jackson*, to the Mavericks' bench, after hitting a lay-up in a 29-point loss

HISTORY:

On this date in 1997 76ers first-year phenom Allen Iverson poured in 44 points in a 126-118 loss to the Bucks. That tied Wilt Chamberlain's rookie record of scoring 40 in three straight games, a streak Iverson would extend to five before it ended.

BIRTHDAY:

Michael Ray Richardson, 1955

TRIVIA:

In 2001, Iverson set an NBA playoff record by scoring 55.7% of his team's points in a game against Toronto. The Answer put up 54 points as his 76ers defeated the Raptors, 97-92, in Game 2 of the Eastern Conference Semifinals.

QUIZ:

Who is the only rookie in NBA history to record a triple-double in his play-off debut?

ANSWER: *Magic Johnson, who in 1980, tallied 13 points, 12 rebounds and 16 assists in a Lakers' win over Phoenix*

TODAY'S THOUGHT:

"Do your best when no one is looking. If you do that, then you can be successful in anything that you put your mind to."
—Bob Cousy

HISTORY:

On this date in 1958 Bob Pettit led the St. Louis Hawks to a 110-109 Game 6 victory over the Boston Celtics for their first NBA championship. Pettit scored 19 of his team's final 21 points to bring his total to 50, tying Bob Cousy's single-game playoff record.

BIRTHDAYS:

Joe Lapchick, 1900; Paul Hoffman, 1922; Larry Cannon, 1947; Brad Miller, 1976

TRIVIA:

The Boston Celtics and St. Louis Hawks met in the NBA Finals four times in five years, beginning in 1957. That year, Boston won its first of a record 16 championships, but it took a 125-123 double overtime victory over the Hawks in Game 7 to do so.

QUIZ:

Who's the only man to be named the Final Four Most Outstanding Player and the NBA Finals Most Valuable Player in back-to-back seasons?

ANSWER: *Magic Johnson, with Michigan State in 1979 and the L.A. Lakers in 1980*

TODAY'S THOUGHT:

"**Y**ou can't get much done in life if you only work when you feel good." *–Jerry West*

HISTORY:

On this date in 1948 the Baltimore Bullets, down 21 points at half-time, defeated the Philadelphia Warriors, 66-63, in one of the greatest single-game comebacks in NBA Finals history. Baltimore would carry that momentum to win three of the next four games and their first championship.

BIRTHDAYS:

Jim Barnes, 1941; Dana Barros, 1967; Bo Outlaw, 1971; Baron Davis, 1979; Quentin Richardson, 1980

TRIVIA:

Exactly 17 years later, the Bullets were the victims of playoff history. Jerry West set an NBA record by averaging 46.3 points per game and reaching 40 in every contest as the Lakers beat the Bullets in six games.

QUIZ:

Three players have been named the NBA Finals MVP in consecutive years. Can you name them?

ANSWER: *Michael Jordan* (1991-93, '96-'98) *Hakeem Olajuwon* (1994-95), *and Shaquille O'Neal* (2000-02)

TODAY'S THOUGHT:

 ou don't have any friends, do you?" –A *reporter* to Alvin Gentry, after Gentry explained how his friends encouraged him to take the Clippers' head coaching job

HISTORY:

On this date in 1962 the Los Angeles Lakers' Elgin Baylor scored an NBA Finals record 61 points and added 22 boards in a 126-121 Game 5 victory over the Celtics. Despite being up three games to two in the series, the Lakers would fall to the Celtics in seven.

BIRTHDAYS:

Cynthia Cooper, 1963; Mark Macon, 1969; Nikoloz Tskitishvili, 1983

TRIVIA:

Los Angeles Clippers general manager Elgin Baylor was named the 2006 NBA Executive of the Year in his 20th year, and only second winning season, with the team. His squad made it to the postseason and won its first playoff series since 1976.

QUIZ:

Elgin Baylor coached what NBA team in the late 1970's?

ANSWER: *The New Orleans Jazz - Baylor compiled an 86-135 record in his three-year stint there.*

TODAY'S THOUGHT:

"It turns out that Iverson doesn't lead the 76ers in steals after all." –Columnist *Dwight Perry*, after John Croce, the brother of Philadelphia 76ers owner Pat Croce, was caught taking money from Allen Iverson's pants

HISTORY:

On this date in 1965 John Havlicek's steal with just seconds left sealed a Celtics 110-109 win over the 76ers in the seventh game of the Eastern Division Finals. Boston would go on to defeat the Lakers once again in the NBA Finals for their seventh straight title.

BIRTHDAYS:

Mahdi Abdul-Rahman, 1942; Michael Cooper, 1956; Rodney Carney, 1984

TRIVIA:

Allen Iverson is the only player to lead the NBA in steals per game for three consecutive years (2001-03). In 1999, The Answer set a playoff record for steals in a single contest with 10 in a game against Orlando.

QUIZ:

Two NBA players share the single-game record for steals, with 11. Larry Kenon is one. Can you name the other?

ANSWER: *Kendall Gill, in 1999*

TODAY'S THOUGHT:

 "Some people want it to happen, some wish it would happen, others make it happen." *–Michael Jordan*

HISTORY:

On this date in 2003 Michael Jordan played in his final NBA game, scoring 15 points in a loss to the 76ers in Philadelphia. After hitting two free throws, he exited with 1:44 remaining to a standing ovation that lasted over three minutes.

BIRTHDAYS:

Dave Gambee, 1937; John Block, 1944; Kareem Abdul-Jabbar, 1947; Walt Williams, 1970; Keon Clark, 1975; Boris Diaw, 1982; Luol Deng, 1985

TRIVIA:

Exactly 16 years earlier, in 1987, Jordan put on one of his finest exhibitions as a pro, scoring 61 points, including a record 23 in a row, in a loss to the Hawks. Jordan's performance put him over the rare 3,000-point mark for the season.

QUIZ:

April 16, 1996 was a historic day for the Chicago Bulls franchise as the team won its record-breaking 70th game of the season. What team did they do it against?

ANSWER: *The Bulls defeated the Bucks in Milwaukee, 86-80.*

TODAY'S THOUGHT:

 "As a basketball player, Julius was the first to actually take the torch and become the spokesman for the NBA...He was the first player I ever remember who transcended sports and was known by one name, 'Doctor.'"

–*Billy Cunningham*, on Julius "Dr. J" Erving

HISTORY:

On this date in 1987 Julius Erving became the first former ABA player, and just the third pro, to score 30,000 career points in the NBA, joining Kareem Abdul-Jabbar and Wilt Chamberlain. Erving netted 38 in the last regular-season home game of his career.

BIRTHDAYS:

Geoff Petrie, 1948; Kevin Porter, 1950; Dwane Casey, 1957; Theo Ratliff, 1973

TRIVIA:

Abdul-Jabbar and Erving, along with several other pros, appeared in the 1979 movie *The Fish That Saved Pittsburgh*, a comedy about a hopeless basketball team that used astrology to win games.

QUIZ:

What former NBA center starred in the movie *My Giant* with Billy Crystal?

ANSWER: *Gheorghe Muresan*

TODAY'S THOUGHT:

 "**W**hat's more important than who's going to be the first black manager is who's going to be the first black sports editor of *The New York Times.*" *–Bill Russell*

HISTORY:

On this date in 1966 following the announcement of Red Auerbach's retirement, center Bill Russell was named the new head coach of the Celtics. As the first black coach in any of the major pro sports, Russell would act as player-coach for three seasons, winning back-to-back titles in 1968 and '69.

BIRTHDAYS:

Don Otten, 1921; Don Ohl, 1936; Michael Bradley, 1979

TRIVIA:

The first black man to be drafted by an NBA team was Duquesne University's Chuck Cooper, who was selected in the second round of the 1950 draft by the Boston Celtics. Cooper would average just under seven points per game in his six-year career.

QUIZ:

After Red Auerbach, the next four Boston coaches were former Celtics. Bill Russell was the first. Can you name the next three?

ANSWER: *In order: Tom Heinsohn, Tom Sanders and Dave Cowens*

TODAY'S THOUGHT:

"e responding to Rodman is like talking to a Bugs Bunny doll. I don't like to talk to Looney Tunes." *–Shaquille O'Neal* on Dennis Rodman, who said that O'Neal does not rebound as well as he should for his size

HISTORY:

On this date in 1992 Dennis Rodman won the first of his record seven consecutive rebounding titles. His average of 18.7 boards per game was the highest in 20 years, and he set a new NBA mark by grabbing 42 percent of the Pistons' total rebounds for the season.

BIRTHDAYS:

Keith Erickson, 1944; Scott Padgett, 1976

TRIVIA:

Rodman, who claims to wear only fake fur, became the first pro athlete to pose for the People for the Ethical Treatment of Animals (PETA) advertisement campaign, "Rather Go Naked Than Wear Fur." Rodman's ad reveals his nude, tatooed body alongside the slogan, "Think Ink, Not Mink."

QUIZ:

When Bill Laimbeer won the NBA rebounding title in the 1985-86 season, he snapped another player's string of five straight titles. Who was it?

ANSWER: *Moses Malone*

TODAY'S THOUGHT:

"I think it's just God disguised as Michael Jordan." *–Larry Bird*

HISTORY:

On this date in 1986 Michael Jordan scored an NBA playoff record 63 points in a 135-131 double overtime loss at Boston. It was the first time Jordan topped the 50-point plateau in his career.

BIRTHDAYS:

Allan Houston, 1971; Lamond Murray, 1973; Danny Granger, 1983

TRIVIA:

In the 1985-86 season, Jordan played in only 18 games and started just 7, the fewest of his career. However, he was not expected to return at all after breaking a bone in his foot in the third game of the season.

QUIZ:

Michael Jordan and Larry Bird played an epic game of H-O-R-S-E in a 1993 Super Bowl commercial promoting what brand?

ANSWER: McDonald's - The prize of the contest: a Big Mac.

TODAY'S THOUGHT:

 inning is like deodorant - it comes up and a lot of things don't stink." *–Doc Rivers*

HISTORY:

On this date in 1996 the Chicago Bulls won their 72nd game of the season, 103-93, over the Washington Bullets. Chicago began the season 41-3 on their way to a 72-10 mark, surpassing the 69-13 record of the 1971-72 L.A. Lakers.

BIRTHDAYS:

Trooper Washington, 1944; Dave Meyers, 1953; Mark Olberding, 1956; Gary Grant, 1965

TRIVIA:

The 1972-73 Celtics squad holds the dubious distinction of having the most regular season wins, 68, without winning an NBA title. In fact, Boston didn't even make it to the championship round that year, losing to the Knicks in the Eastern Conference Finals.

QUIZ:

Only three current teams have played in, and never lost, an NBA Finals series. Can you name them?

ANSWER: *Chicago Bulls (6-0), San Antonio Spurs (3-0) and Miami Heat (1-0)*

TODAY'S THOUGHT:

I've learned I can't help the team sitting on the bench." *–Wilt Chamberlain*, on why he never fouled out of a game in his 14-year NBA career

HISTORY:

On this date in 1947 the Philadelphia Warriors, led by 34 points from Jumpin' Joe Fulks, beat the Chicago Stags, 83-80, in Game 5 to win the first ever NBA championship. At that time, the league was known as the Basketball Association of America.

BIRTHDAYS:

Spencer Haywood, 1949; Phil Smith, 1952; Dennis Hopson, 1965; Bimbo Coles, 1968

TRIVIA:

After averaging two fouls per game in the regular season, Philadelphia big man Art Hillhouse made basketball history by earning five disqualifications against Chicago, fouling out of every game of the Finals.

QUIZ:

What player has committed the most turnovers in NBA playoff history?

ANSWER: *Magic Johnson, with 696*

TODAY'S THOUGHT:

 "He showed a big man was not just a freak, not just some big guy who could hardly walk and chew gum at the same time.**"**
–*Wilt Chamberlain*, on George Mikan

HISTORY:

On this date in 1950 and 1969 two Lakers put on classic NBA Finals performances. In 1950, George Mikan scored 40 points in a 110-95 title-clinching win over the Nationals. 19 years later, Jerry West put up 53 points against Boston in a 120-118 Game 1 victory.

BIRTHDAYS:

Gail Goodrich, 1943; John Bagley, 1960

TRIVIA:

Although the Celtics beat the Lakers in seven games to win the '69 NBA championship, Jerry West was named the Finals MVP, the only player from the losing team to win the award. West had 42 points, 13 rebounds, and 12 assists in the deciding game.

QUIZ:

In 2005, Jerry West's #44 became the first basketball number to be retired by what college?

ANSWER: *West Virginia University*

The Basketball Almanac

TODAY'S THOUGHT:

"**W**ho is Ben Franklin? I sure do see his name a lot around here." *–Marko Milic*, Philadelphia 76ers draft pick

HISTORY:

On this date in 1967 the Philadelphia 76ers, led by Wilt Chamberlain's 24 points and 23 boards, beat the San Francisco Warriors 125-122 to capture the NBA title in six games. It was the only year in the 1960's that the Boston Celtics did not win the championship.

BIRTHDAYS:

Ernie Grunfeld, 1955; Dino Radja, 1967; Eric Snow, 1973

TRIVIA:

Fans voted the 1967 championship 76ers squad, with Wilt Chamberlain, Billy Cunningham, and Hal Greer, as the greatest team in league history during the NBA's 35th anniversary celebration in 1980. That team won 68 regular season games, a record at the time.

QUIZ:

Who is the all-time leading rebounder in the history of the 76ers/Nationals franchise?

ANSWER: Dolph Schayes, with 11,256 boards from 1949-64

TODAY'S THOUGHT:

 "**E**verybody loves Rex. They'll probably rename (the Wildcats) the Rexians." *—Tony Delk*, on fellow Kentucky alum Rex Chapman

HISTORY:

On this date in 1997 Suns guard Rex Chapman set a single-game NBA playoff record, hitting nine three-pointers in a 106-101 win over Seattle. Chapman ended up with a career-high 42 points.

BIRTHDAYS:

Meadowlark Lemon, 1935; Dave Corzine, 1956; Tim Duncan, 1976; Khalid El-Amin, 1979

TRIVIA:

Al McCoy, "The Voice of the Suns," has been uttering his famous catch-phrase "Shazam!" after every three-point basket for over 30 years. McCoy began doing radio broadcasts for Phoenix in 1972, and did not miss a single game until the end of 2005.

QUIZ:

Marvin Philip Aufrichtig was born on June 12, 1941 in Brooklyn, N.Y. You know him better by what name?

ANSWER: *Marv Albert*

TODAY'S THOUGHT:

"**I**t was so small we didn't have a village idiot. My brother and I had to take turns." *–Dick Motta*, on his hometown of Union, Utah

HISTORY:

On this date in 1965 a pair of twins from Indiana made basketball history. With the 13th pick in the NBA Draft, the Knicks selected Dick Van Arsdale. With the very next selection, the Pistons took his twin brother, Tom. The Van Arsdales would eventually play together with Phoenix in 1977, their final season in the NBA.

BIRTHDAYS:

Harry Gallatin, 1927; Bob Boozer, 1937

TRIVIA:

All good things must come in twos, because exactly eight years later, in 1973, John Wooden became the first man to be enshrined in the Basketball Hall of Fame for a second time. He'd made the Hall in 1961 as a player with Purdue, but this time, it was for his tremendous coaching career at UCLA.

QUIZ:

Name the only two other men in the Basketball Hall of Fame to be inducted as both a player and a coach.

ANSWER: *Lenny Wilkens (1989 as a player and 1998 as a coach) and Bill Sharman (1976 as a player and 2004 as a coach)*

TODAY'S THOUGHT:

 hat makes sense. Isn't he part of the Lakers' supporting cast?" *–Lisa Dillman* of *The Los Angeles Times*, after L.A. guard Derek Fisher commissioned Victoria's Secret to make him a designer bra in team colors to auction off for charity

HISTORY:

On this date in 1960 the NBA approved owner Bob Short's bid to move his Minneapolis Lakers to Los Angeles, becoming the league's first west coast team. The move came just two years after the L.A. Dodgers and San Francisco Giants brought Major League Baseball to California.

BIRTHDAY:

George Gervin, 1952

TRIVIA:

Former Lakers owner Jack Kent Cooke disliked the term "purple", even though he liked the actual color. So, under his ownership, the colors he had chosen for his team were referred to as "Forum blue" and gold, as the Lakers played their home games at the Los Angeles Forum.

QUIZ:

Who coached the Lakers to their last NBA championship in Minneapolis in 1954?

ANSWER: *John Kundla*

TODAY'S THOUGHT:

"**S**how me a good loser and I'll show you a loser." *–Red Auerbach*

HISTORY:

On this date in 1966 Red Auerbach ended his coaching career on a high note as the Boston Celtics won their eighth straight NBA title, beating the Los Angeles Lakers, 95-93, in Game 7.

BIRTHDAYS:

Flynn Robinson, 1941; Josh Howard, 1980; Chris Kaman, 1982

TRIVIA:

Before the start of Game 3 of the 1957 NBA Finals, a sold-out crowd saw Red Auerbach punch Hawks owner Ben Kerner in a dispute over the height of one of the baskets. Kerner suffered a bloody nose, Auerbach was fined $300, and St. Louis ended up beating Boston, 100-98.

QUIZ:

What colorful character and former Celtic was nicknamed "Cornbread"?

ANSWER: *Cedric Maxwell*

TODAY'S THOUGHT:

"**I** thought in overtime you got another foul." –76ers coach *John Lucas*, trying to send Shawn Bradley, who had fouled out in the fourth quarter, into an overtime game

HISTORY:

On this date in 1970 Jerry West, the Lakers' "Mr. Clutch," sank a 60-foot desperation shot at the buzzer to send Game 3 of the Finals against the Knicks into overtime. New York, however, would bounce back to win, 111-108, and take the title in seven games.

BIRTHDAYS:

Jason Hart, 1978; David Lee, 1983

TRIVIA:

Unfortunately for the Lakers, West's shot counted as only two points since the NBA would not adopt the three-point rule until 1979. The ABA, however, had used it as a marketing tool since 1967 to compete with its well-established rival.

QUIZ:

Playing by the Rules: From out-of-bounds, Los Angeles Laker Kobe Bryant's throw-in is lobbed above the basket cylinder and swatted away by Tim Duncan of the Spurs. Is this legal?

ANSWER: *Yes*

The Basketball Almanac

TODAY'S THOUGHT:

"**I** like to think an athlete is an athlete." *–Oscar Robertson*

HISTORY:

On this date in 1971 the Milwaukee Bucks won their first NBA title. Led by Oscar Robertson's 30 points and Lew Alcindor's 27, the Bucks completed a four-game sweep over the Baltimore Bullets with a 118-106 victory.

BIRTHDAYS:

Isiah Thomas, 1961; Quinton Ross, 1981

TRIVIA:

The Bucks made sports history by winning the championship in just their third season. Milwaukee finished the year at 66-16, losing only two games in the postseason. They were nearly as impressive the previous year, going 56-26 and reaching the second round of the playoffs.

QUIZ:

Oscar Robertson, who had his #1 retired by the Bucks and #14 by the Kings (formerly the Royals), is one of only two players to have two different numbers retired by teams. Can you name the other?

ANSWER: *Julius Erving, whose #6 is retired by the 76ers and #32 by the Nets*

TODAY'S THOUGHT:

 We're the only team in history that could lose nine games in a row and then go into a slump." *–Bill Fitch*, in his first season of coaching the Cleveland Cavaliers

HISTORY:

On this date in 1988 Michael Jordan became the first player to score 50 or more points in two straight postseason games. Jordan followed a 50-point effort against Cleveland with 55 points in a 106-101 Game 2 first-round win over the Cavs.

BIRTHDAYS:

Frankie Brian, 1923; George Lehmann 1942; Billy Owens, 1969; Austin Croshere, 1975

TRIVIA:

Since joining the league in 1970, the Cleveland Cavaliers have yet to make it to the NBA Finals. In just their sixth year, they reached the Eastern Conference Finals, but lost to the Celtics. In 1992, their only other trip, they were defeated by the Bulls.

QUIZ:

Michael Jordan has scored the most points in NBA playoff history, with 5,987. What big man is second?

ANSWER: *Kareem Abdul-Jabbar, with 5,762*

TODAY'S THOUGHT:

 "**R**esearchers have found that having sex can harm your eyesight. Finally, we know why Wilt Chamberlain was such a terrible free-throw shooter. He couldn't see the rim."
–Comedy writer *Jerry Perisho*

HISTORY:

On this date in 1935 in an AAU-sponsored foul shooting contest, Bunny Levitt shot the lights out, making 499 in a row before his first miss. The contest ended when a player missed two shots, so Bunny made 372 more. His streak ended at 3 a.m. when the janitors turned the gym lights off.

BIRTHDAYS:

Nate Williams, 1950; Jamaal Wilkes, 1953; Roy Hinson, 1961; Brian Cardinal, 1977; Melvin Ely, 1978; Troy Murphy, 1980; Thabo Sefolosha, 1984

TRIVIA:

In 1990, the Nets' Chris Dudley, a career 45.8% shooter from the foul line, set a mark for futility. Dudley bricked 17 of 18 free throws in a single game against the Pacers, including 13 straight misses and an air ball.

QUIZ:

What NBA sharpshooter retired as the all-time leader in free-throw percentage, at 90.4%?

ANSWER: *Mark Price*

TODAY'S THOUGHT:

"**I** was really going to retire, but Mr. Visa and Mr. American Express told me I better stick around another year." *–Joe Kleine*, on why he returned for a final season

HISTORY:

On this date in 1987 Julius Erving's career came to an end when the 76ers were defeated, 102-89, in Game 5 of a playoff series against the Bucks. Dr. J, who announced his retirement at the beginning of the season, finished his last game with 24 points.

BIRTHDAYS:

Gar Heard, 1948; Toby Knight, 1955; Kelvin Ransey, 1958; Jeff Hornacek, 1963; Tyronn Lue, 1977

TRIVIA:

In addition to retired numbers hanging in the rafters, the 76ers have a banner with a microphone on it to honor public address announcer, Dave Zinkoff. Zinkoff was a Philadelphia institution, beginning with the Warriors in 1946 and working for the Sixers until his death in 1985.

QUIZ:

He was an ABA MVP and won NBA titles with the 76ers as both a player and head coach. Name him.

ANSWER: *Billy Cunningham*

TODAY'S THOUGHT:

"**N**obody's as stupid as me. Nobody's going to invest in this team." *–Donald Sterling*, Clippers' owner, on potential investors

HISTORY:

On this date in 1968 the Pittsburgh Pipers won the first ABA title, beating the New Orleans Buccaneers, 122-113, in Game 7 of the Finals. That would be the last winning season for the franchise, which folded in 1972.

BIRTHDAYS:

Reggie Harding, 1942; Butch Beard, 1947; John Hummer, 1948; Dawn Staley, 1970

TRIVIA:

The Oakland Oaks, a charter member of the original American Basketball Association, were owned, in part, by singer Pat Boone.

QUIZ:

What NBA team is owned by a United States Senator?

ANSWER: *The Milwaukee Bucks, owned by Herb Kohl*

TODAY'S THOUGHT:

 "**C**oach Red Auerbach makes mistakes, the entire Boston Celtics team makes mistakes, but they can get away with it because they have the world's largest eraser in center Bill Russell." *–Pepper Wilson*

HISTORY:

On this date in 1969 future Hall of Famers Bill Russell and Sam Jones ended their Celtic playing careers with a 108-106, Game 7 win over the L.A. Lakers in the NBA Finals. It was Boston's 11th title in 13 years.

BIRTHDAYS:

Herm Gilliam, 1946; LaPhonso Ellis, 1970; Harold Miner, 1971; DerMarr Johnson, 1980; P.J. Tucker, 1985

TRIVIA:

Drafted by the Celtics with the eighth pick in 1957, Sam Jones was so sure he wasn't going to make the team that he made plans to become a high school teacher. When the school refused to offer him a $500 salary increase, he decided to go back to basketball.

QUIZ:

Who was the last Boston Celtic to win a single-season scoring title?

ANSWER: *Trick question... No Boston Celtic has ever led the league in scoring.*

TODAY'S THOUGHT:

"**I** remember draft night, I shook David Stern's hand while rocking a red suit with white pinstripes and red gators ... I've always been a trendsetter." *–Jalen Rose*

HISTORY:

On this date in 2000 Reggie Miller and Jalen Rose each scored 40 points to lead the Pacers to a 108-91 win over the 76ers in Game 1 of the Eastern Conference Semifinals. The duo became just the fourth pair of teammates in NBA history to score 40 in the same playoff game.

BIRTHDAYS:

Tom Abernethy, 1954; Chris Paul, 1985

TRIVIA:

The Pacers, who went on to lose to the Lakers in the 2000 Finals, have yet to win an NBA title. In their ABA days, however, they were more successful than any other club, winning three championships in the league's nine-year existence.

QUIZ:

In 2002, Jalen Rose was sent from the Pacers to the Bulls in a trade for two players who would later become teammates on the Sacramento Kings. Name them.

ANSWER: *Ron Artest and Brad Miller*

TODAY'S THOUGHT:

"That play was, 'Give the ball to Michael and everybody else get the #%!#!% out of the way.'" –*Doug Collins*, coach, on Michael Jordan's buzzer-beater against Cleveland

HISTORY:

On this date in 1994 the eighth-seeded Nuggets shocked the top-seeded Sonics with a 98-94 OT win in Game 5 of the first round. By eliminating Seattle from the playoffs, Denver, which had 21 fewer regular-season wins, became the first #8 seed to beat a #1.

BIRTHDAYS:

Louis Orr, 1958; Tony Campbell, 1962; Calvin Booth, 1976; Shawn Marion, 1978; Yaroslav Korolev, 1987

TRIVIA:

In an equally dramatic Game 5 exactly five years earlier, Michael Jordan's hanging foul-line jumper over Cleveland's Craig Ehlo at the buzzer lifted the Bulls over the Cavs, 101-100, and into the second round.

QUIZ:

In 1999, what #8 seed became the second in NBA history to knock off a #1 in the first round?

ANSWER: *The New York Knicks, who defeated the Miami Heat*

TODAY'S THOUGHT:

 hen Willis came out onto the court, it was like the place exploded. Chills were going up and down everyone's spines." –Knicks forward *Bill Bradley*, on Willis Reed's dramatic entrance for Game 7

HISTORY:

On this date in 1970 the New York Knicks won their first NBA title by defeating the Lakers, 113-99, in Game 7 of the Finals. New York was led by guard Walt Frazier, with 36 points and 19 assists, and an effective defense.

BIRTHDAYS:

Mike D'Antoni, 1951; Speedy Claxton, 1978; Keyon Dooling, 1980

TRIVIA:

Before the game, Willis Reed received pain-killing injections for his leg. His only points were the team's first two baskets, but with that momentum, the Knicks never looked back. Reed won the Finals MVP Award despite only four points and three rebounds in the contest.

QUIZ:

With what team did Walt Frazier finish his career?

ANSWER: *The Cleveland Cavaliers*

TODAY'S THOUGHT:

"We don't know where the cutoff is...Maybe if you earn less than $8 million, you'll get a scholarship from the commissioner." *–David Stern*, in response to Marcus Camby's request for a clothing stipend because of the NBA's new dress code

HISTORY:

On this date in 2000 the NBA named Stu Jackson, former general manager of the Vancouver Grizzlies, the Senior Vice President of Basketball Operations. Jackson currently holds one of the highest-ranking African-American positions in U.S. pro sports.

BIRTHDAYS:

Howard Komives, 1941; Calvin Murphy, 1948; Elmore Smith, 1949; Lloyd Batts, 1951; Doug Christie, 1970

TRIVIA:

On the Vancouver Grizzlies' original franchise application to the NBA, the team name was listed as the Mounties. However, the government of Canada took exception to it, claiming the name was trademarked, and forced the team to change it.

QUIZ:

In the summer of 2006, who resigned as the Deputy Commissioner of the NBA after serving in the league office for 30 years?

ANSWER: *Russ Granik*

TODAY'S THOUGHT:

"**I** think the team that wins Game 5 will win the series. Unless we lose Game 5." *–Charles Barkley*

HISTORY:

On this date in 1987 Golden State's Sleepy Floyd set two NBA playoff records, scoring 29 points in the fourth quarter and 39 points in the second half, as the Warriors beat the Lakers in Game 4 of the conference semifinals. Floyd finished with 51 points.

BIRTHDAYS:

Jim Calhoun, 1942; Danny Schayes, 1959; Rony Seikaly, 1965; Jerome Williams, 1973; Nykesha Sales, 1976; Samuel Dalembert, 1981

TRIVIA:

The Suns' Charles Barkley nearly matched Floyd's scoring feats during a 1994 playoff game, ironically against the Warriors. In the Suns' series clincher, Barkley scored 27 points in one quarter and 38 in the half on his way to a career high 56.

QUIZ:

Eric "Sleepy" Floyd began and ended his NBA career with the same team. Name it.

ANSWER: The New Jersey Nets - He played a total of 91 games with the team.

TODAY'S THOUGHT:

"**I** thought, 'What should we do? Should we take the ball out, or should we ask him to do it again?'" –*Magic Johnson*, on Julius Erving's reverse layup during the 1980 NBA Finals

HISTORY:

On this date in 1980 the Philadelphia 76ers defeated Los Angeles, 105-102, in Game 4 of the NBA Finals. But the game itself was upstaged by an acrobatic move of the 76ers' Julius Erving. Dr. J drove baseline and elevated, floating behind the backboard to the other side of the basket before dropping the ball in for two points, much to the dismay of Lakers' center Kareem Abdul-Jabbar.

BIRTHDAYS:

Jack Twyman, 1934; Lauren Jackson, 1981

TRIVIA:

The 76ers are the NBA's oldest franchise. They began play in 1939 as the Syracuse Nationals, an independent professional team. They joined the NBA in 1949 before moving to Philadelphia in 1963 and changing the team name to "76ers".

QUIZ:

Who is the only Philadelphia 76er to lead the NBA in blocks per game in a season?

ANSWER: *Theo Ratliff, in 2001, with 3.74 rejections per contest*

TODAY'S THOUGHT:

"If you don't get lucky, you just sit there looking like a big dork."
–Don Nelson, on the NBA's televised Draft Lottery

HISTORY:

On this date in 1985 the New York Knicks, who finished the season with the league's third-worst record, won the NBA's first Draft Lottery. The Knicks would select Georgetown center Patrick Ewing with the first pick in the June draft.

BIRTHDAYS:

George Karl, 1951; Kevin Grevey, 1953; Keith Bogans, 1980; Mouhamed Saer Sene, 1986

TRIVIA:

Ewing was named Most Outstanding Player in the 1984 NCAA Final Four even though he failed to score more than 10 points in either the national semifinal or championship game.

QUIZ:

Who was selected second after Ewing in the 1985 NBA Draft?

ANSWER: *The Indiana Pacers selected the University of Oklahoma's Wayman Tisdale.*

TODAY'S THOUGHT:

"The word from the NBA is that I'm too controversial. Because I fought the NBA all the way to the Supreme Court...I'm supposed to be erased out of all history - and I have been erased." *–Spencer Haywood*, who sued to allow underclassmen to turn pro

HISTORY:

On this date in 1976 the New York Nets defeated the Denver Nuggets, 112-106, to win the last American Basketball Association championship. The ABA would soon fold, and the Nets and Nuggets would join the NBA along with San Antonio and Indiana.

BIRTHDAYS:

Bill Gabor, 1922; Dennis Rodman, 1961; Mike Bibby, 1978

TRIVIA:

Spencer Haywood spent one year in the ABA after leaving the University of Detroit at the end of his sophomore season. NBA rules kept college players out of the league until their class graduated. Haywood sued, and won, opening the door for underclassmen to be drafted. He then joined the NBA's Sonics in 1970.

QUIZ:

What two cities entered the NBA with Cleveland for the 1970-'71 season?

ANSWER: *Portland and Buffalo*

TODAY'S THOUGHT:

"**A**mbition is the path to success. Persistence is the vehicle you arrive in." *–Bill Bradley*

HISTORY:

On this date in 2003 the NBA lost one of its 50 Greatest Players when former Knick and Piston Dave DeBusschere died at age 62. The eight-time All-Star and six-time All-Defensive first team member averaged 16 points and 11 rebounds over his twelve-year NBA career.

BIRTHDAYS:

Walter Berry, 1964; Pooh Richardson, 1966; Voshon Lenard, 1973; Eddie House, 1978

TRIVIA:

DeBusschere was named player-coach for the Detroit Pistons at age 24, making him the youngest coach in league history. Prior to his NBA career, he spent two seasons in Major League Baseball as a pitcher for the Chicago White Sox.

QUIZ:

DeBusschere wore the same number with basketball's Knicks and baseball's White Sox. What was it?

ANSWER: *22 - His basketball uniform number was retired.*

TODAY'S THOUGHT:

"Iverson goes by the nickname 'The Answer,' so the question must be: 'Will the defendant please rise?'" *–Steve Rosenbloom*, after Allen Iverson was charged with drug and firearm possession

HISTORY:

On this date in 2001 Philadelphia 76ers guard Allen Iverson became both the shortest and lightest player in NBA history to win the Most Valuable Player Award. The six-foot, 165-pound Iverson topped the league in scoring that year and led his team to the NBA Finals.

BIRTHDAYS:

Don Nelson, 1940; Freeman Williams, 1956; Gene Banks, 1959

TRIVIA:

Wes Unseld, in 1969, and Bill Russell, in 1965, are the only two players to win the MVP Award while averaging less than 15 points per game. Both players made their mark on the glass, Unseld grabbing 18.2 rebounds per game and Russell averaging 24.1.

QUIZ:

Who won more MVP Awards, Julius Erving or Moses Malone?

ANSWER: *Malone – Moses won it three times, Erving only once*

The Basketball Almanac

TODAY'S THOUGHT:

"**G**iving Magic the basketball is like giving Hitler an army, Jesse James a gang, or Genghis Khan a horse. Devastation. Havoc."
–*Jim Murray, The Los Angeles Times*

HISTORY:

On this date in 1980 Magic Johnson scored 42 points and grabbed 15 rebounds, leading the Lakers to a 123-107 win over Philadelphia to clinch the NBA title. The rookie wreaked his havoc from the center position, filling in for the injured Kareem Abdul-Jabbar.

BIRTHDAY:

John Salley, 1964; Quincy Douby, 1984

TRIVIA:

In Game 6, Johnson made all 14 of his free throw attempts and scored the most points by a rookie in a single Finals contest. He, of course, was named MVP of the series.

QUIZ:

What Laker recorded his only career triple-double in Game 7 of the 1988 NBA Finals?

ANSWER: Finals MVP James Worthy had 36 points, 16 rebounds and 10 assists in the victory over Detroit.

TODAY'S THOUGHT:

"**A** team should be an extension of the coach's personality. My teams were arrogant and obnoxious." *–Al McGuire*

HISTORY:

On this date in 1993 New York's Pat Riley was named the NBA Coach of the Year in the closest balloting ever, edging Houston's Rudy Tomjanovich by a single vote. Riley's team won 60 games in the regular season, but lost to the Bulls in the Eastern Conference Finals.

BIRTHDAYS:

John Koncak, 1963; Danny Manning, 1966; Hubert Davis, 1970; Tony Parker, 1982; Channing Frye, 1983

TRIVIA:

Riley, who played both football and basketball at Kentucky, was drafted as a flanker by the Dallas Cowboys in the 11th round of the 1967 NFL Draft. He would later be taken by the San Diego Rockets in the first round of the NBA Draft.

QUIZ:

Who coached the Knicks for 59 games after Pat Riley resigned, but before Jeff Van Gundy was hired in 1996?

ANSWER: Don Nelson

TODAY'S THOUGHT:

"**I** knew I was dog meat. Luckily, I'm the high-priced dog meat that everybody wants. I'm the good-quality dog meat. I'm the Alpo of the NBA." *–Shaquille O'Neal*

HISTORY:

On this date in 1987 the Lakers' Magic Johnson won the first of his three MVP Awards, ending a 23-year run in which no guard received the honor. Johnson and Michael Jordan would combine to win the award for the next six seasons.

BIRTHDAYS:

Sam Vincent, 1963; Donyell Marshall, 1973; Ron Mercer, 1976; Reggie Evans, 1980

TRIVIA:

In 2000, the Lakers' Shaquille O'Neal won the MVP Award with the highest percentage of first-place votes in league history. O'Neal received all but one of the 121 possible votes. Allen Iverson was at the top of that other ballot.

QUIZ:

Who is the only other guard besides Johnson and Jordan to win back-to-back MVP Awards?

ANSWER: *Steve Nash, in 2005 and 2006*

TODAY'S THOUGHT:

"**I** saw a quarter, a nickel, and a dime. I could have made forty cents, but it probably would have been an NCAA violation." –UCLA basketball player *Jason Kapono*, after Arizona State fans threw coins on the court doing a loss

HISTORY:

On this date in 1989 the NCAA placed the Kentucky basketball program on probation for three years for numerous recruiting and academic violations. The Wildcats were banned from postseason competition for two seasons and from television appearances for one.

BIRTHDAYS:

Dolph Schayes, 1928; Bill Laimbeer, 1957; Kevin Garnett, 1976; Brian Skinner, 1976

TRIVIA:

Up until 1973, NCAA bylaws stated that incoming freshmen were not allowed to play varsity basketball during their first year in school. The rule was intended to eliminate the pressure to perform and ease their transition to college life.

QUIZ:

Playing by the Rules: During a time-out, Duke coach Mike Krzyzewski leaves the coaching box to confer with the scorekeeper. Is this allowed?

ANSWER: *Yes*

The Basketball Almanac

TODAY'S THOUGHT:

"**I** have one thing to say to those non-believers. ... Don't ever underestimate the heart of a champion." *–Rudy Tomjanovich*, after his Rockets won the 1995 NBA Finals

HISTORY:

On this date in 1995 Mario Elie's three-point shot propelled the Rockets past the Suns, 115-114, and into the Western Conference Finals. Houston became the first team in 13 years to overcome a three games to one deficit in a best-of-seven series.

BIRTHDAYS:

Bill Willoughby, 1957; Terrell Brandon, 1970

TRIVIA:

The 1994-95 Rockets were the first team to defeat four postseason opponents who had 50 or more regular season wins. Houston, which won 47 regular season games, beat Utah, Phoenix, San Antonio, and Orlando to win the NBA title.

QUIZ:

The University of Houston basketball team that featured future NBA stars Hakeem Olajuwon and Clyde Drexler was nicknamed what?

ANSWER: *Phi Slamma Jamma*

TODAY'S THOUGHT:

 "**T**om." –Former Rockets coach *Tom Nissalke*, when asked how he pronounced his name

HISTORY:

On this date in 1986 Houston's Ralph Sampson caught an inbounds pass with one second left and hit a turnaround jumper to stun the Lakers, 114-112, in Game 5 of the Western Conference Finals. That loss kept the Lakers out of the NBA Finals for the only time between 1982 and 1989.

BIRTHDAYS:

Gene Keady, 1936; James Bailey, 1957; Jamaal Magloire, 1978; Zarko Cabarkapa, 1981

TRIVIA:

The Rockets, who at one time played in San Diego, were originally named for the area's motto, "A City in Motion." When the team moved to Houston, home of the NASA Space Center, the nickname fit even better.

QUIZ:

How many team nicknames do not end in the letter "s"?

ANSWER: *Three - Miami Heat, Orlando Magic, and Utah Jazz*

TODAY'S THOUGHT:

"We're shooting 100 percent - 60 percent from the field and 40 percent from the free-throw line."** *—Norm Stewart*, Missouri coach

HISTORY:

On this date in 1975 the Kentucky Colonels won their one and only ABA championship, defeating the Indiana Pacers, 110-105, and winning the series, four games to one. The Colonels' Artis Gilmore scored 28 points and pulled down 31 rebounds.

BIRTHDAYS:

Larry Siegfried, 1939; Roger Brown, 1942; Donald Royal, 1966; Randy Brown, 1968

TRIVIA:

Artis Gilmore remains the only player to average more than 22 points and 22 rebounds in his college career, and is the all-time leader in field goal percentage in both the NBA and ABA. The Jacksonville center was selected by the Bulls in the seventh round of the 1971 NBA Draft, but chose to sign with Kentucky.

QUIZ:

Who won the ABA's first scoring title?

ANSWER: *Connie Hawkins, who averaged 26.8 points per game in 1968 with the Pittsburgh Pipers*

TODAY'S THOUGHT:

"**T**he way my team is doing, we could get Wilt Chamberlain in a trade and find out that he's really two midgets Scotch-taped together." *–Gene Shue*, former NBA coach

HISTORY:

On this date in 1958 University of Kansas All-American Wilt Chamberlain announced his decision to give up his senior year of eligibility to join the Harlem Globetrotters. Chamberlain would barnstorm with the 'Trotters for one year before joining the Philadelphia Warriors in 1959.

BIRTHDAYS:

Jack Coleman, 1924; Rod Thorn, 1941; Rasual Butler, 1979

TRIVIA:

In 1955, the NBA created a "territorial" draft rule to enable a team to claim a local player in exchange for its first-round pick. The Philadelphia Warriors took Chamberlain, arguing that he had grown up and played high school ball in their city. Since there was no NBA team in Kansas, the league allowed their choice.

QUIZ:

A Philadelphia center not named Wilt was the first Warrior to lead the NBA in scoring and rebounding in the same season. Who was it?

ANSWER: *Neil Johnston (22.7 ppg and 15.1 rpg) did it during the 1954-55 season.*

The Basketball Almanac

TODAY'S THOUGHT:

If all I'm remembered for is being a good basketball player, then I've done a bad job with the rest of my life." *–Isiah Thomas*

HISTORY:

On this date in 1999 Chuck Daly resigned as the head coach of the Orlando Magic, ending his 14-year coaching career. Exactly one year later, Isiah Thomas, who played on Daly's two championship Pistons teams in 1989 and '90, was elected to the Hall of Fame.

BIRTHDAYS:

Jim Eakins, 1946; Mitch Kupchak, 1954; Joe Dumars, 1963; Tracy McGrady, 1979

TRIVIA:

Detroit's title in 1989 was its first in 41 years in the league, the longest drought suffered by a team. Originally based in Fort Wayne (IN), the Pistons reached the Finals twice in the '50's without winning.

QUIZ:

After his playing career, Isiah Thomas has held positions with what three NBA teams?

ANSWER: Raptors (part owner, executive VP), Pacers (head coach), and Knicks (President of Basketball Operations, head coach)

TODAY'S THOUGHT:

"It's not that they're the Big Bad Wolf and we're the Three Little Pigs." *–LeBron James*, comparing his Cleveland Cavaliers to the Detroit Pistons during the 2006 NBA Playoffs

HISTORY:

On this date in 1975 Butch Beard scored the final seven points of the game as the Warriors swept the Washington Bullets in the Finals, 96-95. Golden State's Rick Barry was named MVP in only the third sweep in NBA Finals history.

BIRTHDAYS:

Bill Sharman, 1926; K.C. Jones, 1932; Kendall Gill, 1968

TRIVIA:

The Baltimore Bullets shocked everyone when they made it to the 1971 NBA Finals with a regular season mark of 42-40. Their first two playoff series went seven games, before they were swept in four by Milwaukee in the title round.

QUIZ:

In 1982, what unknown college basketball team upset top-ranked Virginia in the Maui Invitational?

ANSWER: *The Division II Chaminade Silverswords defeated Ralph Sampson and the Cavaliers, 77-72.*

TODAY'S THOUGHT:

"**I** 've got a theory that if you give 100 percent all the time, somehow things work out in the end." *–Larry Bird*

HISTORY:

On this date in 1987 the Celtics literally stole Game 5 from the Pistons in the Eastern Conference Finals, 108-107. Boston's Larry Bird intercepted an inbounds pass from Detroit's Isiah Thomas and fed the cutting Dennis Johnson for the winning basket. The Celtics would win the series in seven games, but lose to the Lakers in the Finals.

BIRTHDAYS:

Steve Hawes, 1950; Dan Roundfield, 1953; Willie Burton, 1968; Tom McMillen, 1952; Mehmet Okur, 1979

TRIVIA:

Larry Bird and Dennis Johnson were Celtics teammates from 1983 to '90, and played with the likes of Robert Parish and Kevin McHale. But it's Johnson, the five-time All-Star guard, whom Bird maintains is "the best I've ever played with."

QUIZ:

What 1996 comedy starred Dan Aykroyd and Daniel Stern as obsessed Celtics fans and featured cameos by Bill Walton, Larry Bird, and Bob Cousy?

ANSWER: *Celtic Pride*

TODAY'S THOUGHT:

"**I**t is the second most exciting indoor sport, and the other one shouldn't have spectators." *–Dick Vertleib*, on basketball

HISTORY:

On this date in 1981 Julius Erving, who led his 76ers to a 62-win season, was named the NBA's MVP. He was the first non-center to win the award in 17 years, and the first player to win both the NBA and ABA Most Valuable Player Awards.

BIRTHDAYS:

Dick Schnittker, 1928; Julian Hammond, 1943; Dave Greenwood, 1957; Allan Leavell, 1957; George McCloud, 1967

TRIVIA:

Erving is the father of pro tennis player Alexandra Stevenson. In 1999, Stevenson made her first appearance at Wimbledon and surprised many by advancing to the semifinals, joining Chris Evert and Anna Kournikova as women who got that far in their debuts.

QUIZ:

What NFL team did Grant Hill's father play for?

ANSWER: *Calvin Hill was a Pro Bowl running back for the Dallas Cowboys.*

TODAY'S THOUGHT:

"I once heard that Paul Seymour said as much as winning an NBA championship, he'd like to see the Celtics lose a game after Auerbach brought out the cigar so he could go up to him and stuff the cigar in his face." *–Bob Cousy*

HISTORY:

On this date in 1986 Larry Bird was named the NBA's regular-season Most Valuable Player for the third consecutive year. Bird, who was also the MVP of the Finals that year, joined Bill Russell and Wilt Chamberlain as the only players to win three in a row.

BIRTHDAYS:

Jerry West, 1938; Ben Howland, 1957; Armon Gilliam, 1964; Glen Rice, 1967

TRIVIA:

Bill Russell had a habit of vomiting before virtually every game he played. It became such a routine that, before one game, Boston coach Red Auerbach forbid his team to finish their warm-ups until Russell threw up. When Russell finally came through, the Celtics went on to win.

QUIZ:

Can you name the only man to have been a teammate of both Bill Russell and Larry Bird?

ANSWER: Don Chaney, who played with the Celtics from 1968-75 and again from 1977-80

TODAY'S THOUGHT:

"**T**hey measured me while I was sitting down." *–Manute Bol, 7'7"* center, explaining why his passport listed him at 5'2"

HISTORY:

On this date in 1995 the Pacers' Rik Smits hit the game-winner as Indiana beat Orlando, 94-93, in Game 4 of the Eastern Conference Finals. The lead changed hands four times in the final 14 seconds of the game. The Magic would go on to win the series in seven games.

BIRTHDAYS:

Richie Guerin, 1932; Tate George, 1968; Raef LaFrentz, 1976; Carmelo Anthony, 1984

TRIVIA:

Despite being 7'4", Smits, who is considered one of the Pacers' top players of the '90's, posted career averages of just 1.3 blocks and 6.1 rebounds per game in his 12 years with Indiana.

QUIZ:

Kareem Abdul-Jabbar led the league in blocks four times, tying what other seven-footer for the record?

ANSWER: 7'4", Mark Eaton

TODAY'S THOUGHT:

 hen he's old and in a wheelchair, they're going to roll him out onto the (Madison Square) Garden court and he's still going to hit threes." *–Spike Lee*, on Knick-killer Reggie Miller

HISTORY:

On this date in 1879 the first Madison Square Garden, formerly known as Gilmore's Garden, was officially open to the public at 26th Street and Madison Avenue. The arena was originally built for the sport of track cycling. The Knicks would begin play there in 1946.

BIRTHDAYS:

Billy Donovan, 1965; Rasho Nesterovic, 1976; Eddie Griffin, 1982

TRIVIA:

In arguably his finest Garden moment, Reggie Miller stunned the New York crowd by scoring 8 points in 11 seconds in Game 1 of the 1995 Eastern Conference Semifinals. The Knicks blew a six point lead in under 19 seconds as Miller's two threes and free throws helped the Pacers steal the game.

QUIZ:

How many Madison Square Gardens have there been in New York City?

ANSWER: *Four – The current one is located at 7th Avenue between 31st and 33rd Streets.*

TODAY'S THOUGHT:

"**M**oses Malone used to have them all the time, but we never understood anything he said." *–Jon Koncak*, on Atlanta Hawks team meetings

HISTORY:

On this date in 1983 the Philadelphia 76ers defeated the L.A. Lakers 115-108, to complete a four-game sweep in the NBA Finals. Moses Malone's prediction of three sweeps in the playoffs, "Fo', Fo', Fo'", was just slightly off. The Sixers lost one game en route to their second title.

BIRTHDAYS:

Billy Ray Bates, 1956; Matt Harpring, 1976; Nate Robinson, 1984

TRIVIA:

No NBA team has ever swept every round of the playoffs. The only club other than Philadelphia to surrender just one loss was the 2001 Lakers. L.A. went 15-1 in the postseason, and their lone loss came in Game 1 of the NBA Finals to... the 76ers.

QUIZ:

Moses Malone is second to what player in free throws made in an NBA career?

ANSWER: *Karl Malone*

TODAY'S THOUGHT:

"I told Zollie Volchok we needed an ultrasound machine and he asked me why we needed music in the locker room."
—*Lenny Wilkens*, on the Seattle general manager

HISTORY:

On this date in 1979 Seattle won its fourth straight game, 97-93, after dropping the series opener to Washington in the NBA Finals. The Sonics championship remains the only one, so far, in Seattle professional sports history.

BIRTHDAYS:

Levern Tart, 1942; Smush Parker, 1981

TRIVIA:

When the NBA announced its "50 Greatest Players" in 1996, the only championship club not to have a member represented was that '79 Sonics team. Lenny Wilkens was honored, but he was the coach of Seattle in their title season, not a player.

QUIZ:

What two former Sonics coached Seattle immediately following George Karl's departure in 1998?

ANSWER: *Paul Westphal, who played in 36 games with them in the 1980-81 season, and Nate McMillan*

TODAY'S THOUGHT:

Trust me, it's 360 degrees from where it was." *–Kenyon Martin*, on his improved conditioning and confidence

HISTORY:

On this date in 2000 the New Jersey Nets named Rod Thorn the team's new president and general manager. With the former NBA Executive VP on board, the Nets would go from cellar dwellers to reaching the NBA Finals in 2002 and '03.

BIRTHDAYS:

Al Wood, 1958; Earl Boykins, 1976; Bobby Simmons, 1980

TRIVIA:

Thorn has been in pro basketball for over four decades as a player, coach, general manager and league official. He may be best known as the man who, as the Chicago Bulls' general manager, drafted Michael Jordan.

QUIZ:

The Nets pulled off a rather lopsided deal during the 2001 NBA Draft when they traded what player for Richard Jefferson, Jason Collins, and Brandon Armstrong?

ANSWER: *Eddie Griffin, who was selected seventh overall by New Jersey*

TODAY'S THOUGHT:

I'm often mentioned in the same sentence as Michael Jordan. You know- 'That Scott Hastings, he's no Michael Jordan.'"
–Nuggets center *Scott Hastings*

HISTORY:

On this date in 1992 Michael Jordan lit up the Blazers for six three-pointers and 35 points in the first half as the Bulls defeated Portland, 122-89, in Game 1 of the NBA Finals. Chicago would go on to win the series in six for their second straight title.

BIRTHDAY:

Billy Cunningham, 1943

TRIVIA:

Former Bulls Craig Hodges and Steve Kerr are the only two players in NBA history to lead the league in three-point field-goal percentage more than once. Hodges did it in 1986 and '88, and Kerr in 1990 and '95.

QUIZ:

True or false? Michael Jordan never scored 70 points in an NBA game.

ANSWER: *True - Jordan set career-highs of both points (69) and rebounds (18) against Cleveland in 1990.*

TODAY'S THOUGHT:

"**Y**ou can run a lot of plays when your X is twice as big as the other guys' O. It makes your X's and O's pretty good."
—*Paul Westphal*

HISTORY:

On this date in 1976 the Celtics, led by Jo Jo White's 33 points, defeated the Suns, 128-126, in triple overtime in Game 5 of the NBA Finals. The Celtics would go on to win game six for their 13th NBA championship.

BIRTHDAYS:

Bobby Wanzer, 1921; Xavier McDaniel, 1963; Katie Smith, 1974

TRIVIA:

Down by one point in the second overtime, Phoenix's Paul Westphal, trapped by Boston's defense, called a timeout he knew he didn't have. Although it resulted in a technical foul and gave Boston a two-point lead, it allowed the Suns to make an inbounds pass from midcourt. That led to Gar Heard hitting the buzzer beater that sent the game into a third OT.

QUIZ:

Gar Heard set a Finals record with 61 minutes played in that game. What Sun would surpass that mark in 1993?

ANSWER: *Kevin Johnson, who played 62 minutes in a Game 3 triple overtime win against the Bulls.*

TODAY'S THOUGHT:

If I had caught the shirt, I would have eaten it. Bill's my hero."
—*Maurice Lucas*, after Bill Walton threw his jersey into the crowd when Portland won the NBA title

HISTORY:

On this date in 1977 the Portland Trail Blazers won their first, and only, NBA championship, winning Game 6, 109-107, over Philadelphia. The Trail Blazers were led by Finals MVP Bill Walton, who had 23 rebounds and 8 blocked shots.

BIRTHDAYS:

Zydrunas Ilgauskas, 1975; Kirk Snyder, 1983

TRIVIA:

In 1970, Portland's new NBA franchise held a public "Name the Team" contest. The most popular entry, "Pioneers," was rejected because Portland's Lewis & Clark College was already using the nickname. The team's panel of judges then chose "Trail Blazers."

QUIZ:

Who is the Portland Trail Blazers' all-time leader in rebounds?

ANSWER: *Clyde Drexler - He grabbed 5,339 boards with the team from 1983 to '94.*

TODAY'S THOUGHT:

"Rick Majerus turned down the Golden State Warriors once he learned the team was already over the calorie cap."
–Shaun Powell, The Sporting News

HISTORY:

On this date in 1946 the Basketball Association of America, which would become the NBA three years later, was born. The original charter was signed at the Commodore Hotel in New York, and Maurice Podoloff was declared the league's first president.

BIRTHDAY:

Chuck Williams, 1946

TRIVIA:

The NBA experimented with the salary cap in the 1940's but terminated it after only one year. It was then readmitted in the 1984-85 season to level the playing field. The most a team could spend on its players then was $3.6 million, as compared to roughly $53 million today.

QUIZ:

Of the eleven franchises that began in the BAA, which three still remain in the NBA?

ANSWER: *New York Knicks, Boston Celtics, and Golden State (then Philadelphia) Warriors*

TODAY'S THOUGHT:

"**I**t's too big. Every time I pick my nose it draws too much attention." –*Coach Dick Motta*, on why he doesn't wear his 1977-78 championship ring

HISTORY:

On this date in 1978 Washington's Wes Unseld sank the deciding free throws as the Bullets defeated the Seattle Sonics 105-99, in a rare Game 7 road win in the Finals. The victory gave the franchise its lone NBA championship.

BIRTHDAYS:

Cazzie Russell, 1944; Allen Iverson, 1975

TRIVIA:

Wes Unseld, along with former NBA greats Lenny Wilkens, Walt Bellamy and Quinn Buckner, is a prominent member of Alpha Phi Alpha, the first intercollegiate Greek-letter fraternity established for African-Americans.

QUIZ:

Former Bullets enforcers Rick Mahorn and Jeff Ruland were called what nicknames by former Celtics announcer Johnny Most?

ANSWER: "McFilthy" and "McNasty"

TODAY'S THOUGHT:

"**T**he first thing I would do every morning was look at the box scores to see what Magic did. I didn't care about anything else." *–Larry Bird*

HISTORY:

On this date in 1982 Los Angeles defeated Philadelphia, 114-104, to win the NBA title. Thirteen was the lucky number for Finals MVP Magic Johnson. He posted 13 points, 13 rebounds and 13 assists as L.A. beat the 76ers for the second time in three years in the championship round.

BIRTHDAYS:

Anthony Bonner, 1968; Bryant Reeves, 1973

TRIVIA:

Another title-clinching triple-double was posted exactly four years later when Larry Bird's 29 points, 12 assists and 11 rebounds led Boston to a 114-97 win over Houston in Game 6 to wrap up the Celtics' 16th NBA championship.

QUIZ:

True or false? Magic Johnson and Larry Bird were not drafted in the same year.

ANSWER: *True. Bird was drafted number six in 1978, the year before he played as a fifth-year senior against Magic in the NCAA Championship. Johnson was drafted number one overall in 1979.*

TODAY'S THOUGHT:

"**I** learned to give him the ball." *–Magic Johnson*, on what he learned about basketball playing with Kareem Abdul-Jabbar

HISTORY:

On this date in 1985 Kareem Abdul-Jabbar became the oldest player to win the NBA Finals MVP Award. The 38-year old center led the Lakers past the Celtics in six games. The teams would meet in the Finals for the last time in the 20th century in 1987, with L.A. again besting Boston in six games.

BIRTHDAYS:

Billy Knight, 1952; Wayman Tisdale, 1964; Udonis Haslem, 1980; Sebastian Telfair, 1985

TRIVIA:

The Lakers are the only franchise to post both double-digit wins and losses in the NBA Finals. After being defeated by the Detroit Pistons in 2004, Los Angeles evened its championship round record to 14-14.

QUIZ:

Only two players under the age of 24 have won the NBA Finals MVP Award. Magic Johnson is one. Name the other.

ANSWER: *The Spurs' Tim Duncan in 1999, at 23 years and 2 months old*

TODAY'S THOUGHT:

 alk about making a late-season push." *–Elliot Harris* of *The Chicago Sun-Times*, after Arizona State women's basketball coach Charli Turner Thorne delivered a baby shortly after her team received an NCAA tournament berth

HISTORY:

On this date in 1977 the New Orleans Jazz selected Lucy Harris, a three-time All-American at Delta State, in the seventh round of the NBA Draft. Harris, who would never play a game in the league, is the only woman ever drafted by an NBA team.

BIRTHDAYS:

Jon McGlocklin, 1943; John Gianelli, 1950; Jay Vincent, 1959; Jake Tsakalidis, 1979

TRIVIA:

Nine years later to the day, Nancy Lieberman became the first woman to play in a men's pro league, joining the United States Basketball League's Springfield Fame. In her first game, the Fame defeated Staten Island, 122-107.

QUIZ:

What former female hoops star was married to Dodgers Hall of Fame pitcher Don Drysdale?

ANSWER: Ann Meyers

TODAY'S THOUGHT:

"**I** think this is the best game we played all year." *–Larry Johnson*, after a Knicks' season-opening win

HISTORY:

On this date in 1999 the Knicks defeated the Indiana Pacers, 90-82, in a series-clinching Game 6 of the Eastern Conference Finals. New York became the first eight-seed in history to advance to the NBA Finals, where they would lose to the Spurs in five games.

BIRTHDAYS:

Joey and Stephen Graham, 1982; Diana Taurasi, 1982

TRIVIA:

New York's Larry Johnson was widely criticized during the 1999 NBA Finals for describing his Knicks team as a band of "rebellious slaves." When asked about Spurs point guard Avery Johnson, he said, "That's my man, Ave, because we're from the same plantation. We've both got the Johnson name."

QUIZ:

True or false? The largest crowd in NBA Finals history occurred in 1999 for Game 1 at San Antonio's Alamodome.

ANSWER: *False- The crowd of 39,514 fans was second to the turnout of 41,732 at Detroit's Pontiac Silverdome, when the Pistons beat the Lakers in Game 5 of the 1988 NBA Finals.*

TODAY'S THOUGHT:

 "**P**hil is obviously a good coach. You don't win that many games without being a damn good coach... Remember one thing: He's been very fortunate. He picks his spots. That's all I can say." *–Red Auerbach*, on Phil Jackson

HISTORY:

On this date in 2002 the Lakers won their third consecutive title, completing a sweep of the New Jersey Nets with a 113-107 win. The victory gave Phil Jackson his ninth championship as a head coach, matching the legendary Red Auerbach.

BIRTHDAYS:

Rory Sparrow, 1958; Lee Mayberry, 1970; Jason Caffey, 1973; Kerry Kittles, 1974; Antawn Jamison, 1976; Earl Watson, 1979; Sergio Rodriguez, 1986

TRIVIA:

Phil Jackson's first NBA championship as a head coach came exactly 11 years earlier, ironically, against the Lakers. His Chicago Bulls beat Los Angeles in five games.

QUIZ:

What man's two NBA Coach of the Year Awards were separated by 26 years?

ANSWER: *Hubie Brown, in 1978 with the Hawks, and in 2004 with the Grizzlies*

TODAY'S THOUGHT:

 "Any time Detroit scores more than 100 points and holds the other team below 100 points, they almost always win."
—Former Pistons coach *Doug Collins*

HISTORY:

On this date in 1989 the Detroit Pistons won their first NBA championship, finishing off a sweep of the Lakers with a 105-97 win. The game also marked the end of center Kareem Abdul-Jabbar's illustrious 20-year career.

BIRTHDAYS:

Sarunas Marciulionis, 1964; Linton Johnson, 1980; Steve Novak, 1984

TRIVIA:

In 1988, Detroit's Isiah Thomas scored a Finals record 25 points in the third quarter of Game 6 while playing on a severely sprained ankle. The Pistons, up 3-2 in the series, lost the game by a point. Los Angeles went on to win the seventh game and the title.

QUIZ:

What "Bad Boy" is the Pistons all-time leader in rebounds?

ANSWER: *Bill Laimbeer, with 9,430 boards in his 13 seasons with Detroit*

TODAY'S THOUGHT:

 "The mailman doesn't deliver on Sundays." *–Scottie Pippen*, to Karl Malone, who was at the foul line in the final seconds of a tied Game 1 in 1998 - Malone missed both foul shots and Chicago won at the buzzer.

HISTORY:

On this date in 1998 the Chicago Bulls won their sixth NBA championship in eight years, defeating the Utah Jazz. Michael Jordan ended his Bulls career in dramatic fashion with 45 points, including the final two, in the Bulls' 87-86 Game 6 win. Jordan won his record sixth Finals MVP Award.

BIRTHDAYS:

Pat Summit, 1952; Sam Perkins, 1961; Eric Murdock, 1968; Bruce Bowen, 1971

TRIVIA:

Utah head coach Jerry Sloan was the first player selected by Chicago in their expansion draft in 1966, earning him the nickname "The Original Bull." Sloan played 10 seasons with Chicago before serving as their head coach for three years in the early '80s.

QUIZ:

What Utah defender was the victim of Michael Jordan's famous game-winning shot, falling down after a Jordan crossover?

ANSWER: *Bryon Russell*

The Basketball Almanac

TODAY'S THOUGHT:

 "**T**he L.A. Lakers are so good they could run a fast break with a medicine ball." *–Rich Donnelly*

HISTORY:

On this date in 2001 the Los Angeles Lakers finished off a dominating postseason run, defeating the Philadelphia 76ers, 108-96, in Game 5 for their 13th NBA championship. A Game 1 loss to Philadelphia was the Lakers' only defeat through four rounds of the playoffs.

BIRTHDAYS:

John Brisker, 1947; Michael Doleac, 1977

TRIVIA:

The Lakers' Kobe Bryant was born in Philadelphia in 1978 while his father Joe "Jellybean" Bryant was playing with the 76ers. Kobe would return to Philly in 2002 and win the All-Star Game's MVP. Three years later, Joe would join him in L.A. when he became the head coach of the WNBA's Sparks.

QUIZ:

Who's the only Laker to be a part of the 1987, 1988 and 2000 championship teams?

ANSWER: A.C. Green

TODAY'S THOUGHT:

 "Charles and I have no-trade clauses. His is written in. Mine, well, nobody wants to trade for me." *–Joe Kleine*, Phoenix Suns, on Charles Barkley

HISTORY:

On this date in 1975 Kareem Abdul-Jabbar was dealt by the Bucks to the Los Angeles Lakers for Elmore Smith, Brian Winters, and rookies Dave Meyers and Junior Bridgeman. Abdul-Jabbar claimed the city of Milwaukee did not fit his cultural needs.

BIRTHDAYS:

Rick Adelman, 1946; Al Skinner, 1952; Tree Rollins, 1955; Darrell Griffith, 1958; Anthony Carter, 1975

TRIVIA:

In 1997, Kareem Abdul-Jabbar successfully sued former UCLA running back Karim Abdul-Jabbar (who also wore the #33) for using the famous name. Born Sharmon Shah, the younger Abdul-Jabbar received his new name upon converting to Islam, like the former Lew Alcindor.

QUIZ:

After Kareem Abdul-Jabbar in 1976, two fellow UCLA alumns led the NBA in rebounds per game in 1977 and 1980. Can you name them?

ANSWER: Bill Walton and Swen Nater

TODAY'S THOUGHT:

"**I**'ll always be Number 1 to myself." *–Moses Malone*

HISTORY:

On this date in 1976 the Denver Nuggets, Indiana Pacers, New York Nets, and San Antonio Spurs were officially admitted into the NBA. The expansion, following the demise of the American Basketball Association, raised the league's total to 22 teams.

BIRTHDAYS:

Maurice Stokes, 1933; Edgar Jones, 1956; Popeye Jones, 1970

TRIVIA:

Moses Malone was the last ABA player left in the NBA when he retired in 1995. Malone played the first two seasons of his 21-year career with the Utah Stars and the Spirits of St. Louis before joining the NBA in 1976.

QUIZ:

Who's the only coach in basketball history to lead an ABA team to a title one year and an NBA team to one the next?

ANSWER: Bill Sharman, with the ABA's Stars in 1971 and the NBA's Lakers in 1972

TODAY'S THOUGHT:

"The rule was 'No autopsy, no foul.'" *–Stewart Granger*, on the pickup games he played as a kid

HISTORY:

On this date in 1932 the first International Basketball Conference was held in Geneva, Switzerland. The end result was the formation of the Federation Internationale de Basketball Amateur (FIBA), the world's governing body for basketball.

BIRTHDAYS:

George Mikan, 1924; Eddie Miller, 1931; Bruce Seals, 1953

TRIVIA:

While the NBA is a separate governing body, most of its regulations coincide with FIBA's. However, in international play, the court is actually smaller. FIBA regulations require it to be 91 feet, 10 inches by 49 feet, 2.5 inches, while a standard NBA floor is simply 94' by 50'.

QUIZ:

Playing by the Rules: Ben Wallace of the Bulls is in a downward motion and about to dunk the ball. Minnesota's Kevin Garnett blocks the attempt. Should goaltending be called?

ANSWER: *No - It's legal since the ball had not left Wallace's hand at the time of the block.*

TODAY'S THOUGHT:

I'm just thankful for every day that I wake up." *–LeBron James*

HISTORY:

On this date in 1986 Maryland All-American Len Bias collapsed and died in a university dorm room after overdosing on cocaine. The 22- year old's death came less than 48 hours after being selected by the Boston Celtics with the second pick in the NBA Draft.

BIRTHDAYS:

Skeeter Swift, 1946; Dirk Nowitzki, 1978; Marvin Williams, 1986

TRIVIA:

Tragedy would strike the Boston Celtics franchise, again, seven years later, when All-Star Reggie Lewis died at age 27 of a heart attack suffered during an off-season basketball workout.

QUIZ:

Who is the only Boston Celtic to have his name, rather than his number, retired?

ANSWER: Jim Loscutoff - He asked that his #18 jersey not be retired so that a future Celtic (Dave Cowens) could wear it. In the spaces where the Celtics numbers are retired, Loscutoff's says "Loscy."

TODAY'S THOUGHT:

 "**M**agic Johnson is the best player who plays on the ground, and Michael Jordan is the best player who plays in the air."
–John Paxson

HISTORY:

On this date in 1993 the Chicago Bulls won a third straight title, this time in six games over the Phoenix Suns. John Paxson's three-pointer was the difference in the 99-98 victory, as Michael Jordan was named Finals MVP for the third consecutive year.

BIRTHDAYS:

Rodney Rogers, 1971; Gordan Giricek, 1977; Josh Childress, 1983; Hassan Adams, 1984; Darko Milicic, 1985; Patrick O'Bryant, 1986

TRIVIA:

In Game 2, Michael Jordan and Charles Barkley each scored 42 points, marking the first time in NBA Finals history that opposing players each scored 40 or more in the same game. Jordan averaged a record 41 points per game in the series.

QUIZ:

Which player was selected to more All-Star Games: Michael Jordan or Magic Johnson?

ANSWER: Jordan, with 14 - Magic was picked 12 times.

TODAY'S THOUGHT:

"**I**'m glad you're doing this story on us and not on the WNBA. We're so much prettier than all the other women in sports." –Tennis player *Martina Hingis*, in *Detour Magazine*

HISTORY:

On this date in 1997 the inaugural WNBA season tipped off with the New York Liberty defeating the Los Angeles Sparks, 67-57, in front of 14,284 at the Great Western Forum. Sparks guard Penny Toler gets credit for scoring the first basket in league history.

BIRTHDAYS:

Donald Sidle, 1946; Tom Chambers, 1959; Derrick Coleman, 1967; Loren Woods, 1978; Richard Jefferson, 1980

TRIVIA:

The American Basketball League, the WNBA's main competition, folded after the 1998 season. As a result, many of the ABL's best players, including Olympic gold medalists Nikki McCray and Dawn Staley, joined the rosters of WNBA teams.

QUIZ:

Who was the WNBA's first MVP?

ANSWER: *Cynthia Cooper of the Houston Comets - She also won the 1998 MVP Award.*

TODAY'S THOUGHT:

"alent wins games, but teamwork and intelligence win championships." *–Michael Jordan*

HISTORY:

On this date in 1994 the Rockets became the first professional team from Houston to win a major sports championship. Hakeem Olajuwon scored 25 points and grabbed 10 rebounds in Game 7 to lead the Rockets past New York, 90-84.

BIRTHDAYS:

Pete Maravich, 1947; Clyde Drexler, 1962; Cadillac Anderson, 1964; Darrell Armstrong, 1968

TRIVIA:

Olajuwon's "Dream" season included becoming the first player in NBA history to win Defensive Player of the Year and both the regular season and Finals MVP Awards in the same year.

QUIZ:

In the 1984 NBA Draft, Hakeem Olajuwon went number one and Michael Jordan number three. What two players were selected with the second and fourth picks?

ANSWER: *The Blazers took Sam Bowie second, while the Mavericks grabbed Sam Perkins in the fourth slot.*

TODAY'S THOUGHT:

"**I**'m going to come back and haunt you guys." *–Elvin Hayes*, after being traded by the Rockets

HISTORY:

On this date in 1972 the Houston Rockets traded future Hall of Famer Elvin Hayes to the Baltimore Bullets for Jack Marin. Marin lasted only a season and a half with the Rockets, while Hayes would make the All-Star team eight more times before returning to Houston at the end of his career.

BIRTHDAYS:

Walter Dukes, 1930; LaSalle Thompson, 1961; Mike James, 1975

TRIVIA:

Leroy Ellis and John Q. Trapp went from sky high to rock bottom in one season. After being on the 1972 Lakers squad that won an NBA record 69 games, both were traded to the 76ers, who lost a record-breaking 73 games the following year.

QUIZ:

In 1992, who did the Philadelphia 76ers trade in exchange for Jeff Hornacek, Tim Perry and Andrew Lang?

ANSWER: *Charles Barkley*

TODAY'S THOUGHT:

"**I** made a 1,600 minus 800 minus 200 on the SAT, so I'm very intelligent when I speak." *–Shaquille O'Neal*

HISTORY:

On this date in 1992 Portland's Memorial Coliseum became the first venue outside of New York to host the NBA Draft. The Orlando Magic selected LSU big man Shaquille O'Neal with the first overall pick.

BIRTHDAYS:

Larry Foust, 1928; Sam Jones, 1933; Art Heyman, 1941; J.J. Redick, 1984

TRIVIA:

During the 2004-05 season, the Miami Heat became the first team to have the top three picks of an NBA Draft on their roster at the same time. Besides O'Neal, Alonzo Mourning (picked second by the Hornets) and Christian Laettner (third by the Timberwolves) were chosen in 1992.

QUIZ:

In 2005, the overall number one draft picks in both the NFL and NBA came from the same school, a first. Name that school, along with the players.

ANSWER: *Utah - QB Alex Smith went number one to the San Francisco 49ers while center Andrew Bogut was picked first overall by the Milwaukee Bucks.*

TODAY'S THOUGHT:

"**I** don't think there will ever be another 6' 9" point guard who smiles while he humiliates you." *–James Worthy*, on longtime Lakers teammate Magic Johnson

HISTORY:

On this date in 1981 the Los Angeles Lakers made Magic Johnson a very secure and wealthy young man. Johnson signed a 25-year contract which would pay him $1 million per season beginning in 1984.

BIRTHDAYS:

Willis Reed, 1942; Dell Curry, 1964; Dikembe Mutombo, 1966; Michael Dickerson, 1975

TRIVIA:

In the NBA's first season, the league's top-paid player was Tom King of the Detroit Falcons, who earned $16,500 - but not solely because of his playing ability. He earned $8,000 of his pay as the Falcons' publicity director and business manager.

QUIZ:

What former Laker is the only man to play in the NBA Finals and coach in the Super Bowl?

ANSWER: Bud Grant - He was a reserve forward on the 1949-50 NBA champion Minneapolis Lakers, and later coached the Minnesota Vikings to four Super Bowls.

TODAY'S THOUGHT:

"**H**ouston Rockets No. 1 pick Yao Ming has something in common with most Americans. He'll need an interpreter when he goes to Texas." *—Bob Molinaro* of *The Norfolk Virginian-Pilot*

HISTORY:

On this date in 2002 Yao Ming, who played for China's Shanghai Sharks, was selected first overall by the Houston Rockets in the NBA Draft. It was the first time someone who played neither high school nor college basketball in the U.S. was the top pick.

BIRTHDAYS:

Hal Greer, 1936; Jerome Kersey, 1962; Raymond Felton, 1984; Deron Williams, 1984

TRIVIA:

In 2002, commentator Charles Barkley, unconvinced about the hype surrounding Yao Ming, told TV partner Kenny Smith that he would "kiss [his] ass" if Ming ever scored 20 points in an NBA game. When Yao came through shortly after, Smith brought a live donkey to the set, and Barkley, true to his word, kissed it.

QUIZ:

What two Duke Blue Devils were selected behind Yao with picks two and three?

ANSWER: *The Bulls took Jay Williams second and the Warriors selected Mike Dunleavy, Jr. at number three.*

TODAY'S THOUGHT:

 "**H**e just kept saying 'Michael Jordan (former Wizards president) is going to kill me.'" –*Sgt. Kirk Hartwell*, who arrested Kwame Brown, Washington Wizards, for speeding

HISTORY:

On this date in 2001 Kwame Brown of Georgia's Glynn Academy became the first high school player to be taken with the top pick in the NBA Draft. Brown was selected by the Washington Wizards in what *The Washington Times* called the "worst draft ever."

BIRTHDAYS:

Craig Hodges, 1960; Chuck Person, 1964; Malik Allen, 1978

TRIVIA:

The Chicago Bulls selected track star Carl Lewis in the 10th round of the 1984 NBA Draft. That same year, the Dallas Cowboys picked Lewis in the 12th round of the NFL Draft as a wide receiver. The nine-time Olympic gold medalist stuck to track and field.

QUIZ:

What former Bull is the only player to be picked in the first round of both the NBA and Major League Baseball Drafts?

ANSWER: *Scott Burrell - He was selected 26th by the Mariners in the 1989 MLB Draft and 20th by the Charlotte Hornets in the 1993 NBA Draft.*

TODAY'S THOUGHT:

"**T**he good news is there are a lot of good second round picks. The bad news is a lot will go in the first round." –Former coach *Jerry Reynolds*, on the 1990 NBA Draft

HISTORY:

On this date in 1995 a record NBA Draft crowd gathered at Toronto's SkyDome, home of the expansion Raptors, to see the hometown team take Damon Stoudamire as the first draft pick of the franchise. Joe Smith was chosen as the number one overall pick by Golden State.

BIRTHDAYS:

Tom Owens, 1949; Jeff Malone, 1961; Andrew Lang, 1966; Bobby Hurley, 1971; Rodney White, 1980

TRIVIA:

In 1996, Damon Stoudamire, at 5'10", became the shortest player to win the Rookie of the Year Award. The tallest? 7'4" Ralph Sampson of Houston was the winner in 1984.

QUIZ:

Who did the expansion Vancouver Grizzlies take in that '95 Draft?

ANSWER: *The Grizzlies selected Oklahoma State big man Bryant Reeves with the number six pick.*

TODAY'S THOUGHT:

"I told you I needed to feed my family. They offered me 3 years at $21 million. That's not going to cut it." *—Latrell Sprewell*

HISTORY:

On this date in 1994 the Milwaukee Bucks selected Purdue forward Glenn Robinson with the first pick in the NBA Draft. After threatening to sit out the season if he wasn't paid $100 million, Robinson would end up signing a rookie-record 10-year, $68 million contract.

BIRTHDAYS:

Bob Lavoy, 1926; Gene Littles, 1943; Bob Rule, 1944; Joe Johnson, 1981

TRIVIA:

The 1995 Rookie of the Year Award was shared by the Mavericks' Jason Kidd and the Pistons' Grant Hill. The first time this happened was in 1971, coincidentally in both the ABA (Dan Issel and Charlie Scott) and the NBA (Dave Cowens and Geoff Petrie).

QUIZ:

Who were the last two players to be co-winners of the NBA's Rookie of the Year Award?

ANSWER: *Elton Brand of the Bulls and Steve Francis of the Rockets, for the 1999-2000 season*

TODAY'S THOUGHT:

 "**M**ost teams have a trophy case full of trophies. We have a case filled with ping-pong balls." –Orlando Magic senior VP *Pat Williams*, whose team won the NBA Draft Lottery two years in a row

HISTORY:

On this date in 1993 the Orlando Magic selected Michigan forward Chris Webber with the number one pick, only to trade him to Golden State for the third pick, Anfernee Hardaway. Orlando, the first team in the Draft Lottery era with back-to-back number one picks, took Shaquille O'Neal in 1992.

BIRTHDAYS:

Fred Schaus, 1925; Warren Davis, 1943; Tubby Smith, 1951; Mitch Richmond, 1965; Trevor Ariza, 1985

TRIVIA:

The Magic had the league's second-worst record when they won the Draft Lottery in 1992. But they defied the odds by winning the lottery again the following year, because their mark of 41-41 was the best out of all non-playoff teams in the NBA.

QUIZ:

What player was selected between Webber and Hardaway in 1993?

ANSWER: *The Philadelphia 76ers took 7'6" center Shawn Bradley from Brigham Young.*

TODAY'S THOUGHT:

 "**Y**eah, we players make a lot of money, but we spend a lot of money too." *–Patrick Ewing*, attempting to defend the Players Union position during the NBA lockout

HISTORY:

On this date in 1998 NBA owners imposed a lockout after the Players Association refused their proposal of a new Collective Bargaining Agreement and a hard cap system. The 191-day work stoppage would be the longest in league history, limiting the 1998-99 season to 50 games.

BIRTHDAYS:

Freddie Lewis, 1943; Jim Washington, 1943; Nacy Lieberman, 1958; Bracey Wright, 1984

TRIVIA:

During the 1985-86 season, a contract dispute between Utah's Adrian Dantley and Jazz management led coach Frank Layden to send Dantley home during a road trip. Layden fined the player thirty pieces of silver (three dollars in dimes) for Judas-like betrayal.

QUIZ:

What NBA team finished the lockout-shortened season with just eight wins?

ANSWER: *The Vancouver Grizzlies*

TODAY'S THOUGHT:

"**T**here are two ways to argue with a woman, and neither of them work." –*Carlos Boozer*, after his wife forced him to cancel an interview with *Sports Illustrated*

HISTORY:

On this date in 1997 Rebecca Lobo recorded her 100th consecutive victory when the New York Liberty defeated the Houston Comets, 70-67. The winning streak included Lobo's 35-0 senior season at Connecticut, her 60-0 mark as member of the U.S. Olympic team, and 5-0 WNBA record with the Liberty. The streak would end at 102.

BIRTHDAYS:

Larry Costello, 1931; Curtis Rowe, 1949; Purvis Short, 1957; Clark Kellogg, 1961; Jon Sundvold, 1961

TRIVIA:

Before becoming an official WNBA franchise, the New York Liberty organization purchased all trademark rights to the Liberty Basketball Association to avoid any potential property infringements. The LBA was a women's league that folded after one exhibition game.

QUIZ:

In 2001, what team snapped the Houston Comets' string of four consecutive WNBA championships?

ANSWER: *Los Angeles Sparks*

TODAY'S THOUGHT:

"It's hard to say which city has more to celebrate."
–Steve Abney, San Francisco Chronicle, on the Grizzlies' move from Vancouver to Memphis

HISTORY:

On this date in 2001 the NBA's Board of Governors approved the relocation of the Vancouver Grizzlies to Memphis for the upcoming season. The move would be the NBA's first since the Kings went from Kansas City to Sacramento in 1985.

BIRTHDAYS:

Jamie Feick, 1974; Bostjan Nachbar, 1980

TRIVIA:

Ironically, both the Grizzlies and Charlotte Hornets applied to the NBA for relocation to Memphis, a city often overlooked by sports franchises, on the same day in March of 2001. A year later, the Hornets packed their bags and moved to New Orleans.

QUIZ:

What current NBA team was formerly known as the Dallas Chaparrals?

ANSWER: *San Antonio Spurs*

TODAY'S THOUGHT:

I'm tired of hearing about money, money, money, money, money. I just want to play the game, drink Pepsi, and wear Reebok."
–Shaquille O'Neal

HISTORY:

On this date in 2003 Kobe Bryant was arrested in Eagle, Colorado, on charges that he had sexually assaulted a 19-year old employee at a hotel where Bryant was staying. The Lakers' guard would be released on bond, and the case would eventually be dismissed.

BIRTHDAYS:

Abe Saperstein, 1902; Harvey and Horace Grant, 1965; Adrian Griffin, 1974

TRIVIA:

The accusations against the NBA star proved costly. Bryant lost over $20 million when endorsement deals with McDonald's and Nutella were terminated. Nike, who signed him to a contract right before the incident, kept him on board but waited until 2006 to televise his first ad.

QUIZ:

What hair product did NBA legend Karl Malone endorse in the late 1990's?

ANSWER: Rogaine Extra Strength For Men

TODAY'S THOUGHT:

 "Like I told the team at halftime, Stevie Wonder, Roy Orbison and Ray Charles could have hit some of those shots - or at least come close. We acted like twelve people who were dropped down from outer space, put uniforms on and played like we had never seen one another before." *–Jim Cleamons*

HISTORY:

On this date in 1992 the U.S. Men's Olympic Basketball Team defeated Venezuela,127-80, to win the Tournament of the Americas, a tune-up before the Summer Olympics in Barcelona. Team USA won all six of its games by an average margin of 51.5 points.

BIRTHDAYS:

Eddie Miles, 1940; Joe Hamilton, 1948; Beno Udrih, 1982

TRIVIA:

Utah's John Stockton was the only member of that '92 Olympic squad to wear the same uniform number he wore in the NBA, twelve. International rules restrict any number outside four through fifteen. No one, other than Stockton, wore a number in that range on their NBA uniform.

QUIZ:

What member of the bronze medal-winning Lithuania basketball team at the 2000 Summer Olympics was signed by the Indiana Pacers in 2005?

ANSWER: *Sarunas Jasikevicius*

TODAY'S THOUGHT:

"**I**t's got nothing to do with air, kid. That's just what it feels like playing for the Nuggets." *–The Sporting News*, after NBA rookie Carmelo Anthony compared playing in Denver's mile-high altitude to getting punched in the chest

HISTORY:

On this date in 2000 E. Stanley Kroenke was officially introduced as the new owner of the NBA's Denver Nuggets. Kroenke Sports Enterprises also took over the NHL's Colorado Avalanche and the Pepsi Center, home to both teams.

BIRTHDAYS:

Wally Osterkorn, 1928; Andrew Anderson, 1945; Pau Gasol, 1980

TRIVIA:

Kroenke is also co-owner of a third pro sports franchise - the NFL's Rams. He moved the club to St. Louis in 1995 with Georgia Frontiere, who had inherited the team in 1979. Frontiere was the first female owner of a National Football League franchise.

QUIZ:

True or false? Alex English is the Denver Nuggets' all-time leader in points, rebounds, and assists.

ANSWER: *False - He leads them in points (21,645) and assists (3,679), but Dan Issel is their all-time leader in rebounds (6,630).*

TODAY'S THOUGHT:

I never got a California driver's license. If I ever got stopped, I was going to tell the cop, 'I'm the Clippers coach. I'm not going to be here that long.'" –Former Clippers coach *Bob Weiss*

HISTORY:

On this date in 1978 the NBA approved a trade of *franchises*. John Y. Brown and Harry Mangurian transferred ownership of the Buffalo Braves (now the Los Angeles Clippers) to Irv Levin, in exchange for the Boston Celtics.

BIRTHDAYS:

Jim Barnett, 1944; Rick Roberson, 1947; Ralph Sampson, 1960; Lisa Leslie, 1972; Chris Andersen, 1978

TRIVIA:

Ever since Donald Sterling purchased the Clippers in 1981, he's earned a reputation as a frugal spender. In his first cost-cutting move, Sterling wanted to fire a team trainer, so he asked coach Paul Silas if Silas could tape the players' ankles instead.

QUIZ:

Ross Perot Jr., the son of the former presidential candidate, was the majority owner of what NBA franchise from 1996-2000?

ANSWER: *The Dallas Mavericks, who were later bought by Marc Cuban*

TODAY'S THOUGHT:

"**L**ike I told the guys earlier, once he turns 21 and is able to drink, it's over." *–Jalen Rose*, after 20-year old LeBron James scored 56 points on his Raptors

HISTORY:

On this date in 2003 18-year old LeBron James made his pro debut in an NBA summer league game against the Magic. James delighted the near-capacity crowd in Orlando with 14 points, 7 rebounds, and 6 assists in a Cleveland victory.

BIRTHDAYS:

Bucky Bockhorn, 1933; Wang Zhizhi, 1977; Hakim Warrick, 1982

TRIVIA:

Summer league games are usually played without a lot of fanfare, but not that night. Five hours before tip-off, a traffic jam had formed around the arena while $5 tickets were being scalped for $80.

QUIZ:

Who's the youngest player in NBA history to play in a regular season game?

ANSWER: *The Lakers' Andrew Bynum, in 2005, at 18 years and 6 days old*

TODAY'S THOUGHT:

 he man who won't loan money isn't going to have many friends - or need them." *–Wilt Chamberlain*

HISTORY:

On this date in 1968 the Philadelphia 76ers traded future Hall of Famer Wilt Chamberlain to the Los Angeles Lakers for Jerry Chambers, Archie Clark and Darrall Imhoff. Chamberlain would finish his career in Los Angeles, winning his second NBA championship in 1972.

BIRTHDAYS:

Jim Pollard, 1922; Jim Paxson, 1957

TRIVIA:

Jerry Chambers is the only man in NCAA tournament history to win the Most Outstanding Player Award as a member of a fourth-place team. In 1966, his Utah squad lost the semifinal game to Texas Western and the consolation game to Duke. But Chambers' 70 points and 35 rebounds in those two losses were enough to win the award.

QUIZ:

What player made 21 of 22 shots in the 1973 NCAA Championship Game?

ANSWER: *Bill Walton of UCLA, who scored 44 points and grabbed 13 rebounds in the win over Memphis State*

TODAY'S THOUGHT:

"**O**fficiating is the only occupation in the world where the highest accolade is silence." *–Earl Strom*

HISTORY:

On this date in 1994 former NBA referee Earl Strom died at age 66 after a losing bout with brain cancer. Strom served as an official from 1957-90, calling 2,400 regular-season games and 29 NBA and ABA Finals. He was posthumously elected to the Basketball Hall of Fame in 1995.

BIRTHDAYS:

Pete Carril, 1930; Cliff Meely, 1947; Ken Charles, 1951

TRIVIA:

In 1958, referee Jim Duffy threw the St. Louis Hawks' Clyde Lovellette out of an exhibition game for arguing a call. Lovellette got even later that night when he showed up at Duffy's motel room with a pair of six-shooters loaded with blanks. Duffy ran for cover, to say the least.

QUIZ:

Playing by the Rules: On a throw-in, Tony Parker steps on the end line. Is this a violation?

ANSWER: *No - He's allowed to step on the line, but not over it.*

TODAY'S THOUGHT:

"We all get heavier as we get older because there's a lot more information in our heads." *–Vlade Divac*, explaining why he reported to training camp 15 pounds overweight

HISTORY:

On this date in 1996 the Hornets officially completed a trade with the Lakers that sent 18-year old Kobe Bryant to Los Angeles in exchange for center Vlade Divac. Charlotte had selected the Lower Merion (PA) High School guard with the 13th pick of the NBA Draft.

BIRTHDAYS:

Woody Sauldsberry, 1934; Clem Haskins, 1943; Lou Hudson, 1944; Rod Strickland, 1966; Eduardo Najera, 1976

TRIVIA:

In 1998, Dallas general manager Don Nelson found two franchise players in a matter of hours. On draft day, he traded 6th pick Robert Traylor to the Bucks for 9th pick Dirk Nowitzki and Pat Garrity. Garrity, the 19th selection, was then sent to Phoenix with a future draft pick for Steve Nash. That future pick, by the way, was Shawn Marion.

QUIZ:

The NBA Draft: Who's the odd man out, and why?
a. John Starks b. Bruce Bowen c. Brad Miller d. Andre Miller

ANSWER: *d. Actually, Andre is the only man "in" – in the NBA Draft, that is. Miller was picked 8th overall by Cleveland in 1999. The others were not selected in the draft.*

TODAY'S THOUGHT:

I started out my athletic career as the ball. My brothers used to toss me around the room." *–Danny Ainge*

HISTORY:

On this date in 1955 a feather in the cap of Celtics player Gene Conley was in order - a baseball cap! The dual-sport performer, pitching for the NL as a member of the Braves in the All-Star Game, struck out the side in the 12th inning and was the game's winning pitcher when Stan Musial homered in the bottom of the inning.

BIRTHDAYS:

Ray Scott, 1938; Paul Silas, 1943; Travis Best, 1972

TRIVIA:

Conley is the only person to win a world championship in both the NBA and Major League Baseball. He was a member of the World Series champs, the Milwaukee Braves, in 1957 and was a three-time champion with the Boston Celtics from 1959-'61.

QUIZ:

What basketball All-American at Duke was voted the National League MVP in 1960, the same year he won a World Series with the Pirates?

ANSWER: *Dick Groat*

The Basketball Almanac

TODAY'S THOUGHT:

"**A**nd in related headlines: 'Sky likely blue again,' 'Bengals likely bad again,' and 'Israelis, Palestinians likely mad at each other again.'" *–Mike Bianchi*, after his newspaper, *The Orlando Sentinel*, proclaimed "Grant Hill likely out again"

HISTORY:

On this date in 2006 the Chicago Bulls signed All-Star center Ben Wallace to a a four-year, $60 million contract. The four-time Defensive Player of the Year helped lead the Detroit Pistons to their third NBA championship in 2004.

BIRTHDAYS:

Frank Ramsey, 1931; Bob Kauffman, 1946; David Thompson, 1954; Spud Webb, 1963

TRIVIA:

Wallace went undrafted in 1996, playing for the Bullets and Magic before being dealt with Chucky Atkins to Detroit for Grant Hill. The two were considered minor parts of the trade, a move designed to clear salary cap room for Hill to sign with Orlando.

QUIZ:

When the NBA's Defensive Player of the Year Award was first established, what player claimed back-to-back honors in 1983 and '84?

ANSWER: *Sidney Moncrief*

TODAY'S THOUGHT:

"**I**'m strong, I'm tough, I still wear my eyeliner." *–Lisa Leslie*

HISTORY:

On this date in 1999 the WNBA held its inaugural All-Star Game at Madison Square Garden in New York. The capacity crowd watched the West beat the East, 79-61, as the Los Angeles Sparks' Lisa Leslie earned MVP honors with 13 points in just 17 minutes.

BIRTHDAYS:

Harold Pressley, 1963; Eric Dampier, 1974; Renaldo Balkman, 1984

TRIVIA:

WNBA teams were owned collectively by the NBA until 2002, when they were either sold to their NBA counterparts in the same city or to a third party. As a result, two teams moved and two were forced to suspend operations before the following season began.

QUIZ:

How many of the eight original WNBA teams can you name?

ANSWER: *New York Liberty, Houston Comets, Charlotte Sting, Cleveland Rockers, Los Angeles Sparks, Phoenix Mercury, Sacramento Monarchs and Utah Starzz*

TODAY'S THOUGHT:

" **I** ncompetence should not be confined to one sex." *–Bill Russell*, on female officiating

HISTORY:

On this date in 1991 Sandhi Ortiz-DelValle became the first woman to officiate a men's professional basketball game when she refereed a United States Basketball League contest between the New Haven Skyhawks and the Philadelphia Spirit.

BIRTHDAY:

Archie Clark, 1941

TRIVIA:

In 2002, the all-female crew of Mona Miller, Erica Bradley and Leigh Anne Webb made history when they officiated a regular season men's college basketball game between Martin Methodist and Atlanta Christian in Pulaski, Tennessee.

QUIZ:

In 1997, these two women became the first female referees in the NBA. Name them.

ANSWER: *Violet Palmer and Dee Kantner - Palmer was also the first woman to ref an NBA playoff game, in 2006.*

TODAY'S THOUGHT:

"**T**he newest Laker, Karl Malone, said he joined the team because he wanted to get a ring. So I guess he's hoping that Kobe cheats on him too." *–Jay Leno*, after Kobe Bryant bought his wife a $4 million ring to make amends for cheating on her

HISTORY:

On this date in 2003 the Los Angeles Lakers signed free agents Gary Payton and Karl Malone, who took big pay cuts with the hope of winning their first NBA title. The Lakers' season, however, would end with a loss to Detroit in the 2004 NBA Finals.

BIRTHDAYS:

Charles Smith, 1965; Chris Mihm, 1979; Zach Randolph, 1981; Solomon Jones, 1984

TRIVIA:

The 1962-63 Boston Celtics roster featured eight future Hall of Famers, more than any other single-season squad. They were: Bill Russell, Bob Cousy, John Havlicek, Sam Jones, Tom Heinsohn, Frank Ramsey, K.C. Jones, and Clyde Lovellette.

QUIZ:

Who is the only member of the Basketball Hall of Fame whose last name begins with the letter "U?"

ANSWER: *Wes Unseld*

TODAY'S THOUGHT:

"How can you foul out when you don't guard anyone?"
–Syracuse coach *Jim Boeheim*, to his player, Lawrence Moten

HISTORY:

On this date in 2003 the Denver Nuggets signed Carmelo Anthony to his first professional contract, a three-year deal worth more than $9 million. His real payday, though, would come in 2006 when he signed a five-year, $80 million extension.

BIRTHDAYS:

Connie Hawkins, 1942; Calbert Cheaney, 1971; Eric Williams, 1972

TRIVIA:

Anthony scored 53 points combined in the two Final Four games of the 2003 NCAA Tournament, leading Syracuse to the title. He was only the second freshman, following DePaul's Mark Aguirre, to put up 50 total points in the Final Four.

QUIZ:

What player has scored the most career points in NCAA tournament play?

ANSWER: *Christian Laettner of Duke, who tallied 407 points in 23 games*

TODAY'S THOUGHT:

"**I**t was like the Red Sox selling off Babe Ruth. They had the curse of the Bambino, and we had the curse of Shaq." *–Pat Williams*, Magic senior vice president, on losing Shaquille O'Neal to free agency

HISTORY:

On this date in 1996 the Los Angeles Lakers signed unrestricted free agent Shaquille O'Neal to a seven-year, $120 million contract. O'Neal would go on to lead L.A. to three titles, while his former team, Orlando, would quickly return to mediocrity.

BIRTHDAYS:

Donnie Freeman, 1944; Mike Gale, 1950; Wally Walker, 1954; Anfernee Hardaway, 1971; Derek Anderson, 1974

TRIVIA:

When Lakers legend George Mikan died in 2005, his family, faced with some financial difficulties, accepted a generous offer from O'Neal to cover the late center's funeral expenses.

QUIZ:

Who coached Shaquille O'Neal at Louisiana State University from 1989-92?

ANSWER: *Dale Brown*

TODAY'S THOUGHT:

"**H**is initials are PG, but I want him to be rated R." *–Damon Stoudamire*, on toughening up Grizzlies teammate Pau Gasol

HISTORY:

On this date in 2001 Atlanta and Memphis finalized a deal that sent Lorenzen Wright, Brevin Knight and the draft rights to #3 pick Pau Gasol to the Grizzlies for Shareef Abdur-Rahim. Gasol would win Rookie of the Year and, in 2004, lead Memphis to its first playoff appearance.

BIRTHDAY:

Alvan Adams, 1954; Adam Morrison, 1984; LaMarcus Aldridge, 1985

TRIVIA:

Shareef Abdur-Rahim had played the second most career NBA games (744) without making a postseason appearance. Abdur-Rahim, who finally made it to the playoffs with Sacramento in 2006, is surpassed only by Tom Van Arsdale, who in his entire 12-year career of 929 games, never made it to the postseason.

QUIZ:

Brevin Knight's brother, Brandin, played college basketball at what Big East school?

ANSWER: *University of Pittsburgh*

TODAY'S THOUGHT:

"I heard they used to." –Indiana Pacers coach *Larry Bird*, asked if he was aware when he took the job that NBA head coaches speak to the media every day

HISTORY:

On this date in 2000 Isiah Thomas was named head coach of the Indiana Pacers, replacing Larry Bird. Like Bird, the Indiana job was Thomas' first coaching experience, and, like Bird, the Pacers would make the playoffs in each of his three years there.

BIRTHDAYS:

Chuck Daly, 1930; Mel Daniels, 1944; Nick Weatherspoon, 1950; Ray Allen, 1975

TRIVIA:

Bob Davies was a standout coach at Seton Hall and a player with the National Basketball League's Rochester Royals - at the same time. He led the Pirates to a 24-3 record during the 1947 season, and was voted the NBL MVP while playing for Rochester.

QUIZ:

Coach Billy Donovan, who led the Florida Gators to a national title in 2006, played briefly for what NBA team?

ANSWER: *He played 44 games with the New York Knicks in the 1987-88 season.*

TODAY'S THOUGHT:

 year ago he was the All-Star coach. And now people are talking about firing him? It's like your wife, man. You can't love her when she's got makeup on, (and when) she takes the makeup off you hate her." *–Kevin Garnett*, on Flip Saunders

HISTORY:

On this date in 2005 Flip Saunders was named successor to Larry Brown as coach of the Detroit Pistons. Saunders, who served as coach of the Minnesota Timberwolves for 10 years, would lead Detroit to a franchise record 64 wins in 2006.

BIRTHDAYS:

Fred Hetzel, 1942; Tamika Catchings, 1979; Paul Davis, 1984

TRIVIA:

Paul Westphal, who led the Phoenix Suns to 62 wins in the 1992-93 season, holds the record for the most victories in a season by a rookie coach. He followed that up with 56 wins in 1994 and 59 in '95.

QUIZ:

Can you name the first man to be voted Coach of the Year with a losing team? (Hint: The team remains the only first-year club to make the NBA playoffs.)

ANSWER: *Johnny "Red" Kerr, who led the expansion Chicago Bulls to a record of 33-48 in 1967*

TODAY'S THOUGHT:

"**I** have a God-given talent. I got it from my dad." –*Julian Wakefield,*
Missouri basketball player

HISTORY:

On this date in 1993 James Jordan, father of Michael, disappeared in North
Carolina. Two weeks later, investigators found Jordan's body, determined
that he was murdered, and charged two local teens with the crime.

BIRTHDAYS:

Slick Watts, 1951; Bird Averitt, 1952; Alvin Robertson 1962

TRIVIA:

Bobby Knight's son, Pat, was a member of the Indiana basketball team
from 1991-95, though he saw little playing time. Pat now serves as an
assistant to his father at Texas Tech, which has signed a contract designat-
ing the younger Knight as head coach when Bobby retires.

QUIZ:

What former NBA player was coached by his father at the University of
Tennessee in the early 1990's?

ANSWER: *Allan Houston, who was coached by his father, Wade*

TODAY'S THOUGHT:

I 'm just glad it wasn't Detroit. I don't like anybody there."
—J.R. Reid, after being traded to the San Antonio Spurs

HISTORY:

On this date in 2003 heads were spinning as four teams were involved in a five-player trade. Minnesota dealt Terrell Brandon to Atlanta and Marc Jackson to Philadelphia, while getting Latrell Sprewell from New York. The 76ers, in turn, received Glenn Robinson from the Hawks after sending Keith Van Horn to the Knicks.

BIRTHDAYS:

Antoine Carr, 1961; Micheal Williams, 1966; Elden Campbell, 1968; Gary Payton, 1968; Darvin Ham, 1973; Gerald Wallace, 1982; Brandon Roy, 1984

TRIVIA:

During their inaugural season, the Timberwolves played their home games in the Minneapolis Metrodome. Despite a 22-60 mark for the 1989-90 campaign, the team set an NBA attendance record, averaging over 26,100 fans per game, including a crowd of 49,551 for their home finale.

QUIZ:

Quick! How many teams are there in the NBA?

ANSWER: *Thirty*

TODAY'S THOUGHT:

It's not going to be peaches and gravy all the time."
–Brad Miller, on the Indiana Pacers' inconsistency

HISTORY:

On this date in 2003 trade winds continued to blow in the NBA, as Indiana, San Antonio, and Sacramento completed a deal. When the smoke had cleared, Indiana ended up with Scot Pollard and Danny Ferry, San Antonio had Hedo Turkoglu and Ron Mercer, and Sacramento received Brad Miller.

BIRTHDAYS:

Chuck Noble, 1931; Walt Bellamy, 1939; Joe Barry Carroll, 1958; Karl Malone, 1963; Rick Fox, 1969; Rafer Alston, 1976

TRIVIA:

Bruce Jenner was labeled the "World's Greatest Athlete" after winning the gold medal in the decathalon at the 1976 Olympics. Apparently the Kansas City Kings thought so, choosing Jenner with their seventh round pick in the 1977 NBA Draft.

QUIZ:

What UCLA standout did the Kings select with their second round pick in the 1995 NBA Draft?

ANSWER: *Tyus Edney*

TODAY'S THOUGHT:

"**W**e're going to be exciting. Of course, it was exciting when the Titanic went down." —coach *Bob Weiss*, on the Hawks' prospects for the 1992-93 season

HISTORY:

On this date in 1988 the Atlanta Hawks became the first NBA team to play an official exhibition game outside North America, defeating the Soviet Georgia All-Stars, 85-84 in the Soviet Union. The Hawks would also play the Soviet National Team twice on their tour, winning one and losing the other.

BIRTHDAYS:

Nate Thurmond, 1941; Jon Barry, 1969; Tracy Murray, 1971; Kenny Thomas, 1977; Nenad Krstic, 1983

TRIVIA:

The Atlanta Hawks' nickname traces back to the days when they were known as the Tri-Cities Blackhawks. The three cities referred to Moline and Rock Island, Illinois, and Davenport, Iowa, the region where the Blackhawk War was fought in 1831. The name was shortened to "Hawks" in 1951 when the team moved to Milwaukee.

QUIZ:

Three Atlanta Hawks have won the NBA Slam Dunk Contest. How many can you name?

ANSWER: *Dominique Wilkins (1985, '90), Spud Webb (1986), and Josh Smith (2005)*

TODAY'S THOUGHT:

"I may not be a class act, but I'm an American." *–Ron Artest*, on wanting to play for the Olympic team

HISTORY:

On this date in 2004 Team USA Basketball began its quest for another Olympic gold medal when it opened training camp at the University of North Florida in Jacksonville. The U.S. would come away with a disappointing bronze medal the following month in Athens.

BIRTHDAYS:

Gary Bradds, 1942; Mike Davis, 1946; Earl Tatum, 1953; Joe Smith, 1975; Delonte West, 1983

TRIVIA:

Perhaps the worst team in Olympic basketball history was the 1948 Iraqi squad. Playing in only five games, Iraq's average margin of defeat was 86 points, including two losses by 100 points each to Korea and China.

QUIZ:

Who was the only member of the 2004 U.S. Olympic squad that had yet to play in an NBA game?

ANSWER: *The Charlotte Bobcats'* Emeka Okafor

TODAY'S THOUGHT:

 "**A**nyone else remember when the only labor issues facing the WNBA involved Sheryl Swoopes having a baby?" *–Jeff McDonald* of *The San Angelo Standard Times*, on a near strike in the WNBA

HISTORY:

On this date in 1999 the Houston Comets' Sheryl Swoopes recorded the first triple-double in WNBA history. She finished with 14 points, 15 rebounds and 10 assists as her Comets destroyed the Detroit Shock, 85-46.

BIRTHDAYS:

Mack Calvin, 1947; Marvin Barnes, 1952; Moochie Norris, 1973; Mwadi Mabika, 1976

TRIVIA:

WNBA star Cheryl Ford averaged a double-double as a rookie in 2003, leading the Detroit Shock to their first championship. Ford is the daughter of former NBA great Karl Malone, and like dad, played her college ball at Louisiana Tech.

QUIZ:

What 2002 WNBA Rookie of the Year had a father that played in the NBA from 1975-85?

ANSWER: *Tamika Catchings, daughter of Harvey Catchings*

TODAY'S THOUGHT:

"**I** told them we're bowl-eligible. We've got seven wins."
—*Larry Brown*, on his New Year's message to the Knicks

HISTORY:

On this date in 2005 Larry Brown signed a five-year, $50 million contract with the New York Knicks to become the highest-paid coach in NBA history. Brown would lead New York to 59 losses, the most in team history, before being replaced by Isiah Thomas.

BIRTHDAYS:

Bill Bradley, 1943; Doug Collins, 1951; Manu Ginobili, 1977; Willie Green, 1981

TRIVIA:

Brown must have been smarter in 1992 when he took over as coach of the Los Angeles Clippers at mid-season. L.A. won 23 of its final 35 games to finish with a 45-37 mark, ending a record streak of missing the playoffs for 15 straight years.

QUIZ:

I'm the only coach to take over two different teams after the beginning of the season and lead them to NBA titles. Who am I?

ANSWER: Pat Riley - He did it in 1982 with the Lakers and in 2006 with the Heat.

TODAY'S THOUGHT:

None of the guys like the city of Utah." *–Vernon Maxwell*, on playing the Jazz

HISTORY:

On this date in 2004 the Utah Jazz signed restricted free agent Carlos Boozer to a controversial six-year, $68 million deal. Reportedly, Boozer had a verbal agreement with his former team, Cleveland, to sign a new contract with them after they let him out of the final year of his old deal.

BIRTHDAYS:

Gene Moore, 1945; Neal Walk, 1948; Scott Wedman, 1952; Ronald Murray, 1979

TRIVIA:

In 2006, Boozer filed a lawsuit against musician, Prince, concerning a home owned by Boozer in California that was being leased by the rock star. Prince was accused of making unauthorized changes to the house, such as painting the exterior with purple striping.

QUIZ:

What NBA player made a rap album entitled *Misunderstood* under the moniker "Jewelz?"

ANSWER: Allen Iverson - The CD contained such obscene language that it was never released to stores.

TODAY'S THOUGHT:

"**E**very obnoxious fan has a wife home who dominates him.**"**
–Al McGuire

HISTORY:

On this date in 2002 L.A. Sparks center Lisa Leslie became the first WNBA player to dunk in a game when she threw down a one-handed, fastbreak jam in front of a celebratory Staples Center crowd. That was the highlight for the Sparks in an 82-73 loss to Miami.

BIRTHDAYS:

Billy Paultz, 1948; Bill Cartwright, 1957; Chris Mullin, 1963; Carlos Arroyo, 1979; Kevin Pittsnogle, 1984

TRIVIA:

In 2004, womens' hoops star Candace Parker became the first female winner of the McDonald's High School Slam Dunk Contest. The 17-year old beat out five male competitors for the title, completing every dunk she attempted.

QUIZ:

What woman was named the Most Outstanding Player of the NCAA Tournament in both 1983 and '84?

ANSWER: *Cheryl Miller, with USC*

TODAY'S THOUGHT:

"I didn't tell him 'yes.' I told him, 'Hell, yes!'" *–Mark Cuban*, Dallas Mavericks owner, when asked to be a celebrity judge in the Miss America pageant

HISTORY:

On this date in 1958 Dallas Mavericks owner Marc Cuban was born. The exuberant and outspoken billionaire amassed his fortune in the high-tech industry and bought the Mavs in 2000, transforming them from a mediocre team to a perennial title contender.

BIRTHDAYS:

Mike Jackson, 1949; Marc Cuban, 1958; Ruben Patterson, 1975

TRIVIA:

In one of Cuban's outbursts, he ridiculed the NBA director of officials, Ed Rush, saying he "wouldn't hire him to manage a Dairy Queen." When Dairy Queen officials took offense to the comment, Cuban humbly worked for a day at a Coppell, Texas DQ, where he waited on eager fans.

QUIZ:

What former Oakland A's baseball owner purchased the ABA's Memphis Pros in 1972 and renamed them the Tams?

ANSWER: *Charlie O. Finley - The name "Tams" was an acronym for Tennessee, Arkansas and Mississippi, the states in which the franchise's fans were located.*

TODAY'S THOUGHT:

"I t would have been less if I'd been playing." –Former Nets center *Todd MacCulloch*, on having to get twenty tickets for family members for a road game, even though he sat out with an injury

HISTORY:

On this date in 1973 the Virginia Squires traded Julius Erving and Willie Sojourner to the New York Nets for George Carter, the draft rights to Kermit Washington, and cash. Erving would guide the Nets to their last title before being sold to the 76ers in 1976.

BIRTHDAYS:

Maurice McHartley, 1942; Roy Williams, 1950; Kiki Vandeweghe, 1958; Stacey Augmon, 1968

TRIVIA:

On today's birthday list is Kiki Vandeweghe, a 14-year NBA veteran from 1980-93. He's the son of former NBA player Ernie Vandeweghe and Colleen Kay Hutchins, who was Miss America in 1952. Kiki is also the nephew of another hoopster, four-time NBA All-Star Melvin Hutchins.

QUIZ:

Towards the end of his career, Kiki Vandeweghe played several seasons with the club his dad played for his entire NBA career. Name the team.

ANSWER: *The New York Knicks*

TODAY'S THOUGHT:

"I cherished getting kicked out of school. It was a great thing. I became a millionaire." –Miami's *Jason Williams*, on what he liked most about his days at the University of Florida

HISTORY:

On this date in 2005 the largest trade in NBA history was made. The five-team deal involved the Heat, Celtics, Grizzlies, Hornets, and Jazz. Antoine Walker, James Posey, Jason Williams (all sent to Miami), and Eddie Jones (to Memphis) were among the thirteen players in the swap.

BIRTHDAYS:

Bob Netolicky, 1942; Cedric Ceballos, 1969

TRIVIA:

Miami point guard Jason Williams and NFL star wide receiver Randy Moss were teammates on DuPont High School's basketball squad in Belle, West Virginia. Moss was twice named the state's basketball player of the year, and ended his career with a school-record 1,713 points.

QUIZ:

The first trade Jason Williams was involved in occurred in 2001 when he was dealt from the Sacramento Kings to the Grizzlies for what fellow point guard?

ANSWER: *Mike Bibby*

TODAY'S THOUGHT:

"**G**uys aren't able to get $15 or $20 million a year anymore, so you have to play for the love of the game." *–Anfernee Hardaway,* in 1999, after the NBA capped player salaries

HISTORY:

On this date in 1949 the Basketball Association of America (BAA) and the National Basketball League (NBL) merged to form the NBA. The new league expanded to seventeen teams, but would consolidate until 1954, when only eight remained.

BIRTHDAYS:

Pete Newell, 1915; Mike Gminski, 1959; Nate McMillan, 1964; Viktor Khryapa, 1982; Chris Wilcox, 1982

TRIVIA:

Trenton routed the Brooklyn YMCA, 16-1, in the first professional basketball game, which took place November 7, 1896 in Trenton, N.J. The players were paid $15 each, except for Fred Cooper. As captain of the winning team, he received a one-dollar bonus, raising his share to $16.

QUIZ:

Which of the following was *not* a real team in the 1949-50 NBA season?
a. St. Louis Bombers b. Rocky Mountain Falcons c. Sheboygan Redskins d. Waterloo Hawks

ANSWER: *b. Rocky Mountain Falcons*

TODAY'S THOUGHT:

 "**M**aybe he saw our new ticket prices." –Atlanta Hawks president *Stan Kasten*, on a mugger who attacked him

HISTORY:

On this date in 2004 the Dallas Mavericks traded Antoine Walker and Tony Delk to the Atlanta Hawks for Jason Terry, Alan Henderson, and a draft pick. Walker and Terry would go on to meet in the 2006 NBA Finals after Walker was traded to the Heat in '05.

BIRTHDAYS:

Caldwell Jones, 1950; Mardy Collins, 1984; Ha Seung-Jin, 1985

TRIVIA:

For the 2002-03 season, confident Atlanta management offered a $125 refund to each of its season ticket holders if the Hawks didn't make the playoffs. The team didn't. The brainstorm of coach Lon Kruger backfired, and the Hawks had to refund $500,000 to some 4,000 customers. Kruger was gone long before the payout. He was fired in mid-season.

QUIZ:

The 2006 NBA title, won by the Heat over the Mavericks, marked the second time the two Finals teams came from Florida and Texas. The first was in 1995, when what two squads faced off?

ANSWER: *The Rockets and Orlando Magic, in a series that was swept by Houston*

TODAY'S THOUGHT:

 he game is in the refrigerator. The door is closed, the lights are out, the eggs are cooling, the butter is getting hard, and the Jell-O is jiggling." *–Chick Hearn*, after a game's outcome had been all but determined

HISTORY:

On this date in 2002 legendary Los Angeles Lakers broadcaster Chick Hearn died at the age of 85. During his 42 years on the job, Hearn called 3,338 consecutive games for the franchise. Evidence of his popularity was that Hearn's broadcasts were simulcast on both radio and television.

BIRTHDAYS:

Patrick Ewing, 1962; Otis Thorpe, 1962

TRIVIA:

Chick, born Francis Dayle Hearn, got his nickname while playing AAU basketball in his home state of Illinois. His teammates once played a prank by handing him a shoebox which contained not sneakers, but rather a dead chicken.

QUIZ:

What NBA coach and TV analyst was nicknamed "The Czar of the Telestrator" by Marv Albert?

ANSWER: *Mike Fratello*

TODAY'S THOUGHT:

"**C**harles joined my family for a day at the beach and my children asked if they could go in the ocean. I had to tell them, 'Not right now, kids. Charles is using it.'" *–Pat Williams*, Philadelphia 76ers GM, on 260-pound rookie Charles Barkley

HISTORY:

On this date in 1963, after the franchise's move from Syracuse to Philadelphia, a contest was held to re-name the club known as the Nationals. Out of 500 entries, Walt Stahlberg's was chosen as the winner among several others who picked the name "76ers."

BIRTHDAYS:

Mike Green, 1951; Darwin Cook, 1958; Dale Ellis, 1960; David Robinson, 1965; Alvin Williams, 1974

TRIVIA:

In 1982, Sylvester Stallone donated a statue of his character in the *Rocky* movies, boxer Rocky Balboa, to the city of Philadelphia. The statue was placed in front of the Spectrum, the 76ers' former home and the site of Rocky's first fight with Apollo Creed. It has since been moved to other locations throughout the city.

QUIZ:

He ended his 16-year Hall of Fame career as a player while doubling as coach of the 76ers in their inaugural year in Philly in 1963-64. Name him.

ANSWER: *Dolph Schayes*

TODAY'S THOUGHT:

"**I** know one thing. Wives and girlfriends would be saying, 'No way are you going to that team.'" –*Horace Grant*, Chicago Bulls, on Madonna's comments that she wanted to own an NBA team

HISTORY:

On this date in 1996 Val Ackerman was named the first president of the WNBA. In eight seasons on the job, she became the first female to successfully launch a women's team-oriented sports league. In 2005, Ackerman became the first female president of USA Basketball and was replaced in the WNBA's top spot by Donna Orender.

BIRTHDAY:

Fred Brown, 1948

TRIVIA:

In 1991, Susan O'Malley became the first female president of an NBA franchise when she took the position with the Washington Bullets (now Wizards). In her first season handling off-court activities, the team experienced the largest ticket revenue increase in the history of an NBA franchise.

QUIZ:

How long is a quarter of play in the WNBA?

ANSWER: *Ten minutes*

TODAY'S THOUGHT:

"**L**ook, show me something for about $300 from a sheep that's fooled around a little." *–Chuck Daly*, NBA coach, after being shown a $1,000-plus virgin wool suit

HISTORY:

On this date in 1992 the U.S. Olympic men's basketball team won the gold medal at the Barcelona Olympics, defeating Croatia, 117-85. The Chuck Daly-coached "Dream Team" featured NBA stars on the Olympic roster for the first time.

BIRTHDAYS:

Jerry Tarkanian, 1930; Bill Hewitt, 1944; Rashard Lewis, 1979

TRIVIA:

Team USA embarrassed its opponents in Barcelona in '92, going 8-0 in competition while scoring an Olympic record 117.3 points a game. The team's defeat of Croatia by 32 points was their smallest margin of victory, almost 12 under their average of 43.8 points per game.

QUIZ:

Can you name the only member of the 1992 Dream Team who had yet to play in an NBA game?

ANSWER: *Duke's Christian Laettner, who had just been drafted by Minnesota that June*

TODAY'S THOUGHT:

"**I** don't know anything about Angola, but I know they're in trouble."
–Dream Team member *Charles Barkley*, in 1992, before the USA's first game, against Angola (They won 116-48.)

HISTORY:

On this date in 1936 the U.S. Olympic basketball team played their way to their first victory ever in the Games with a 52-28 trouncing of Estonia. Basketball became an Olympic sport for the first time at the Berlin Games in 1936.

BIRTHDAYS:

Bob Cousy, 1928; Hot Rod Williams, 1962; Vinny Del Negro, 1966; Derek Fisher, 1974; Chamique Holdsclaw, 1977; Jarvis Hayes, 1981

TRIVIA:

The win over Estonia was technically the second Olympic triumph for the U.S. Spain was actually America's first opponent, but because of the Spanish Civil War, the team never showed up. The United States was credited with a 2-0 victory.

QUIZ:

Can you name the first international player to be named the NBA's Rookie of the Year?

ANSWER: *Spain's Pau Gasol, with the Grizzlies in 2002*

TODAY'S THOUGHT:

"To a father, when a child dies, the future dies; to a child, when a parent dies, the past dies." *–Red Auerbach*

HISTORY:

On this date in 1970 Joe Lapchick died at the age of 70. The Hall of Famer starred on the Original Celtics in the 1920's and '30's before coaching at the college and pro levels. Lapchick led St. John's to four NIT championships, and the Knicks to three straight NBA Finals appearances in the early 1950's.

BIRTHDAYS:

Red Holzman, 1920; Ralph Simpson, 1949; Don Buse, 1950; John Starks, 1965; Marcus Fizer, 1978

TRIVIA:

Just hours before the 1980 Louisville-UCLA National Championship Game, Cardinals star forward Wiley Brown, who cut off his thumb with a knife at the age of four, realized he'd left his artificial thumb on the breakfast table at the team's hotel. A team trainer found it in the garbage, retrieved it in the nick of time, and the title was thumbs up for Louisville.

QUIZ:

In 1939, H.V. Porter, an official with the Illinois High School Association, came up with what phrase to commemorate a basketball tournament?

ANSWER: *March Madness*

TODAY'S THOUGHT:

 We can't win at home and we can't win on the road. My problem as a general manager is I can't think of another place to play." *–Pat Williams*, Orlando Magic general manager

HISTORY:

On this date in 2001 the Los Angeles Sparks became the first WNBA team to go undefeated at home. The team, coached by former Lakers player Michael Cooper, had a perfect 16-0 regular season record at the Staples Center en route to winning their first championship.

BIRTHDAY:

Craig Ehlo, 1961

TRIVIA:

2001 WNBA Finals MVP Lisa Leslie once scored 101 points in a high school game - in one half! With her team, Inglewood Morningside, ahead 102-24 at halftime, the opponent, South Torrance, refused to play the second half. Leslie was just shy of Cheryl Miller's high school record of 105.

QUIZ:

Muffet McGraw was the head coach of what college basketball team that won the first women's NCAA title of the 21st century?

ANSWER: *Notre Dame, in 2001*

TODAY'S THOUGHT:

"**I** love Sam Cassell, he's a great guy... but he does look like E.T."
—*Charles Barkley*

HISTORY:

On this date in 2005 the Minnesota Timberwolves traded Sam Cassell and a future draft pick to the Clippers for Marko Jaric and Lionel Chalmers. While Minnesota's season would be a disappointment, Cassell and the reborn Clippers went on to win 47 games and their first playoff series in 20 years.

BIRTHDAYS:

Cornell Warner, 1948; George McGinnis, 1950; Antoine Walker, 1976; Rafael Araujo, 1980

TRIVIA:

In 1973-74, when the Clippers were known as the Buffalo Braves, the franchise played nine home games in Canada at Toronto's Maple Leaf Gardens. After just 21 wins the previous year, their plan worked, as attendance increased and the 42-40 Braves made the playoffs for the first time.

QUIZ:

Two Minnesota players in the team's 1989-90 expansion season later became head coaches in the NBA. Can you name either one?

ANSWER: *Sidney Lowe (Wolves and Grizzlies) and Sam Mitchell (Raptors)*

TODAY'S THOUGHT:

"**H**e's so tall that if he falls down, he'd be halfway home."
–Darryl Dawkins, on the 7'7" Manute Bol

HISTORY:

On this date in 1948 Team USA, led by 7'0" Bob Kurland, once again swept the competition, winning eight straight games. The last, a 65-21 rout of France, gave the team the gold medal in London.

BIRTHDAY:

Gary Gregor, 1945

TRIVIA:

While playing at Oklahoma A&M, Bob Kurland was such a prolific shot blocker that the NCAA introduced a new rule prohibiting shots from being blocked on downward arcs. We know it today as goaltending. Kurland's dominance was such that, even after the rule went into effect, an official was often perched on a platform directly above the basket for the sole purpose of watching him.

QUIZ:

Playing by the Rules: Your throw-in from the sidelines goes over the intended receiver's head and hits the rim. A teammate then catches it. Is this allowed?

ANSWER: *Yes*

TODAY'S THOUGHT:

"**I** am sure that no man can derive more pleasure from money or power than I do from seeing a pair of basketball goals in some out of the way place - deep in the Wisconsin woods an old barrel hoop nailed to a tree, or a weather-beaten shed on the Mexican border with a rusty iron hoop nailed to one end." –*James Naismith*

HISTORY:

On this date in 1936 the United States won the first Olympic gold medal awarded in basketball, defeating the Canadians, 19-8, in Berlin, Germany. Team USA's Joe Fortenberry matched Canada's output of 8 points in a game played in heavy rain on an outdoor clay court.

BIRTHDAYS:

Frank Brickowski, 1959; Magic Johnson, 1959; Fred Roberts, 1960; Ed O'Bannon, 1972; Chucky Atkins, 1974

TRIVIA:

The 1936 U.S. basketball team earned more than just an Olympic gold medal. Each of the players also received a handshake and a laurel wreath from the inventor of basketball, James Naismith.

QUIZ:

Who was the President of the United States when basketball was invented in 1891?

ANSWER: *Benjamin Harrison*

TODAY'S THOUGHT:

 ou wonder why parents do that to a kid. But he points out there's no quit in sophomore Sur Render." —Gunnison (CO) High School athletic director *Larry Mims*, on the basketball team's scrappy 5'6" point guard with the unfortunate name

HISTORY:

On this date in 2002 Chamique Holdsclaw of the Washington Mystics became the first WNBA player to lead the league in both points and rebounds per game. She finished the season averaging a double-double with 19.9 points and 11.6 rebounds a contest.

BIRTHDAYS:

Bob Wilkerson, 1954; Kenny Carr, 1955; David Harrison, 1982

TRIVIA:

Holdsclaw attended Christ the King Regional High School in Queens, New York, where she led the women's basketball team to four straight state titles. She then went on to Tennessee and guided the Lady Vols to three consecutive NCAA women's basketball championships from 1996-98.

QUIZ:

Can you name the Basketball Hall of Famer who was cut from the Baton Rouge High School basketball team in his freshman and sophomore years?

ANSWER: *Bob Pettit*

TODAY'S THOUGHT:

 e'd hand them a caramel candy, and if they took the wrapper off before they ate it, they'd get a basketball scholarship. If they ate the caramel with the paper still on it, we'd give them a football scholarship." *–Frank Layden*, on a test he used to give recruits when he coached at Niagara

HISTORY:

On this date in 1862 Amos Alonzo Stagg was born. Renowned as a collegiate football player and coach, Stagg was an overall athletic pioneer. As the athletic director and basketball coach at the University of Chicago, Stagg was responsible for developing the sport as a five-player game. He was a member of the inaugural Basketball Hall of Fame class of 1959.

BIRTHDAYS:

Amos Alonzo Stagg, 1862; George King, 1928; Charlie Tyra, 1935; Les Hunter, 1942; Sonny Dove, 1945; James Donaldson, 1957

TRIVIA:

In 1962, Heisman Trophy-winning quarterback Terry Baker and his Oregon State Beavers led the nation in total offense. The following year, Baker was the second-leading scorer on OSU's basketball team, which went all the way to the Final Four.

QUIZ:

Can you name the Heisman Trophy-winning quarterback who was drafted by the New York Knicks in 1994?

ANSWER: *Florida State's Charlie Ward*

TODAY'S THOUGHT:

"It was the first time in my life I was happy to see a zero after my name." *–Tom McMillen*, Maryland congressman and former NBA player, after he was absolved of any wrongdoing in the 1992 House banking scandal

HISTORY:

On this date in 1951 a New York grand jury indicted three Bradley basketball players and eight gamblers on bribery and conspiracy charges. The betting scandal, which reached seven schools and thirty-two players around the country, nearly destroyed college basketball.

BIRTHDAYS:

Red Kerr, 1932; Kenny Sears, 1933; Mike Brooks, 1958; Christian Laettner, 1969; Dee Brown, 1984; Rudy Gay, 1986; Tyrus Thomas, 1986

TRIVIA:

In 2003, Yao Ming sued Coca-Cola for using his image without permission on Coke bottles that sold in China. The Rockets star, who had just signed an international deal with Pepsi, demanded twelve cents in damages and an apology. The soft drink giant eventually backed down, paid up and said they were sorry.

QUIZ:

In a 2006 interview with ESPN, what Basketball Hall of Famer revealed that he'd lost roughly $10 million from gambling?

ANSWER: *Charles Barkley*

TODAY'S THOUGHT:

"**L**arry, you only told me one lie. You said there will be another Larry Bird. Larry, there will never, ever be another Larry Bird." —*Magic Johnson*, at Bird's retirement party

HISTORY:

On this date in 1992 Boston Celtics forward Larry Bird announced his retirement from the game at the age of 35. Bird, who along with Magic Johnson was credited with reviving the slumbering NBA, was Rookie of the Year in 1980 and a three-time MVP.

BIRTHDAYS:

Rickey Green, 1954; Fat Lever, 1960; Kenny Walker, 1964; Isaac Austin, 1969

TRIVIA:

There were more than 4,000 people on hand to see their hometown boy, Larry Bird, play his final high school game at Springs Valley High in French Lick, Indiana. The crowd was more than twice the population of the entire town.

QUIZ:

What NBA player has been on the cover of *Sports Illustrated* more than any other person?

ANSWER: *Michael Jordan*

TODAY'S THOUGHT:

"**I** don't care what people think; people are stupid." *–Charles Barkley*

HISTORY:

On this date in 1996 the Houston Rockets traded Robert Horry, Sam Cassell, Chucky Brown and Mark Bryant to the Phoenix Suns for All-Star forward Charles Barkley. Sir Charles would wind up his NBA journey playing with the likes of Hakeem Olajuwon and Clyde Drexler, but would fail to win an NBA title in his career.

BIRTHDAYS:

Stew Johnson, 1944; Ricky Pierce, 1959

TRIVIA:

Charles Barkley missed the 1994-95 season opener because of a rather bizarre ailment. Sir Charles was at an Eric Clapton concert where the bright stage lights caused Barkley to rub his eyes. He ended up burning the first layer of his corneas because of a chemical reaction from hand lotion he'd been using.

QUIZ:

Can you name the all-time leading scorer for the Phoenix Suns?

ANSWER: *Walter Davis, with 15,666 points from 1977-88*

TODAY'S THOUGHT:

"**I**'m in favor of drug tests, just so long as they are multiple choice." *–Kurt Rambis*, former NBA player

HISTORY:

On this date in 2002 the Portland Trail Blazers waived Shawn Kemp, ending his last significant stint with an NBA squad. Once regarded as a premier forward as a Supersonic in the 1990's, the troubled Kemp would play one more year before being let go by the Magic in 2003.

BIRTHDAYS:

Si Green, 1933; Quinn Buckner, 1954

TRIVIA:

In 2002, Portland's Qyntel Woods was stopped by police for speeding. When he rolled down the window of his car, police smelled marijuana, searched the vehicle, and found the drug. When they asked Woods for proof of license and insurance, the Trail Blazer had neither, so he produced the next best thing for ID - his basketball card.

QUIZ:

In his 1975 book *Maverick: More Than a Game*, what player (more famous now as a coach) claimed that LSD enhanced his play?

ANSWER: *Phil Jackson*

TODAY'S THOUGHT:

"**I** look back and know that my last seven years in the league versus my first seven years were a joke in terms of scoring. I stopped shooting - coaches asked me to do that, and I did. I wonder sometimes if that was a mistake." *–Wilt Chamberlain*

HISTORY:

On this date in 1936 Wilt Chamberlain was born. The Big Dipper was simply one of the most dominant sports figures of all-time, from his high school days in Philadelphia, where he once scored 60 points in ten minutes, to the NBA and his 100-point performance in 1962.

BIRTHDAY:

Wilt Chamberlain, 1936

TRIVIA:

Chamberlain's career scoring split shows a remarkable disparity- He averaged 40 points per game during the first half of his NBA career, and less than 20 in the second half, for a total scoring average of 30.06.

QUIZ:

True or false? In Chamberlain's 14th, and final, NBA season, he led the league in scoring.

ANSWER: *False - But he did lead the league in rebounding with an 18.6 per game average, and shot an NBA-record 72.7% from the field.*

TODAY'S THOUGHT:

"**A** tough day at the office is even tougher when your office contains spectator seating." *–Nik Posa*

HISTORY:

On this date in 1951 in Berlin, West Germany, 75,052 people turned out to watch the Harlem Globetrotters perform at Olympic Stadium. At the time, it was the largest crowd to ever attend a basketball game.

BIRTHDAYS:

Terry Catledge, 1963; Michael Curry, 1968; Andray Blatche, 1986

TRIVIA:

The Pistons were the first NBA team to go over a million in attendance, with 1,066,505 fans in 1987-88, going to the Finals before losing to L.A. The next year, Detroit won the NBA title, but attracted 190,000 fewer fans. The reason: They had moved from the cavernous Pontiac Silverdome to the 21,000-seat Palace of Auburn Hills, which they would sell out for five straight years.

QUIZ:

A simple yes or no- Is Meadowlark Lemon in the Basketball Hall of Fame?

ANSWER: *Yes*

TODAY'S THOUGHT:

"**I**sn't he that guy with Felix Unger?" –*Charles Barkley*, on Brazilian basketball star Oscar Schmidt

HISTORY:

On this date in 1987 Brazil's Oscar Schmidt scored 46 points to lead his team to a 120-115 upset over the United States in the Pan American gold medal game. Brazil came back from a 14-point halftime deficit to deny the U.S. the gold for just the second time in the 36-year history of the Pan Am games.

BIRTHDAYS:

Rick Smits, 1966; Lawrence Frank, 1970; Pat Garrity, 1976; Kobe Bryant, 1978

TRIVIA:

Oscar Schmidt was selected by the Nets in the sixth round of the 1984 NBA Draft. New Jersey spent years trying to convince him to come to the NBA, but Schmidt refused, fearing he would get little playing time. He explained, "My friend played a year in Phoenix. The guards did not like him, they don't pass him the ball."

QUIZ:

What international distinction does Henry Biasatti own?

ANSWER: He was the first Italian, and first foreign-born player, in the NBA. Biasatti played for the Toronto Huskies in 1946.

TODAY'S THOUGHT:

"**I**t was so quiet you could hear a rat pee on cotton." *-Reggie Miller*, after hitting a game-winning shot against the Suns

HISTORY:

On this date in 1965 Reggie Miller was born. The UCLA product, taken with the 11th pick of the 1987 NBA Draft by Indiana, would go on to play his entire 18-year career with the Pacers. Famed for his long range shooting, Miller has more three-pointers than anyone in NBA history (2,560).

BIRTHDAYS:

Will Frazier, 1942; Wes Matthews, 1959; Reggie Miller, 1965; Michael Redd, 1979; Charlie Villanueva, 1984

TRIVIA:

Miller was born with a hip deformity that caused severely splayed feet, making it hard for him to walk. For four years as a child, he wore leg braces to correct the problem, and doctors questioned if he would ever walk unassisted.

QUIZ:

Reggie Miller played more games with the same team than all but two players in NBA history. Who are they? (Hint: They're from the same team.)

ANSWER: *John Stockton and Karl Malone of the Utah Jazz*

TODAY'S THOUGHT:

 "fter I played him for the first time, I said, 'Let's see. He's four or five inches taller. He's 40 or 50 pounds heavier. His vertical leap is at least as good as mine. He can get up and down the floor as well as I can. And he's smart. The real problem with all this is I have to show up.'" *–Bill Russell*, on Wilt Chamberlain

HISTORY:

On this date in 1965 Bill Russell's contract demand to be paid one more dollar than his rival, Wilt Chamberlain, was met by the Boston Celtics. His upcoming salary for the year, the highest in the NBA, would be $100,001.

BIRTHDAYS:

Robert Horry, 1970; Damon Jones, 1976

TRIVIA:

Russell was teammates with baseball legend Frank Robinson on the McClymonds High School basketball squad in Oakland, CA. Russell, however, was by no means the star. In his junior year, he was cut from the junior varsity team. He played varsity ball just one season, and no college recruited him. The University of San Francisco offered him a scholarship only after he tried out.

QUIZ:

Can you name the shortest player to be selected as the MVP of the NBA in the 20th century?

ANSWER: 6'1" Bob Cousy, in 1957

TODAY'S THOUGHT:

"**I**f I was going to get beat up, I wanted to be indoors where it was warm." *–Tom Heinsohn*, on why he picked basketball over football at Holy Cross

HISTORY:

On this date in 1934 Tom Heinsohn was born. Heinsohn was a part of the Celtics' glory years, playing with Boston when they won eight NBA titles in nine years, including seven in a row between 1959 and '65. The Hall of Famer later coached the team to NBA crowns in 1974 and '76.

BIRTHDAYS:

Tom Heinsohn, 1934; Leon Douglas, 1954; Kelvin Cato, 1974; Morris Peterson, 1977

TRIVIA:

In Game 3 of the 2002 Eastern Conference Finals, the Celtics made the largest fourth-quarter comeback ever in an NBA playoff game. The victim, the New Jersey Nets, led 74-53 going into the final period. In the fourth, Boston rallied behind 19 points from Paul Pierce to outscore the Nets, 41-16, for a 94-90 win.

QUIZ:

The Nets, in 2002 and '03, are the last team to lose in consecutive NBA Finals. What two teams defeated them?

ANSWER: *Los Angeles Lakers in 2002 and San Antonio Spurs in '03*

TODAY'S THOUGHT:

"**H**e's just like me- except he's seven foot six and Chinese."
–Steve Francis, on former Rockets teammate Yao Ming

HISTORY:

On this date in 1999 the Grizzlies, Rockets and Magic pulled off an eleven-player, three-team deal. The lone big name in the trade, Steve Francis, was sent to Houston after publicly announcing he didn't want to play in Vancouver. The Grizzlies had selected Francis with the #2 pick in the draft.

BIRTHDAY:

Otto Moore, 1946

TRIVIA:

Yao Ming's father, 6'8" Yao Zhi Yuan, and mother, 6'2" Fang Feng Di, were both Chinese national team basketball players. In 2006, author Brook Larmer released *Operation Yao Ming*, a controversial book in which he claims Yao's parents were "encouraged" to wed to produce a tall, athletic superstar.

QUIZ:

In the 2004 trade that landed the Rockets Tracy McGrady, Steve Francis was shipped to Orlando with what Houston backcourt mate?

ANSWER: *Cuttino Mobley*

TODAY'S THOUGHT:

"**I**t will work out, somehow. That's a hell of a duo right there, Marbury, Crawford and Houston." *–Carmelo Anthony*, assessing the future of the 2004-05 Knicks

HISTORY:

On this date in 1983 Gerry McNamara was born. One of the most beloved players ever to wear the orange for Syracuse, McNamara started in all 135 games he played in his four years there (2002-06). He helped the school win its first national championship in 2003.

BIRTHDAYS:

John Long, 1956; Matt Carroll, 1980; Gerry McNamara, 1983

TRIVIA:

Syracuse coach Jim Boeheim has spent his entire college basketball career (player, assistant coach, and head coach) at the school. He enrolled at Syracuse in 1962 as a student, played on the basketball team as a walk-on until 1966, and in 1969 was hired as a graduate assistant. He's been with the program ever since.

QUIZ:

In his senior season, Jim Boeheim was a co-captain for Syracuse along with what future Basketball Hall of Famer?

ANSWER: *Dave Bing*

TODAY'S THOUGHT:

"I'd say I gave it the old college try, except that I never went to college.**"** *–Darryl Dawkins*

HISTORY:

On this date in 1974 Moses Malone, a Petersburg (VA) High School star, signed a seven-year contract with the ABA's Utah Stars. The 6'11" phenom, who had committed to the University of Maryland, changed his mind and became the first player to jump straight from high school to the pros.

BIRTHDAYS:

Warren Jabali, 1946; Darnell Hillman, 1949; Rodney McCray, 1961; Will Perdue, 1965; Devean George, 1977; David West, 1980; Carlos Delfino, 1982

TRIVIA:

The 1975 NBA Draft marked the first time a high school player was taken in the first round, when Darryl Dawkins was selected by the 76ers with the fifth pick. In the second round, another high schooler, Bill Willoughby, was chosen by Atlanta.

QUIZ:

The NBA's New Jersey Nets were formerly the New York Nets of the ABA who were formerly the ABA's New Jersey…?

ANSWER: *Americans*

TODAY'S THOUGHT:

"**I**t was like Hamlet. Suspense, a thriller, and then I killed them."
—Quentin Richardson, on hitting a game-winning shot

HISTORY:

On this date in 1997 the Houston Comets defeated the New York Liberty, 65-51, to become the first WNBA champions. Regular season MVP Cynthia Cooper, who led the way with 25 points, won the first of her four consecutive Finals MVP Awards.

BIRTHDAYS:

Pop Gates, 1917; Ted McClain, 1946; Bill Keller, 1947; Robert Parish, 1953; Robert Reid, 1955

TRIVIA:

In Game 2 of the 1999 WNBA Finals, the Comets were ready to celebrate another championship at the expense of the Liberty. But spoiling the party was New York guard Teresa Weatherspoon, who connected on a half-court buzzer beater to give New York a 68-67 win. Houston, however, would take the title in the deciding Game 3.

QUIZ:

Can you name the Basketball Hall of Famer who was the first head coach of the WNBA's Phoenix Mercury in 1997?

ANSWER: *Cheryl Miller*

TODAY'S THOUGHT:

 "**P**laygrounds are the best place to learn the game because if you lose, you sit down." –*Gary Williams*, college basketball coach

HISTORY:

On this date in 1990 Nat "Sweetwater" Clifton died at the age of 67. Clifton was the first African-American to sign an NBA contract. After stints with the New York Rens and the Harlem Globetrotters, Clifton signed with the New York Knicks in 1950.

BIRTHDAYS:

Mickey Johnson, 1952; Chris Duhon, 1982

TRIVIA:

The New York Rens began play in 1922 as the first all-black professional basketball team. A creation of Bob Douglas, the name came from Harlem's Renaissance Casino, which gave the team a place to play in return for publicity. In nearly 30 years in existence, the Rens won over 2,000 games.

QUIZ:

Name the former New York City playground legend, and St. John's star, who led both the NCAA and NBA in regular season assists.

ANSWER: *Mark Jackson*

TODAY'S THOUGHT:

"**I**f NBA Commissioner David Stern is really committed to bringing fans closer to the action, why not invite them to arraignments?"
–Peter Vecsey

HISTORY:

On this date in 1963 Walter Kennedy was named the NBA's second commissioner, replacing Maurice Podoloff. The league was struggling with only nine teams, but by the time Kennedy retired in 1975, the NBA had doubled in size, landed a lucrative television contract and tripled its attendance figures.

BIRTHDAYS:

Guy Rodgers, 1935; Vinnie Johnson, 1956; Tim Hardaway, 1966; Cuttino Mobley, 1975; Ryan Gomes, 1982

TRIVIA:

Before Walter Kennedy's career in the NBA front office began, he had some experience with a different breed of basketball, touring the world with the Harlem Globetrotters as their publicity director in the 1950's. Shortly after he returned home to Connecticut, Kennedy was elected the mayor of Stamford.

QUIZ:

Though not a prominent NBA name, what former Pacer and Bull was nicknamed "The Mayor?"

ANSWER: *Fred Hoiberg, who earned the moniker from his college days at Iowa State due to his extreme popularity in his hometown of Ames, Iowa*

TODAY'S THOUGHT:

"**A** champion needs a motivation above and beyond winning."
–Pat Riley

HISTORY:

On this date in 1995 Pat Riley took over the reigns as the team president and head coach of the Miami Heat. After only one winning season in their seven-year history prior to his arrival, Riley led Miami to four consecutive Atlantic Division titles from 1997-2000 and, ultimately, to the NBA crown in 2006.

BIRTHDAYS:

Adolph Rupp, 1901; Ed Conlin, 1933; John Thompson, 1941; Nate "Tiny" Archibald, 1948; Harvey Catchings, 1951; Sam Mitchell, 1963

TRIVIA:

As the head coach of the Lakers in 1986, Riley led L.A. to the largest total margin of victory in a single NBA playoff series. In a first round match-up against the Spurs, Los Angeles posted victories of 135-88, 122-94, and 114-94, totaling a 95-point disparity.

QUIZ:

Who led the Lakers to their lone NBA Finals appearance of the 1990's? (It wasn't Riley.)

ANSWER: *Mike Dunleavy, in 1991-L.A. lost to the Bulls in five games.*

TODAY'S THOUGHT:

"**I** read over the years that I was as much a Bay Area landmark as the Golden Gate Bridge. But I'm going and that bridge isn't going anywhere." –*Nate Thurmond*, after being traded from the Warriors to the Bulls

HISTORY:

On this date in 1974 the Golden State Warriors traded Hall of Famer Nate Thurmond to the Chicago Bulls for Clifford Ray. The Warriors then went on to defeat the Bulls for the Western Conference crown before sweeping the Washington Bullets in the NBA Finals.

BIRTHDAYS:

Chris Gatling, 1967; George Lynch, 1970; Damon Stoudamire, 1973

TRIVIA:

When the Warriors traded Rick Barry to the Rockets in 1978, he found himself in a dilemma. He no longer could wear his No. 24, as it belonged to Houston's Moses Malone. Barry solved the problem by wearing the No. 2 at home games and the No. 4 on the road.

QUIZ:

The Chicago Bulls and baseball's Cubs have both retired the number 10. Can you name the players they honored?

ANSWER: *Bob Love for the Bulls and Ron Santo for the Cubs*

TODAY'S THOUGHT:

"**T**here was no place I could go to cut classes." –*Marvin Barnes*, a Providence standout who led a troubled career, on why he earned a lot of college credits while in prison

HISTORY:

On this date in 1993 the University of Southern California welcomed back Cheryl Miller to its basketball program, naming her the new women's basketball coach. Miller led USC to back-to-back NCAA titles in 1983 and '84 as a player. In two seasons as a coach, her Trojans made two tournament appearances.

BIRTHDAYS:

Ben Warley, 1936; Lloyd Daniels, 1967

TRIVIA:

Lloyd "Swee'pea" Daniels, one of today's birthday boys, had a pretty miraculous basketball career considering the circumstances. A New York City playground legend, in 1989 Daniels was shot three times in the chest and survived. Though he never played in college nor was he drafted, he managed to play five NBA seasons for six teams.

QUIZ:

Can you name the former NBA head coach who was a tennis All-American at Maryland?"

ANSWER: *John Lucas*

The Basketball Almanac

TODAY'S THOUGHT:

 "We're not a very good basketball team right now. We couldn't hit a bull in the butt with a bass fiddle.**"** *–Rick Carlisle,* Pacers head coach

HISTORY:

On this date in 1979 Ann Meyers became the first woman to sign a contract with an NBA team, the Indiana Pacers. Meyers had previously been the first female to sign a four-year athletic scholarship, at UCLA, where she became the first four-time All-American. Her NBA career, however, would end after a week of training camp.

BIRTHDAYS:

Mike Barrett, 1943; Charles Williams, 1943; Julius Keye, 1946; Ken Norman, 1964; Dennis Scott, 1968; Nazr Mohammed, 1977

TRIVIA:

Penny Ann Early became the nation's first licensed female jockey in 1968, but the boys at Churchill Downs didn't take to her too kindly and boycotted the races she entered. The ABA's Kentucky Colonels saw it as a promotional opportunity and hired her for one night, for one inbound pass, making Early the first female ABA player in history.

QUIZ:

This man coached the Indiana Pacers in all but one of the team's nine ABA seasons. Do you know him?

ANSWER: *Slick Leonard*

TODAY'S THOUGHT:

"**I**f all his girlfriends buy it, it'll be a best-seller." *–Hot Rod Hundley's* ex-wife, on his autobiography

HISTORY:

On this date in 1946 Ron Boone was born. Boone, a 13-year pro, was known best for his eight seasons in the ABA, where he was a four-time All-Star and scored 12,153 points, good for third all-time. Over the past decade, Boone and broadcasting partner Hot Rod Hundley have become known as the voices of the Utah Jazz.

BIRTHDAYS:

Ron Boone, 1946; Kevin Willis, 1962; Anthony Goldwire, 1971

TRIVIA:

Another one of today's birthday boys, Kevin Willis, led a lengthy 20-year NBA career. Willis finally won his first championship ring at the age of 40, with the San Antonio Spurs. The 19-year wait, from 1984-2003, was the longest ever by an NBA player in search of his first title.

QUIZ:

This NBA Hall of Famer was a three-time MVP in the ABA. Can you name him?

ANSWER: *Julius Erving, who won the award in 1974, '75, and '76 (and in 1981 in the NBA)*

TODAY'S THOUGHT:

"**I**'ve won at every level, except college and pro." —*Shaquille O'Neal*, in the 1990's, on his lack of championships

HISTORY:

On this date in 1929 Clyde Lovellette was born. The Basketball Hall of Famer owns the distinction of being the first player ever to play on an NCAA, Olympic and NBA championship team. He won in 1952 with the Kansas Jayhawks and the U.S. Olympic squad, and claimed NBA titles with Minneapolis in '54 and Boston in '63 and '64.

BIRTHDAYS:

Al McGuire, 1928; Clyde Lovellette, 1929; Bob Verga, 1945; Antonio McDyess, 1974; Mateen Cleaves, 1977

TRIVIA:

Unfortunately, Lovellette cannot say he was a champion at *every* level of his basketball career. As a junior in 1947, his Garfield High School team in Terre Haute, Indiana, fell one game short of a state championship.

QUIZ:

Who's the only foreign-born player to win an Olympic gold medal (not with the U.S.) and an NBA championship ring?

Manu Ginobili, who won two titles with the Spurs (2003 and '05) and a gold medal for Argentina in Athens in 2004

TODAY'S THOUGHT:

 "**P**eople will look up at me and say, 'Oh, my God.' I'll tell 'em, 'No, I'm your center.'" *–7'5" Chuck Nevitt*

HISTORY:

On this date in 2004 the Bulls traded Dikembe Mutombo to the Rockets for Adrian Griffin, Eric Piatkowski and Mike Wilks. Mutombo, who had been dealt to Chicago from New York the previous month, joined his fifth team since 2001, as his days as a four-time Defensive Player of the Year appeared to be behind him.

BIRTHDAYS:

Jim Krebs, 1935; Maurice Cheeks, 1956; Latrell Sprewell, 1970; Clarence Weatherspoon, 1970; Jason Collier, 1977; Will Blalock, 1983

TRIVIA:

Even longer than the 7'2" Mutombo is his full name: Dikembe Mutombo Mpolondo Mukamba Jean Jacque Wamutombo. The 48 letters are more than twice the size of Mutombo's size-22 shoes.

QUIZ:

Of Georgetown big men Patrick Ewing, Alonzo Mourning and Dikembe Mutombo, which was selected to the most NBA All-Star teams?

ANSWER: *Ewing, with 11 – Mutombo has 8 and Mourning 7.*

TODAY'S THOUGHT:

"**I** have placed it in my will that my wife and my children can never, ever receive that medal from the '72 Olympic Games." –U.S. Team Captain *Kenny Davis*

HISTORY:

On this date in 1972 the U.S. basketball team's 63-game Olympic winning streak came to a controversial end when they lost to the Soviet Union, 51-50, in the gold medal contest in Munich. Because of issues with the game clock and horn going off, the Soviets were given three chances to convert a last-second inbound pass for the winning bucket.

BIRTHDAYS:

Walter Davis, 1954; Dan Majerle, 1965; B.J. Armstrong, 1967; Shane Battier, 1978

TRIVIA:

Following the game, Team USA filed a formal protest with the International Basketball Federation, but the panel ruled in favor of the Soviets. After refusing to accept a second-place finish, their silver medals sit unclaimed in a vault in Lausanne, Switzerland, to this day.

QUIZ:

What player hit the two free throws that put the U.S. ahead by one over the Soviets with three seconds left?

ANSWER: *Doug Collins*

TODAY'S THOUGHT:

 "Pat Knight is a living example of why some animals eat their young." *–Bobby Knight*, following his son's arrest for public intoxication

HISTORY:

On this date in 2000 Indiana University President Myles Brand fired Bobby Knight after the controversial coach violated the school's "zero tolerance" policy. Knight reportedly grabbed student Kent Harvey by the arm and scolded him after Harvey said, "Hey Knight, what's up?"

BIRTHDAYS:

Bob Lanier, 1948; Mike Glenn, 1955; Sedale Threatt, 1961; Matt Geiger, 1969; Ben Wallace, 1974; Jay Williams, 1981

TRIVIA:

In 1974, Larry Bird briefly attended Indiana University. Hailing from the small town of French Lick, the 17-year old Bird could not get used to the massive IU campus, and left before attending a single basketball practice. He worked as a garbage collector before attending the smaller Indiana State the next fall.

QUIZ:

Can you name the only college basketball coach to reach the NCAA Final Four in four different decades?

ANSWER: *Dean Smith of North Carolina, in the '60's, '70's, '80's, '90's*

The Basketball Almanac

TODAY'S THOUGHT:

"**I**t wasn't a fight. He punched me one time, that's all. I don't fight at 30,000 feet. I have an education." –Duke grad *Christian Laettner*, on a reported fight on an airplane between him and then-team-mate Jerry Stackhouse (from rival UNC, who left school early)

HISTORY:

On this date 2002 the Wizards and Pistons swapped swingmen. As part of a six-player deal, Washington sent Richard Hamilton to Detroit for Jerry Stackhouse. Hamilton would play a key role in Detroit's 2004 title-run, while Stackhouse would also make a Finals appearance, but with the Mavs in '06.

BIRTHDAYS:

Johnny Neumann, 1951; Gerald Wilkins, 1963; Ike Diogu, 1983; Shaun Livingston, 1985

TRIVIA:

Since NBA players cannot use their uniforms for advertising, Richard Hamilton decided to use his head. For several games in 2005, Goodyear Tire and Rubber Company paid the Pistons guard to braid his hair in the style of the tread pattern of their Assurance TripleTred product.

QUIZ:

In the 1999 NBA Draft, a record four players from Duke were selected among the top 15 picks. How many can you name?

(#14)

ANSWER: *Elton Brand (#1), Trajan Langdon (#11) Corey Maggette (#13), and William Avery*

TODAY'S THOUGHT:

 "**W**hat do you have when you've got an agent buried up to his neck in sand? Not enough sand." *–Pat Williams*, Orlando Magic general manager, following a contract dispute with one of his players

HISTORY:

On this date in 1984 the Chicago Bulls signed their No. 1 draft choice, Michael Jordan, to an NBA contract, locking up the North Carolina product for the next seven years. As they say, the rest is history.

BIRTHDAYS:

Phil Jordon, 1933; Clemon Johnson, 1956; Vernon Maxwell, 1965; Terry Dehere, 1971; Yao Ming, 1980; Zoran Planinic, 1982

TRIVIA:

Michael's first Nike sneaker, the Air Jordan, was a big hit among fans. However, it created controversy during the NBA season. In 1985, the league fined M.J. $1,000 for every game in which he wore his red-and-black Air Jordans. Although they matched the Bulls uniform, NBA rules stated that no player could wear sneakers different from his teammates.

QUIZ:

Who was the last man to lead the NBA in scoring before Michael Jordan's seven-year streak from 1987-93?

ANSWER: *Dominique Wilkins*

TODAY'S THOUGHT:

 "**T**here was no evidence of him being under the influence. And we won't charge him with murder for killing the hydrant." *—Sgt. John Edmundson*, after Shawn Kemp crashed his car into a fire hydrant and a stop sign

HISTORY:

On this date in 2002 DerMarr Johnson, the Hawks' No. 1 draft pick out of Cincinnati in 2000, suffered a broken neck in a near-fatal car accident in south Atlanta. Miraculously, Johnson was back on the court within a year, and completed his return in 2004 by playing in 21 games with the Knicks.

BIRTHDAYS:

Willie Murrell, 1941; Nene, 1982

TRIVIA:

In a scary moment during a 1988 Kings-Blazers game, Sacramento coach Jerry Reynolds, known to pull pranks, suddenly collapsed in front of his team's bench. An official, thinking Reynolds was mocking his calls, even gave him a technical foul. When it became evident that Reynolds had in fact passed out, he was rushed to a hospital. He would be fine.

QUIZ:

After leaving Cincinnati, what college basketball team did Bob Huggins become the head coach of in 2006?

ANSWER: *Kansas State University*

TODAY'S THOUGHT:

"**I**t's been consistent. When thing aren't looking good, you can look at Doug and feel good about yourself." *–Larry Brown*, on his relationship with former NBA coach Doug Moe

HISTORY:

On this date in 1940 Larry Brown was born. The well-traveled coach became the first to lead both a college team, Kansas University in 1988, and an NBA club, Detroit Pistons in 2004, to championships. He's also the first NBA coach to guide seven different franchises to the playoffs.

BIRTHDAYS:

Larry Brown, 1940; Alvin Scott, 1955; Pete Chilcutt, 1968

TRIVIA:

In 1983, a Blazers blowout win over Doug Moe's Nuggets was all but complete- until Moe called timeout with a minute to play. Moe instructed his squad to stop playing defense and let the Blazers get the team scoring record they were closing in on. After five uncontested baskets, Portland set their new mark, winning 156-116. Moe's act of kindness cost him $5,000 and a two-game suspension.

QUIZ:

True or false? Larry Brown has never won the NBA's Coach of the Year Award.

ANSWER: *False - He won it once, when he led the 76ers to the Finals in 2001.*

TODAY'S THOUGHT:

 "Saltwater taffy."** *–Caldwell Jones*, former NBA center, naming his favorite seafood

HISTORY:

On this date in 1982 the Rockets executed a sign-and-trade with the 76ers, re-signing restricted free agent Moses Malone and shipping him to Philadelphia for Caldwell Jones and a first-round draft pick. The following season, Malone would lead Philly to the NBA title and win his second straight MVP Award.

BIRTHDAYS:

Mike Davis, 1960; Sherman Douglas, 1966; Jason Terry, 1977; Mike Dunleavy Jr., 1980

TRIVIA:

A former 76ers teammate of Malone's, Charles Barkley is known to many as the "Round Mound of Rebound." To others, he's "Sir Charles." And because of Barkley's ferocious appetite, to golf's Tiger Woods, he's "Sir Cumference."

QUIZ:

Who are Hondo, The Microwave, and The Boston Strangler?

ANSWER: *John Havlicek, Vinnie Johnson and Andrew Toney*

TODAY'S THOUGHT:

 "He would drive people insane and then just walk away. He was like Gandhi." *–Chuck Daly*, on his former player, Bill Laimbeer

HISTORY:

On this date in 2003 a record WNBA crowd of 22,076 was on hand at the Palace of Auburn Hills to watch the Detroit Shock win their first WNBA title. Detroit defeated the Sparks, 83-78, in a deciding Game 3, denying Los Angeles their third consecutive championship.

BIRTHDAYS:

Elgin Baylor, 1934; Bill McGill, 1939; Ron Brewer, 1955; Greg Buckner, 1976; Dan Dickau, 1978

TRIVIA:

The 2003 WNBA Finals featured a match up of two former NBA players both coaching in their respective NBA cities- the L.A. Sparks' Michael Cooper and the Detroit Shock's Bill Laimbeer. Cooper's Lakers and Laimbeer's Pistons battled in two NBA Finals in 1988 and '89, each winning one.

QUIZ:

Can you name the man who was named the WNBA Coach of the Year in the league's first three seasons?

ANSWER: *Van Chancellor, with the Houston Comets*

TODAY'S THOUGHT:

 e don't see ourselves as four All-Stars. We see our-selves as one unit. It's like five fingers on a hand. You can do more damage together as a fist than spread out flat." *–Rasheed Wallace*, on being one of four Pistons selected to the 2006 All-Star team

HISTORY:

On this date in 1974 Rasheed Wallace was born. Often a cause of controversy, the former Trail Blazer resurrected his NBA career with the Pistons. Along with the since-departed Ben Wallace, the duo formed the core of Detroit's smothering defense, a key ingredient in their 2004 championship season.

BIRTHDAYS:

Phil Jackson, 1945; Kermit Washington, 1951; Junior Bridgeman, 1953; Rasheed Wallace, 1974

TRIVIA:

As a thank you to their fans, Detroit decided to give one lucky person an authentic $15,000 Pistons championship ring. Dave Muehring, the winner of the 25,000-entry drawing, received his ring along with the Detroit players and executives before the start of the team's 2004-05 season opener against Houston.

QUIZ:

With what team did 2004 NBA Finals MVP Chauncey Billups begin his NBA career?

ANSWER: *The Boston Celtics, in 1997*

TODAY'S THOUGHT:

 "**T**hey talk about the economy this year. Hey, my hairline is in recession, my waistline is in inflation. All together, I'm in a depression." *–Rick Majerus*, former Utah head coach

HISTORY:

On this date in 1952 Rick Pitino was born. While Pitino coached with mixed results on the pro level with the Knicks and Celtics, he remains a top coach in the college game. He led Kentucky to a 1996 NCAA championship, and guided three different teams (Louisville, Kentucky, and Providence) to the Final Four.

BIRTHDAYS:

Red Rocha, 1923; Rick Pitino, 1952; Dennis Johnson, 1954; Toni Kukoc, 1968; Travis Outlaw, 1984

TRIVIA:

Former Michigan star Chris Webber bought himself a self-deprecating reminder of the infamous timeout he tried to call during the 1993 NCAA Championship Game against North Carolina- vanity plates that read "Timeout." He also formed a charitable organization appropriately named the Timeout Foundation.

QUIZ:

Because it does not have a postseason tournament, what league's conference champion receives an automatic bid to The Big Dance?

ANSWER: *The Ivy League*

TODAY'S THOUGHT:

"**I** love the tension. I love when everything's going wrong ... In the NBA, they don't promote guys like me. They like guys who like Cheerios, good guys." *—Ron Artest*

HISTORY:

On this date in 2005 the NBA announced a new affiliation system for its Development League. NBA clubs would now be assigned a specific D-League team to which they could send any rookie and second-year players. The move was made by Commissioner David Stern in hopes of creating a true minor league farm system for the NBA.

BIRTHDAYS:

Brian Hill, 1947; Sidney Wicks, 1949; Raja Bell, 1976

TRIVIA:

In 1998, Isiah Thomas became the owner of the Continental Basketball Association, the former minor leagues of the NBA. Two years later, the league was forced into bankruptcy and folded. The blame is often attributed to Thomas for his poor management skills and spending habits.

QUIZ:

The fourth pick in the 2000 NBA Draft, this huge bust in the pros was the D-League's MVP for the 2005-06 season. Who is he?

ANSWER: *Marcus Fizer*

TODAY'S THOUGHT:

 "**T**he Boston Celtics are not a basketball team; they are a way of life." *–Red Auerbach*

HISTORY:

On this date in 1917 Red Auerbach was born. The Hall of Famer began coaching in the NBA in its inaugural season, 1946, and joined the Celtics in 1950, where he's remained with the team in some capacity ever since. He coached Boston to nine championships, eight consecutively, up until 1966, and later won seven titles as a member of the Celtics' front office.

BIRTHDAYS:

Red Auerbach, 1917; Dave Twardzik, 1950

TRIVIA:

The Boston Celtics' famous logo of a winking leprechaun was designed by Zang Auerbach, Red's brother, in the early 1950's. Zang had previously worked as a political cartoonist at the now-defunct *Washington Star*.

QUIZ:

Can you name the last Celtics coach to lead Boston to a 50-win season?

ANSWER: Chris Ford, in 1991-92 (Boston went 51-31.)

TODAY'S THOUGHT:

"**I**'m quitting this team for the Olympic swim team. I'm going to the pool as long as there are babes with no tops. You'll think I'm Mark Spitz before this week is over." –*Charles Barkley*, on women sunbathing topless in Monte Carlo, site of the 1992 U.S. Olympic team training camp

HISTORY:

On this date in 1991 the "Dream Team", the first-ever USA Basketball squad comprised of NBA players, was officially announced. The collection of twelve superstars to play in the 1992 Olympics would be headed by Michael Jordan, Larry Bird, and Magic Johnson.

BIRTHDAYS:

Doug Moe, 1938; Joe Strawder, 1940; Artis Gilmore, 1948; Bob Huggins, 1953; Sidney Moncrief, 1957; Rick Mahorn, 1958; Bryce Drew, 1974

TRIVIA:

Two Dream Team members, Charles Barkley and Scottie Pippen, played together on Houston in 1999 after Barkley took a pay cut so the Rockets could acquire Pippen from the Bulls. Things didn't work out, Houston made a quick exit from the playoffs, and Pippen complained of Barkley's "sorry, fat butt." Three days later, Scottie's butt was headed for Portland.

QUIZ:

Scottie Pippen was originally drafted by what NBA team?

ANSWER: *Seattle Sonics, with the 5th pick in 1987- He was then traded to the Bulls for their draft choice, Olden Polynice, selected at #8.*

TODAY'S THOUGHT:

"**I** knew that if he shot off his mouth long enough, he'd say something right." *–Billy Tubbs*, former Oklahoma college basketball coach, on the garrulous Dick Vitale calling him an offensive genius

HISTORY:

On this date in 1934 Lute Olson was born. The longtime head coach of the Arizona Wildcats has made five Final Four appearances (including one from his days with Iowa) and won it all in 1997. That year, Arizona had the unprecedented distinction of defeating three number one seeds in the same tournament.

BIRTHDAYS:

Lute Olson, 1934; Larry Jones, 1942; David Stern, 1942; Gary Trent, 1974; Swin Cash, 1979; Jannero Pargo, 1979

TRIVIA:

Arizona's basketball program has been called "Point Guard U" because of all the players who've excelled at the "1" spot- among them Steve Kerr, Mike Bibby, Gilbert Arenas, Jason Terry and Damon Stoudamire.

QUIZ:

Mike Krzyzewski was Army's captain and point guard in his junior and senior year. Who was Coach K's coach?

ANSWER: *Bobby Knight*

TODAY'S THOUGHT:

" **A** bsolute silence – that's one thing a sportswriter can quote accurately." *–Bobby Knight*

HISTORY:

On this date in 2003 Rebecca Lobo, one of the WNBA's original players, retired from the league. Lobo played most of her pro career with the New York Liberty, but may be remembered best for her college days at UConn. In 1995, she led the undefeated Huskies to a national championship, and was named the Women's Player of the Year.

BIRTHDAYS:

Eric Montross, 1971; Ricky Davis, 1979

TRIVIA:

Lobo is married to *Sports Illustrated* writer Steve Rushin. Rushin, who writes the weekly column "Air and Space" for the magazine, was named the 2005 National Sportswriter of the Year by the National Sportscasters and Sportswriters Association.

QUIZ:

In 2006, who broke the WNBA's single-game scoring record by pouring in 47 points in a triple-overtime contest?

ANSWER: *The Phoenix Mercury's Diana Taurasi, in a 111-110 win over the Houston Comets*

TODAY'S THOUGHT:

I 've had to overcome a lot of diversity." –Cavaliers forward *Drew Gooden*, on the ups and downs of his NBA career

HISTORY:

On this date in 1983 Randy Foye was born. The former Villanova guard was the Big East Player of the Year in 2006. Selected by the Boston Celtics with the 7th overall pick in that same year, Foye eventually wound up with the Minnesota Timberwolves after a series of trades.

BIRTHDAYS:

Ron Williams, 1944; Drew Gooden, 1981; Randy Foye, 1983

TRIVIA:

Randy Foye reportedly has the rare condition situs inversus, which means his organs are arranged as the mirror image of a normal person's. For example, his heart is on the right side rather than the left. This condition, however, is not expected to impact his health or his game.

QUIZ:

The college basketball facility in Baton Rouge, Louisiana, is named for what former player?

ANSWER: *Pete Maravich (LSU Pete Maravich Arena)*

TODAY'S THOUGHT:

 o be successful you have to be selfish, or else you never achieve. And once you get to your highest level, then you have to be unselfish. Stay reachable. Stay in touch. Don't isolate." *–Michael Jordan*

HISTORY:

On this date in 2001 Michael Jordan announced he was leaving the Washington Wizards front office to come out of retirement (for a second time) and play for the team. Jordan would donate his entire $1 million salary to victims of the 9/11 terrorist attacks that occurred just weeks earlier.

BIRTHDAYS:

Carl Braun, 1927; Hubie Brown, 1933; Bob McAdoo, 1951; Scottie Pippen, 1965; Chauncey Billups, 1976; Rashad McCants, 1984

TRIVIA:

Jordan played his first game for the Wizards in New York. To raise money for a recently created 9/11 charity, celebrity Knicks fan Spike Lee sold one of his courtside seats on an Internet auction. The anonymous winner, who paid $101,300 for the seat, gave the ticket to a child of one of the firefighters who died in the World Trade Center tragedy.

QUIZ:

Can you name the only North Carolina player other than Michael Jordan to win an NBA MVP?

ANSWER: *Bob McAdoo, in 1975*

TODAY'S THOUGHT:

"**I** don't have the first clue who he's talking about because all I worry about is Jerome." *–Jerome James*, in response to Sonics coach Nate McMillan calling him selfish

HISTORY:

On this date in 1973 Wilt Chamberlain signed a contract to take over the coaching reins of the ABA's San Diego Conquistadors. His tenure would last for just one season as San Diego finished with a 37-47 record, yet still made the playoffs.

BIRTHDAYS:

Mike Farmer, 1936; Lucius Allen, 1947; John Roche, 1949

TRIVIA:

Originally, Chamberlain signed on as a player-coach with the Conquistadors. However his former NBA team, the Lakers, claimed Chamberlain still owed L.A. the final year on his previous contract. They sued and won the case, and Chamberlain was forbidden to play on any team but the Lakers, despite the fact that he was now in a different league.

QUIZ:

This Basketball Hall of Famer coached ten seasons in the NBA, but his first head-coaching job came with the Conquistadors in 1972. Who is he?

ANSWER: K.C. Jones

TODAY'S THOUGHT:

T "he main ingredient of stardom is the rest of the team."
—John Wooden

HISTORY:

On this date in 2002 the Harlem Globetrotters were enshrined in the Basketball Hall of Fame as a team. Since Abe Saperstein originated the comedic club in Chicago in 1927, the Globetrotters have won more than 22,000 games and once had an 8,829 game winning streak.

BIRTHDAY:

Steve Kerr, 1965

TRIVIA:

The first Globetrotter-NBA team match-up occurred in 1948 when the barnstorming club took on the George Mikan-led Minneapolis Lakers. With the score tied at 59 and less than a minute to go, Trotters' ball handling wizard Marques Haynes dribbled down the clock and then flipped the ball to Ermer Robinson, who hit a buzzer-beater for the win.

QUIZ:

What state currently has the most NBA teams?

ANSWER: *California, with four (Clippers, Kings, Lakers and Warriors)*

TODAY'S THOUGHT:

"Did you know James Naismith came up with the game (of basketball) as a way to keep young men away from women and out of trouble? Well, that sure worked well!" *–Jay Leno*

HISTORY:

On this date in 2002 the Naismith Memorial Basketball Hall of Fame opened up its third home, one day after welcoming its newest class. The brand-new $45 million, 80,000 square foot shrine in Springfield, Massachusetts is located right on the Connecticut River and just south of the previous Hall of Fame.

BIRTHDAYS:

Randolph Mahaffey, 1945; Mitchell Wiggins, 1959; Johnny Dawkins, 1963; Bonzi Wells, 1976; Jose Calderon, 1981; Emeka Okafor, 1982; Anderson Varejao, 1982

TRIVIA:

James Naismith's 13 Original Rules of "Basket Ball" were published in January of 1892 in the Springfield College school newspaper, *The Triangle*. "Basketball" was originally two words until it was changed much later in the game.

QUIZ:

Playing by the Rules: You take a shot which hits the rim, bounces up and rolls along the top of the backboard. Is the ball out of play?

ANSWER: *No – It's still in play.*

TODAY'S THOUGHT:

"**N**o, Reggie, that's just your ego." *–Cheryl Miller*, to her brother, about his claim that his Olympic gold medal was bigger than hers

HISTORY:

On this date in 1988 the U.S. Women's Olympic basketball team won the gold medal in Seoul with a 77-70 victory over Yugoslavia. Team USA was led by 18 points from Teresa Edwards as it finished off its second consecutive sweep of the Summer Games.

BIRTHDAY:

Hersey Hawkins, 1966

TRIVIA:

In the '88 Games, the U.S. women's squad went over the century mark for the first time in their Olympic basketball history, with a 101-74 win over Yugoslavia. When they again topped 100 just two games later, they posted their first-ever victory over the Soviet Union in Olympic competition.

QUIZ:

In what state is the Women's Basketball Hall of Fame located?

ANSWER: *Tennessee (in Knoxville)*

TODAY'S THOUGHT:

 "**G**ood, better, best. Never let it rest. Until your good is better and your better is best." *–Tim Duncan*, on his approach to basketball

HISTORY:

On this date in 2000 the U.S. men's basketball team captured its 12th gold medal in 14 Olympic competitions after defeating France, 85-75, in Sydney, Australia. Team USA showed signs of weakness by barely surviving their semifinal game, winning 85-83, only after Lithuania missed a three-pointer at the buzzer.

BIRTHDAYS:

Red Robbins, 1944; John Drew, 1954; Jerome Whitehead, 1956; Eric Piatkowski, 1970

TRIVIA:

Larry Brown is the only man to both play and coach for the United States in the Olympics. He was a player on the 1964 squad that beat the Soviet Union to win the gold in Tokyo. Then in Athens in 2004, Brown coached Team USA to their disappointing bronze medal, as Argentina claimed its first gold.

QUIZ:

What Basketball Hall of Famer coached the USA to the gold at the 1996 Summer Games in Atlanta?

ANSWER: Lenny Wilkens, then the head coach of the Atlanta Hawks

TODAY'S THOUGHT:

The older I get, the better I used to be." –NBA Hall of Famer *Connie Hawkins*

HISTORY:

On this date in 1999 Boston Celtics forward Kevin McHale and Georgetown coach John Thompson headlined a class of five that was enshrined into the Naismith Basketball Hall of Fame in Springfield (MA). McHale, a seven-time All-Star, won three titles with the Celtics. Thompson reached the NCAA Final Four three times with the Hoyas, winning one championship.

BIRTHDAY:

Alton Lister, 1958

TRIVIA:

Wayne Embry, another member of that class, became the NBA's first black general manager in 1971 when he took over the Milwaukee Bucks. Embry was also the league's first black team president, taking the helm of the Cleveland Cavaliers in 1994.

QUIZ:

Who is the only NBA player in the Basketball Hall of Fame whose last name begins with the letter "I"?

ANSWER: *Dan Issel*

TODAY'S THOUGHT:

"**D**ennis ain't as crazy as he seems. I would leave my kids with him." *–John Lucas*, former Spurs coach, on Dennis Rodman

HISTORY:

On this date in 1995 the San Antonio Spurs traded Dennis Rodman to Chicago for Will Perdue. The controversial rebounding machine would win a title in each of his three years with the Bulls before brief stints with the Lakers and Mavericks in 1999 and 2000.

BIRTHDAYS:

Dick Barnett, 1936; Connie Dierking, 1936; Tom Boswell, 1953; Aaron Williams, 1971; Aaron McKie, 1972; Anthony Johnson, 1974; Primoz Brezec, 1979; Tyson Chandler, 1982

TRIVIA:

In 1953, Bill Chambers of William and Mary became the first player in NCAA history to pull down 50 rebounds in a single game, grabbing 51 against Virginia. Over a half-century later, his record has yet to be broken.

QUIZ:

At what NAIA school did Dennis Rodman play his college ball?

ANSWER: *Southeastern Oklahoma State University*

TODAY'S THOUGHT:

 "He was the one who fouled me...I wouldn't have blown the game if it hadn't been for (Jerry) West." –Chicago Bulls rookie *Tom Boerwinkle*, after missing three straight last-second foul shots and costing his team a shot at the playoffs

HISTORY:

On this date in 1974 Jerry West, the Lakers' "Mr. Clutch" for 14 NBA seasons, announced his retirement. L.A.'s all-time leading scorer earned his nickname by averaging over 29 points per game in 153 playoff contests.

BIRTHDAY:

Greg Foster, 1968

TRIVIA:

West was dubbed "Zeke from Cabin Creek" because of his West Virginia roots, but the Hall of Famer was not too fond of the nickname. West actually grew up in Cheylan, although his family received its mail in the town of Cabin Creek.

QUIZ:

Two men from West Virginia have been selected first overall in the NBA Draft. The first was Mark Workman in 1952 by the Hawks. Can you name the second?

ANSWER: *Hot Rod Hundley, by the Cincinnati Royals in 1957 — West was the second overall pick in 1960.*

TODAY'S THOUGHT:

"**I** really didn't want it, but now that I've won it, it's nice. It's an honor. It's nice to know people don't think you're a total idiot. ... It must have been a poor year for coaches."
–Doug Moe, named 1988 NBA Coach of the Year

HISTORY:

On this date in 2001 84-year old Red Auerbach was once again named the president of the Boston Celtics, a title he held for 27 years before giving it up in 1997. In Auerbach's first year back, the Celtics would reach the Conference Finals for the first time since 1988.

BIRTHDAYS:

Hub Reed, 1936; Truck Robinson, 1951; Jim McElroy, 1953; A.C. Green, 1963; Kurt Thomas, 1972; James Jones, 1980

TRIVIA:

Despite winning nine NBA championships as the head coach of the Celtics, Auerbach was named Coach of the Year only once, in 1965. Ironically, the award is now called the Red Auerbach Trophy.

QUIZ:

Can you name the only one of the Top 10 Coaches (as named by the league in 1996) to have never won an NBA championship?

ANSWER: Don Nelson

TODAY'S THOUGHT:

"**I**'m getting awfully tired of this baloney. Every kid who can dribble a ball gets called 'as good as Cousy.' Well, I've got news for you. There ain't nobody as good as Cooz. There never was."
–*Red Auerbach*, on Bob Cousy

HISTORY:

On this date in 1950 players from the defunct Chicago Stags were dispersed to NBA teams in a drawing. The Boston Celtics, disappointed that first choice Max Zaslofsky was picked by New York, pulled the name of Bob Cousy from the hat.

BIRTHDAYS:

Adrian Smith, 1936; Aaron James, 1952; Kelvin Sampson, 1955; Rex Chapman, 1967; Grant Hill, 1972

TRIVIA:

General Manager Red Auerbach passed on Cousy with the first pick of the 1950 NBA Draft, opting to select center Chuck Share of Bowling Green. When the media criticized his choice, Auerbach explained, "Little men are a dime a dozen. I'm supposed to win, not go after local yokels."

QUIZ:

What brewery owned the Boston Celtics for two years in the late 1960's?

ANSWER: Ballantine, from 1968-69

TODAY'S THOUGHT:

"**N**o comment." *–Michael Jordan*, asked for his response to making the All-Interview Team

HISTORY:

On this date in 1993 30-year old Michael Jordan announced his retirement from the NBA at a Chicago news conference, citing a lost desire to play the game.

BIRTHDAYS:

Stan McKenzie, 1944; Wendell Ladner, 1948; Ricky Berry, 1964; Rebecca Lobo, 1973

TRIVIA:

Standing at the foul line in a game against Denver in 1991, Jordan was kiddingly asked by Nuggets rookie Dikembe Mutombo if he could make a free throw with his eyes closed. Jordan shut his eyes, swished the shot, turned to Mutombo and said, "Welcome to the NBA."

QUIZ:

True or false? Michael Jordan's career scoring average is below 30 points per game.

ANSWER: *False - It's 30.1.*

TODAY'S THOUGHT:

"**L**eft hand, right hand, it doesn't matter. I'm amphibious."
–*Charles Shackleford*, former NBA player

HISTORY:

On this date in 1985 Lynette Woodard, a former Kansas All-American and 1984 Olympic gold medalist, became the first female member of the famed Harlem Globetrotters. Woodard would play two seasons with the 'Trotters before moving to Italy to play professionally.

BIRTHDAY:

Willie Naulls, 1934

TRIVIA:

Woodard's cousin, Hubert "Geese" Ausbie, played with the Globetrotters for 24 years, serving as the team's "Clown Prince" from 1961 until 1985. In 1994, he was given a Globetrotters "Legends" ring, an honor shared by a select few.

QUIZ:

Who is the only NBA Hall of Famer to have his Harlem Globetrotters uniform number retired?

ANSWER: *Wilt Chamberlain, #13*

TODAY'S THOUGHT:

 Fans never fall asleep at our games, because they're afraid they might get hit by a pass." *–George Raveling,* college basketball coach

HISTORY:

On this date in 1975 the Louisiana Superdome, which would soon become the home of the New Orleans Jazz, hosted its first-ever basketball game. The San Antonio Spurs, then with the ABA, defeated the NBA's Atlanta Hawks, 109-107, in an exhibition contest.

BIRTHDAY:

Monty Williams, 1971

TRIVIA:

From 1973-92, the Spurs played their home games at HemisFair Arena, which had an original capacity of 10,000. To create more seats, the roof of the arena was raised, but it created another problem. The new support beams for the upper deck obstructed views from seats in the lower levels.

QUIZ:

What's the largest arena in the NBA?

ANSWER: *The Palace of Auburn Hills, home of the Detroit Pistons, has a capacity of 22,076.*

TODAY'S THOUGHT:

"Michael, if you can't pass, you can't play." *–Dean Smith*, to freshman Michael Jordan

HISTORY:

On this date in 1997 the legendary Dean Smith announced his retirement at the Dean Dome, the North Carolina court named in his honor. In 36 years, Smith coached the Tarheels to 879 wins, 11 Final Four appearances, and two NCAA championships.

BIRTHDAYS:

Arnie Risen, 1924; Kenny Anderson, 1970; Juan Dixon, 1978; Darius Miles, 1981

TRIVIA:

After graduating college, Smith served a stint in the United States Air Force in Germany. From 1955-58 he served as an assistant basketball coach and also the head coach of the baseball and golf teams at the Air Force Academy.

QUIZ:

Baseball Hall of Famer Sandy Koufax played one season of college basketball at what university?

ANSWER: *Cincinnati*

TODAY'S THOUGHT:

"**T**he Knicks recently retired Patrick Ewing's jersey. In keeping with tradition, it will disappear in the fourth quarter."
—Steve Rosenbloom

HISTORY:

On this date in 2001 the Knicks' Larry Johnson announced that chronic back problems were forcing him to retire from the NBA. Selected by Charlotte as the first pick overall in the 1991 draft, Johnson averaged 16.2 points and 7.5 rebounds per game in his 10-year career.

BIRTHDAYS:

Gus Williams, 1953; Derrick McKey, 1966; Yinka Dare, 1972; Joel Przybilla, 1979; Ryan Hollins, 1984

TRIVIA:

The Knicks retired "613" in honor of coach Red Holzman. That's the number of games Holzman won in his 14 seasons with the team. When New York raised it to the rafters, it became the highest number to be retired by any club in NBA history.

QUIZ:

With what two teams did Patrick Ewing finish his career after leaving the Knicks in 2000?

ANSWER: *Seattle Supersonics and Orlando Magic*

TODAY'S THOUGHT:

 e couldn't beat ... us. We couldn't even beat us. I was trying to think of somebody bad, and I couldn't think of anybody else." *–Tim Legler,* after a Mavericks' blowout loss to the Spurs

HISTORY:

On this date in 1980 the expansion Dallas Mavericks kicked off their inaugural NBA season with a surprising 103-92 win over the San Antonio Spurs. The Mavs, however, would lose 15 of their next 16 games and finish the year at 15-67.

BIRTHDAYS:

Norm Nixon, 1955; Desmond Mason, 1977; Salim Stoudamire, 1982

TRIVIA:

During the 1992-93 season, the Mavericks were on a pace to match the 1973 76ers for the worst record in league history. Dallas stood at 4-57 after 61 games, but managed to split their final six contests to finish at 11-71, missing the record by two games.

QUIZ:

Can you name the last NBA team to lose 70 or more games in a single season? (It happened in 1997-98.)

ANSWER: *The Denver Nuggets, with a mark of 11-71*

TODAY'S THOUGHT:

"**W**e have a great bunch of outside shooters. Unfortunately, all our games are played indoors." *–Weldon Drew*, former college basketball coach

HISTORY:

On this date in 1979 the Celtics' Chris Ford scored the first three-point basket in NBA history with 3:48 left in the first quarter of a victory over the Rockets at Boston Garden. The historic game also marked the professional debut of Larry Bird.

BIRTHDAYS:

Jack Marin, 1944; Charlie Ward, 1970; Marko Jaric, 1978

TRIVIA:

Thanks in large part to Larry Bird, the Celtics experienced one of the NBA's best single-season turnarounds in the 1979-80 campaign. They went from 29-53 the previous year to 61-21, the league's best record, in Bird's rookie season.

QUIZ:

Who is the tallest player to win an NBA Three-Point Shootout?

ANSWER: *Seven-footer Dirk Nowitzki, in 2006*

TODAY'S THOUGHT:

" **I** 'm an optometrist. I always believe in good - well you know what I mean. I believe in good stuff." *–Mychal Thompson*, former NBA player turned optimist and, sometimes, eye doctor

HISTORY:

On this date in 1967 the first game in ABA history tipped off, as the Oakland Oaks defeated the Anaheim Amigos, 134-129. Of the 11 teams in the league, the Oaks and Amigos would be the only two to lose more than 50 games that season.

BIRTHDAYS:

Nathaniel Clifton, 1922; Reggie Theus, 1957; Derek Harper, 1961; Doc Rivers, 1961; Paul Pierce, 1977; Jermaine O'Neal, 1978

TRIVIA:

When the ABA folded in 1976, two of its six remaining teams were not invited to join the NBA. One owner accepted $3 million in compensation. Ozzie and Dan Silna, owners of the St. Louis Spirits, fought for a share of TV revenues from the four teams entering the NBA. So far they've collected over $160 million, with more coming every season.

QUIZ:

Two players in ABA history won the All-Star Game and regular season MVP Awards in the same year. Can you name them?

ANSWER: *Spencer Haywood (1970) and Mel Daniels ('71)*

TODAY'S THOUGHT:

 "H e doesn't shine them ... he sends them through a car wash."
—*Lynn Shackelford*, former UCLA forward, describing the size-22 shoes worn by Bob Lanier

HISTORY:

On this date in 1970 two future Hall of Famers made their NBA debuts. Bob Lanier took the floor for the Detroit Pistons in a victory over Seattle, while Nate "Tiny" Archibald and the Cincinnati Royals lost at home against New York.

BIRTHDAYS:

John Wooden, 1910; Ray Williams, 1954; P.J. Brown, 1969; Jim Jackson, 1970

TRIVIA:

When Bob Lanier hung up his basketball shoes in 1984 after 14 years in the NBA, he joked that he did so only because the Milwaukee Bucks had finally found another player, Alton Lister, who could literally fill Lanier's size-22 sneakers.

QUIZ:

With what team did Celtics legend Bill Sharman begin his NBA career?

ANSWER: *The Washington Capitols, before they folded midway through the 1950-51 season*

TODAY'S THOUGHT:

 "Coaches who start listening to fans wind up sitting next to them." *–Johnny Kerr,* former NBA coach

HISTORY:

On this date in 1966 Bill Russell made his debut as the NBA's first black head coach. Russell, serving a dual role as a player-coach, led the Celtics to a 121-113 win over the San Francisco Warriors. Boston would finish the year at 60-21, but lose in the second round of the playoffs.

BIRTHDAYS:

Ron Anderson, 1958; Fred Hoiberg, 1972

TRIVIA:

In 1911, it was illegal to coach during a basketball game, even during time-outs. An initial violation led to a warning, with subsequent infractions resulting in free throws for the opposing team. Not until 1949 were coaches allowed to speak to their players during a timeout.

QUIZ:

What other two NBA teams did Bill Russell coach in his career?

ANSWER: *Seattle Supersonics and Sacramento Kings*

TODAY'S THOUGHT:

"**I** come from New York, where if you fall down, someone will pick you up by the wallet." *–Al McGuire*

HISTORY:

On this date in 1968 the Harlem Globetrotters finally played their first game in Harlem, New York. It had been 41 years and more than 9,500 games since the team debuted in Hinckley, Illinois.

BIRTHDAYS:

Dave DeBusschere, 1940; Mel Counts, 1941; John Mengelt, 1949; Manute Bol, 1962; Tom Tolbert, 1965; Sue Bird, 1980; Alan Anderson, 1982

TRIVIA:

The Globetrotters were actually formed from Chicago's Wendell Phillips High School. The team played in the Negro American Legion League as the "Giles Post," and in 1927 turned professional as the Savoy Big Five under manager Dick Hudson.

QUIZ:

What is the Harlem Globetrotters' theme song?

ANSWER: *Sweet Georgia Brown*

TODAY'S THOUGHT:

 o for the moon. If you don't get it, you'll still be heading for a star." –*Willis Reed*

HISTORY:

On this date in 1964, '68, and '70, three of the NBA's 50 Greatest Players saw their first professional action. In 1964, Willis Reed debuted for the New York Knicks; in 1968, Elvin Hayes began his career with the Houston Rockets; and, in 1970, Pete Maravich saw his first NBA action with the Atlanta Hawks.

BIRTHDAYS:

Steve Jones, 1942; Jay Humphries, 1962; Danny Ferry, 1966

TRIVIA:

In 1971, Atlanta teammates and future Hall of Famers "Pistol" Pete Maravich and Walt "Bells" Bellamy became the first NBA players to put their nicknames on the back of their jerseys.

QUIZ:

This future NBA Coach of the Year was a college teammate of Elvin Hayes at Houston and, like Hayes, was a first round pick in the 1968 draft. Name him.

ANSWER: *Don Chaney, who was taken by the Boston Celtics*

TODAY'S THOUGHT:

 "**A**lert NBA statisticians immediately credited Forte with the off-season's first trouble-double." *–Dwight Perry* of the *Seattle Times*, on the Sonics' Joe Forte being charged with speeding, drug possession, and illegal gun possession all in one day

HISTORY:

On this date in 1974 Chicago center Nate Thurmond, in his first game with the Bulls, recorded the NBA's first quadruple-double. Thurmond's 22 points, 14 rebounds, 13 assists and 12 blocks led the Bulls to a 120-115 overtime win against Atlanta.

BIRTHDAYS:

John Johnson, 1947; Terry Furlow, 1954; Anthony Avent, 1969

TRIVIA:

Wilt Chamberlain is the only player in NBA history to record a double-triple-double (20 points, 20 rebounds, 20 assists in one game). In a 76ers' win over the Pistons in 1968, the Big Dipper logged an astounding 22 points, 25 rebounds and 21 assists.

QUIZ:

Can you name the only two players with over 100 career triple-doubles?

ANSWER: *Oscar Robertson (181) and Magic Johnson (138)*

TODAY'S THOUGHT:

"I don't think we learned a lesson; I think it was a learning experience for us." *–Shaquille O'Neal*, to Jim Gray, after a 2001 NBA Finals Game 4 win

HISTORY:

On this date in 1960 the Lakers began their first season in Los Angeles, falling to the Cincinnati Royals, 140-123. The team had spent the previous 12 years in Minneapolis. The contest also marked the NBA debuts of future Hall of Famers Oscar Robertson and Jerry West.

BIRTHDAYS:

Bill Melchionni, 1944; Lionel Hollins, 1953; Lonnie Shelton, 1955; Bruce Weber, 1956; Brad Daugherty, 1965

TRIVIA:

The Great Western Forum, home to the Lakers from 1967 through 1999, was purchased by the Faithful Central Bible Church in 2000. The church holds its regular service there each Sunday morning and makes the building available for rent on other days.

QUIZ:

Statues of two sports greats, one from the NBA and the other from the NHL, are outside the Staples Center in Los Angeles. Neither of the superstars played in the building. Can you name them?

ANSWER: *Magic Johnson of the Lakers and Wayne Gretzky of the Kings*

TODAY'S THOUGHT:

 e got the Babe Ruth of basketball." –76ers general manager *Pat Williams*, after acquiring Julius Erving

HISTORY:

On this date in 1976 the New York Nets, unable to resolve a salary dispute with Julius Erving, sold his contract to the Philadelphia 76ers for $3 million. The Nets, having won the ABA championship the previous year with Erving, would finish their first season in the NBA with the league's worst record.

BIRTHDAYS:

Ed Mikan, 1925; Ronald Franz, 1945; Eddie Jones, 1971; Lawrence Roberts, 1982

TRIVIA:

In 1968, the Nets were known as the Americans and played their home games in the Teaneck (NJ) Armory. The team was forced to forfeit a playoff game that year because a circus had already booked the building for the date in question.

QUIZ:

What NBA team made Julius Erving the 12th pick overall in the 1972 draft?

ANSWER: *Milwaukee Bucks*

TODAY'S THOUGHT:

 "The referees have asked that, regardless of how terrible the officiating is, please don't throw things on the floor." —Oklahoma coach *Billy Tubbs*, addressing the crowd right before he received a technical foul

HISTORY:

On this date in 1972 the Buffalo Braves proved that what goes around comes around, scoring an NBA record-low four points in the third quarter of a 91-63 loss to Milwaukee. One day earlier, the Braves set an NBA record with 58 points in the fourth quarter of a loss to the Celtics.

BIRTHDAYS:

Vern Mikkelsen, 1928; Johnny Davis, 1955; James White, 1982; Shelden Williams, 1983

TRIVIA:

Towns County High School lost to Rabum County, 129-41, according to the scoreboard. But Towns County actually scored 97 points in the contest! Its players were so upset with the game's officiating that they decided to shoot at their opponent's basket, scoring 56 points for Rabum.

QUIZ:

When an NBA official pats himself on the head, what violation is he calling?

ANSWER: *24-second, or shot clock, violation*

TODAY'S THOUGHT:

 "**M**y whole family likes to play basketball. George II plays for his high school team and George III and George IV and George V are going to be good players. One day we're going to have a team and call it Georgetown." *–George Foreman*

HISTORY:

On this date in 1976 brothers Tom and Dick Van Arsdale became the first pair of identical twins to play for the same NBA team. The pair suited up for the Phoenix Suns' season opener, a 111-98 loss to the New Orleans Jazz.

BIRTHDAYS:

Slater Martin, 1925; Drazen Petrovic, 1964; Jeff McInnis, 1974; Dion Glover, 1978

TRIVIA:

Current NBA twins Jason and Jarron Collins attended the same college (Stanford) and were drafted in the same year (2001). Jason was taken 18th by the Rockets and traded to New Jersey, while brother Jarron was picked 53rd by the Jazz.

QUIZ:

True or false? Twins Harvey and Horace Grant never attended college.

ANSWER: *False - Harvey went to the University of Oklahoma while Horace went to Clemson.*

TODAY'S THOUGHT:

"**D**etroit Shock forward Astou Ndiaye-Diatta gave birth to triplets in April, one year after the Cleveland Rockers' Helen Darling did the same. Alert statisticians immediately credited the WNBA with pro basketball's first triplet-double." *–Dwight Perry*, of the *Seattle Times*

HISTORY:

On this date in 1996 Sheryl Swoopes became the first player signed by the WNBA, agreeing to a deal with the Houston Comets. One of the top players in the league, Swoopes became the WNBA's first three-time MVP in 2005.

BIRTHDAY:

Keith Van Horn, 1975

TRIVIA:

The Comets are also in the league's history book for making the WNBA's first draft pick. In 1997, Houston tabbed USC's Tina Thompson with the number one overall selection. Thompson was named to the All-WNBA First Team the first two years of her career.

QUIZ:

Who was the last woman to be named college basketball's Player of the Year twice in a row?

ANSWER: *Seimone Augustus of LSU, in 2005 and 2006*

TODAY'S THOUGHT:

 "**Y**oung man, you have the question backwards." *—Bill Russell,* when asked how he would have fared against Kareem Abdul-Jabbar

HISTORY:

On this date in 1959 Wilt Chamberlain made one of the most impressive debuts in NBA history. The rookie center scored 43 points and pulled down 28 rebounds as his Philadelphia Warriors beat the New York Knicks, 118-109.

BIRTHDAY:

Doug Lee, 1964

TRIVIA:

Amazingly, Wilt Chamberlain had a better career field goal percentage (.540) than free throw percentage (.511). As a result, also amazing is the fact that he shot 28 for 32 from the foul line in his 100 point game in 1962. The Big Dipper would finish that year with a career best 61.3% from the stripe.

QUIZ:

Kareem Abdul-Jabbar has won more regular season MVP Awards than anyone in NBA history. How many?

ANSWER: *Six*

TODAY'S THOUGHT:

 ou have some clouds in your coffee sometimes. It's not easy right now." *–Kevin Garnett*, on Minnesota's struggles

HISTORY:

On this date in 2000 the Minnesota Timberwolves were found guilty of entering into a secret contract agreement with forward Joe Smith. NBA Commissioner David Stern punished the team by fining them, taking away three future first-round draft picks, suspending GM Kevin McHale, and voiding Smith's contract.

BIRTHDAYS:

Zelmo Beaty, 1939; Bobby Knight, 1940; Dave Cowens, 1948; Dan Issel, 1948; Mike Sweetney, 1982

TRIVIA:

A series of foolish trades in the early '80's by owner Ted Stepien cost Cleveland a number of first round draft picks. The NBA eventually forced Stepien to sell the Cavaliers, and created a rule, in his name, which prohibits teams from dealing future first-rounders in consecutive years.

QUIZ:

In 2005, with one of their reinstated first-round selections, Minnesota took what North Carolina product with the 14th pick in the NBA Draft?

ANSWER: *Rashad McCants*

TODAY'S THOUGHT:

"**T**here's nobody you'd rather beat than your good friend."
—*Charles Barkley*, on playing against Michael Jordan

HISTORY:

On this date in 1984 future Dream Team members Charles Barkley, Michael Jordan and John Stockton all made their NBA debuts. Barkley's 76ers and Jordan's Bulls were both victorious, while Stockton tasted defeat in his first game with the Jazz.

BIRTHDAYS:

Joe Fulks, 1921; Hot Rod Hundley, 1934; Tom Meschery, 1938; Darel Carrier, 1940; Joe Meriweather, 1953; John Williams, 1966; Nick Collison, 1980; Andrea Bargnani, 1985; Monta Ellis 1985

TRIVIA:

When Jordan dunked on the smaller Stockton in a game in Utah, Jazz owner Larry Miller yelled at him, "Dunk on someone your own size!" On the very next possession, Jordan threw one down over 6'11" Melvin Turpin. He then looked over at Miller and asked, "Was he big enough?"

QUIZ:

When John Stockton dished out 24 assists in a 1988 playoff game, he tied the postseason record held by the man he was playing against. Can you name him?

ANSWER: *Magic Johnson of the Lakers*

TODAY'S THOUGHT:

 "**Y**ou can't compare preseason to regular season. Preseason is just a way to screw fans out of money." *–Charles Barkley*

HISTORY:

On this date in 1992 the NBA played its first game in Latin America as the Dallas Mavericks defeated the Houston Rockets, 104-102. The preseason contest was held before a crowd of 19,527 at the Mexico City Sports Palace.

BIRTHDAYS:

Rick Carlisle, 1959; Predrag Drobnjak, 1975; Andrew Bynum, 1987

TRIVIA:

In 1997, Horacio Llamas became the first Mexican-born player to appear in an NBA game after signing with the Phoenix Suns. The city's large Hispanic population made Llamas a crowd favorite, but his play caused him to be released after just 28 games with the Suns.

QUIZ:

In 1996-97, the Phoenix Suns set a record for the most consecutive losses to begin a season and yet make the NBA playoffs. Do you know how many straight losses they endured?

ANSWER: *They began the year 0-13.*

TODAY'S THOUGHT:

"**T**he idea is not to block every shot. The idea is to make your opponent believe that you might block every shot."
—Bill Russell

HISTORY:

On this date in 1973 Elmore Smith blocked an NBA record 17 shots for the Lakers in a 111-98 win over Portland. Smith would go on to average a career best and league-leading 4.9 blocked shots per game for the season.

BIRTHDAYS:

Lenny Wilkens, 1937; Dwight Davis, 1949; Randy Wittman, 1959; Jarrett Jack, 1983

TRIVIA:

Former NBA center Manute Bol, at 7'7", was known to block a few shots in his career. The Sudan-born Bol wasn't introduced to the game of basketball until coming to the U.S. at the age of 18. The first time he tried to dunk the ball, he chipped a tooth on the rim.

QUIZ:

Only one ABA and one NBA player have ever averaged more than five blocks per game in a season. Can you name either?

ANSWER: The ABA's Artis Gilmore, with 5.02 in 1972, and the NBA's Mark Eaton, with 5.56 in 1985

TODAY'S THOUGHT:

 "**E**very night, when you lay your head on your pillow, you say, 'Wow, I'm one of 300.' Of course, 50 of us are real bad." –*Scott Hastings*, on being an NBA player

HISTORY:

On this date in 1996 the 50 Greatest Players in NBA History were announced in celebration of the league's 50th season. Commissioner David Stern unveiled the list at a hotel luncheon in New York City at the site where the original NBA charter was signed.

BIRTHDAY:

Dick Garmaker, 1932

TRIVIA:

When the 50 Greatest were named, only three players out of the NBA's top 20 career leaders in points did not make the cut: Alex English, Dominque Wilkins, and Adrian Dantley.

QUIZ:

Can you name the only person to be one of the NBA's 50 Greatest Players and Top 10 Coaches?

ANSWER: *Lenny Wilkens*

TODAY'S THOUGHT:

"**W**e have to play hard for the full 40 minutes." After being informed a game goes for 48 minutes: "48? Oh, that's right. 12-minute quarters." *–Mikki Moore* (unintentionally explaining the Pistons' troubles during that season)

HISTORY:

On this date in 1954 the new NBA season began with two major rule changes to speed up the game. The league adopted the 24-second shot clock, an invention of Syracuse Nationals owner Danny Biasone. It also put into effect a limit of six team fouls allowed per quarter before sending the opponent to the foul line.

BIRTHDAYS:

George Peeples, 1943; Glen Combs, 1946; Phil Chenier, 1950; Terry Tyler, 1956; Kevin Edwards, 1965; Maurice Taylor, 1976; Kareem Rush, 1980

TRIVIA:

Biasone came up with 24 seconds by dividing 2,880 (the number of seconds in a game) by 120 (the average number of shots in a game). His Nationals went on to win the NBA title in the shot clock's inaugural season.

QUIZ:

Playing by the Rules: Mavs coach Avery Johnson elects to call a time-out as Dallas forward Dirk Nowitzki is bringing the ball upcourt. Is this allowed?

ANSWER: *No*

TODAY'S THOUGHT:

"**R**ed had such a high degree of intelligence. But at the same time, he just wanted to win. It didn't matter if it was at basketball or anything else. We used to play racquetball and he would cheat and be foaming at the mouth." *–K.C. Jones,* on Red Auerbach, whose Celtic teams broke several color barriers

HISTORY:

On this date in 1950 Earl Lloyd became the first black man to play in an NBA game when he suited up for the Washington Capitols in a 78-70 road loss to the Rochester Royals. Lloyd would play nine years in the league, averaging 8.4 points per game.

BIRTHDAYS:

Blue Edwards, 1965; Antonio Davis, 1968; Steven Hunter, 1981

TRIVIA:

Two other black players, Chuck Cooper of the Celtics and Nat "Sweetwater" Clifton of the Knicks, made their NBA debuts days later. It was only because Lloyd's team played its season opener first that he was the one to make history.

QUIZ:

In 1958, Sweetwater Clifton and what former Harlem Globetrotters teammate joined the Detroit Clowns baseball team in the Negro Leagues?

ANSWER: *Reece "Goose" Tatum*

TODAY'S THOUGHT:

"Quick guys get tired. Big guys don't shrink." *–Marv Harshman*, 1950's college basketball coach, on speed vs. size

HISTORY:

On this date in 1946 Canada's Maple Leaf Gardens was the site of the first NBA game, as the New York Knicks defeated the Toronto Huskies, 68-66. Fifty years later to the day, in 1996, New York played the Raptors in Toronto, and again the Knicks won, 107-99.

BIRTHDAYS:

Joe Caldwell, 1941; Derek Smith 1961; Jake Voskuhl, 1977

TRIVIA:

For that inaugural game, Toronto allowed any fan taller than George Nostrand, the Huskies' six-foot eight-inch center, to get in for free. Meanwhile, regular tickets were priced from seventy-five cents to $2.50. In all, the game drew a solid crowd of over 7,000 fans.

QUIZ:

In the 1987-88 season, what team featured both the tallest and shortest players in NBA history at the same time?

ANSWER: *The Washington Bullets, featuring 7'7" Manute Bol and 5'3" Muggsy Bogues*

TODAY'S THOUGHT:

"**C**oach told us, 'Don't get into a track meet.' We got into a track meet with Marion Jones and Carl Lewis - and we're running like Bill Cosby." *–Olden Polynice*, Utah Jazz, after a 107-77 loss to Dallas

HISTORY:

On this date in 1990 defense took the night off as Golden State and Denver set a new NBA record for the most points scored by two teams in a non-overtime game. The Warriors opened the season by edging the Nuggets, 162-158.

BIRTHDAYS:

Whitey Skoog, 1926; Bernie Bickerstaff, 1944; Dave Wohl, 1949; Ron Lee, 1952; Rodney Buford, 1977

TRIVIA:

On that same day in '90, the NBA became the first American pro sports league to play a regular season game outside North America. Phoenix and Utah began a two-game set at the Tokyo Metropolitan Gymnasium with the Suns winning, 119-96. The Jazz gained a split of the series the following night, winning 102-101.

QUIZ:

He became the first Chinese man to play in an NBA game when he took the floor with the Dallas Mavericks in 2001. Can you name him?

ANSWER: *Wang Zhizhi*

TODAY'S THOUGHT:

"We left a lot of roadkill on this trip. We killed some Bucks, some Wolves. We missed out on the bear, the Grizzly bear. We got a Raptor, took care of that."
–Quentin Richardson, commenting on the Suns' road trip

HISTORY:

On this date in 1995 Canada's two new NBA teams, the Toronto Raptors and Vancouver Grizzlies, both made successful debuts. The Grizzlies defeated the Trail Blazers, 92-80, in Portland, while the Raptors beat the Nets, 94-79, in their first home game.

BIRTHDAYS:

George Yardley, 1928; Steve Johnson, 1957

TRIVIA:

Toronto finished the 1995-96 campaign at 21-61, but they did have one unforgettable moment to relish. They were one of just nine teams to defeat the Bulls in Chicago's record-breaking 72-10 season. The expansion Raptors hung on for a 109-108 win, dropping the Bulls to 60-8.

QUIZ:

Can you name the two men who served as the first head coaches for the Toronto and Vancouver franchises?

ANSWER: *Brendan Malone for Toronto and Brian Winters for Vancouver*

TODAY'S THOUGHT:

 **"Y**our team is by far the worst in the NBA. Your star player has said he has trouble caring. You fired your coach and demoted the general manager. Naturally, it's time to raise prices."** –*Jonathan Feigen, Houston Chronicle*, on the Orlando Magic's plan to raise ticket prices in 2004

HISTORY:

On this date in 1988 and 1989 the Eastern Conference of the NBA welcomed two new teams. In '88, the Hornets opened their first season losing to Cleveland, 133-93. The Orlando Magic didn't have any more success than Charlotte the following year. They lost their home opener, 111-106, to New Jersey.

BIRTHDAYS:

Bill Calhoun, 1927; Dick Groat, 1930; Em Bryant, 1938; Randy White, 1967; Mikki Moore, 1975; Lorenzen Wright, 1975

TRIVIA:

The new franchise in Charlotte was originally named the Charlotte Spirit, but the moniker didn't catch on with the home folks. The name "Hornets" came from the city's fierce resistance to British occupation during the Revolutionary War, leading General Cornwallis to refer to the area as a "Hornets' Nest."

QUIZ:

Along with the Magic, what other franchise made its NBA debut during the 1989-90 season?

ANSWER: *Minnesota Timberwolves*

TODAY'S THOUGHT:

 "**T**he Chocolate Thunder Flying Robinzine Crying, Teeth Shaking, Glass Breaking, Rump Roasting, Bun Toasting, Wham, Bam, I Am Jam." *–Darryl Dawkins*, describing his backboard-breaking dunk

HISTORY:

On this date in 1946 Boston's Chuck Connors broke the first backboard in NBA history while warming up before a Celtics game. Connors' weapon of choice was not a dunk, but a deadly two-hand set shot that hit the basket where a piece of protective rubber was missing.

BIRTHDAYS:

Bill Walton, 1952; Jerry Stackhouse, 1974; Keith McLeod, 1979

TRIVIA:

Connors left the Celtics to try his hand at professional baseball. In 1952, while playing for the minor-league Los Angeles Angels, Connors was spotted by an MGM casting director. Bit by the acting bug, he left the sports world, eventually landing the TV role that made him famous as *The Rifleman*.

QUIZ:

In 1979, what Hall of Famer became the first basketball player to host *Saturday Night Live*?

ANSWER: *Bill Russell*

TODAY'S THOUGHT:

"**I**t's what you learn after you know it all that counts." *–John Wooden*

HISTORY:

On this date in 1999 the Indiana Pacers christened their brand new home, Conseco Fieldhouse, by defeating the Boston Celtics, 115-108. Legendary coach John Wooden served as the honorary scorer, while broadcaster Bob Costas handled the player introductions.

BIRTHDAYS:

Dr. James Naismith, 1861; John Tresvant, 1939; Steve Kuberski, 1947; Charlie Criss, 1948; Lamar Odom, 1979; Luke Jackson, 1981

TRIVIA:

Before his coaching days, John Wooden was a standout player at Purdue University, earning the nickname "Indiana Rubber Man" for his dives on the hardcourt. In the early 1930's, Wooden played professionally for the Indianapolis Kautskys, once connecting on 138 consecutive free throws over a period of games.

QUIZ:

He was once an assistant to John Wooden at UCLA. Then, as a head coach in 1980, his team beat the Bruins in the NCAA Championship Game. Do you know who it is?

ANSWER: *Denny Crum, of Louisville*

TODAY'S THOUGHT:

"**Y**ou can't be Dr. J or the Big E. They're both taken. Can I call you Magic?" *–Lansing State Journal* sportswriter *Fred Stabley*, asking high school star Earvin Johnson about a potential nickname

HISTORY:

On this date in 1991 Magic Johnson shocked basketball fans around the world, announcing his retirement from the NBA because he was HIV positive. A member of the original Dream Team, Johnson became the Lakers' all-time assists and steals leader while winning five championships in his twelve seasons with the team.

BIRTHDAYS:

Al Attles, 1936; Tony Jackson, 1942

TRIVIA:

Brooklyn playground legend and NBA star Lloyd "World" B. Free claims his nickname came from his high school days, when he showed off with his 44-inch vertical leap and 360-degree dunks. While playing with the Warriors in 1982, the flamboyant player had his name legally changed to World B. Free.

QUIZ:

What former NBA center was nicknamed "The Human Eraser?"

ANSWER: *Marvin Webster*

TODAY'S THOUGHT:

"The trouble with officials is they just don't care who wins."
—*Tommy Canterbury*, college basketball coach

HISTORY:

On this date in 1978 Philadelphia and New Jersey began a game that, because of a protest, wouldn't end until four months later. Nets coach Kevin Loughery and player Bernard King were mistakenly given third technical fouls, so the league ordered the teams to replay the final 17:50 of the game. The 76ers came out on top when the contest finally ended in March, 1979.

BIRTHDAYS:

Frank McGuire, 1916; Tom Sanders, 1938; Wilbur Holland, 1951; Geoff Huston, 1957; Brevin Knight, 1975; Maurice Evans, 1978

TRIVIA:

When the game started, Harvey Catchings and Ralph Simpson were playing for the 76ers and Eric Money and Al Skinner were on the Nets. By the time the game resumed, the players had been traded for each other, marking the first time in pro sports that someone played for both teams in the same game.

QUIZ:

Playing by the Rules: During a timeout, Duke coach Mike Krzyzewski leaves the coaching box to confer with the scorekeeper. Is this allowed?

ANSWER: *Yes*

TODAY'S THOUGHT:

 "The Sonics are 19-0 in games they lead after the fourth quarter." –Sonics public relations director *Rick Moxley*

HISTORY:

On this date in 1989 it took Milwaukee five overtime periods to defeat Seattle, 155-154, in the NBA's longest game in the shot-clock era. The Supersonics' Dale Ellis scored 53 points while playing 69 of a possible 73 minutes in the loss.

BIRTHDAYS:

Frank Selvy, 1932; J.R. Smith, 1985

TRIVIA:

During the 1986-87 campaign, Seattle's Dale Ellis, Tom Chambers and Xavier McDaniel became the first three teammates in NBA history to each average at least 23 points per game. Ellis led the way with 24.9 ppg, Chambers posted a 23.3 average, and McDaniel scored exactly 23 points per game.

QUIZ:

Only Reggie Miller and this active player rank above Dale Ellis in career three-point field goals made. Can you name him?

ANSWER: *Ray Allen*

TODAY'S THOUGHT:

 We've turned more corners this season than a New York cab driver." *—Dan Issel*, Nuggets head coach, when asked if he felt his team had turned a corner

HISTORY:

On this date in 1990 Phoenix and Denver gave new meaning to the term "high-scoring." The Suns tied the 1959 Boston Celtics for the most points scored by one team in a non-overtime game, beating the Nuggets, 173-143. The team's 107 first–half points also broke the record of 90 set a few days earlier by...the Denver Nuggets.

BIRTHDAYS:

Gene Conley, 1930; John Williamson, 1951; Craig Smith, 1983; Kendrick Perkins, 1984

TRIVIA:

Suns coach Cotton Fitzsimmons made history of his own in the record-setting game by picking up his 700th career coaching victory. He became just the seventh NBA coach to reach the milestone.

QUIZ:

When Denver began play in the ABA in 1967, their nickname was one used by a current NBA team. Do you know it?

ANSWER: *Rockets*

TODAY'S THOUGHT:

"**I**f we stay free of injuries, we'll be in contention to be a healthy team." *–Chris Morris*, Nets forward

HISTORY:

On this date in 1993 the New Jersey Nets retired the uniform number (#3) worn by the late Drazen Petrovic. The Croatian guard, who was killed in a car accident in Germany earlier in the year, had led the Nets in scoring the past two seasons.

BIRTHDAYS:

Rudy LaRusso, 1937; Brendan Haywood, 1979

TRIVIA:

The band Pearl Jam was originally named "Mookie Blaylock," paying homage to the NBA point guard. The group even included his trading card with their first demo CD. Although trademark issues necessitated a change after they were signed to a recording contract, Pearl Jam's first album was titled *Ten*, Blaylock's uniform number.

QUIZ:

While I was addressing the Democratic National Convention at Madison Square Garden in 1992, my retired jersey could be seen overhead. Who am I?

ANSWER: *Former U.S. Senator Bill Bradley, whose Knicks uniform number 24 is retired*

TODAY'S THOUGHT:

"I told one player, 'Son, I couldn't understand it with you. Is it igno-rance or apathy?' He said, 'Coach, I don't know and I don't care.'"
—*Frank Layden*, former Jazz coach

HISTORY:

On this date in 1986 the Celtics and Bucks went into battle without their head coaches, an NBA first. Boston's K.C. Jones and Milwaukee's Don Nelson were both too ill to attend the game, won by Boston, 124-116. It was the Celtics' 44th straight home win.

BIRTHDAYS:

Gene Wiley, 1937; Dale Schlueter, 1945; Corey Maggette, 1979

TRIVIA:

Frank Layden played college basketball at Niagara University, where he roomed with teammate, and future NBA coach, Hubie Brown. Brown would coach the New York Knicks from 1982-86, the same team that Scott Layden, Frank's son, would become the president of in 1999.

QUIZ:

What former NBA guard had a son who was the second pick in the 1998 NBA Draft and a brother who pitched a no-hitter in the majors?

ANSWER: Henry Bibby – Son, Mike, was selected by the Vancouver Grizzlies in '98, while broth-er, Jim, threw a no-hitter for the Texas Rangers in 1973.

TODAY'S THOUGHT:

"**I**'ve been here so long that when I got here the Dead Sea wasn't even sick." *–Wimp Sanderson*, on his lengthy coaching career at the University of Alabama

HISTORY:

On this date in 1998 Hall of Fame coach William "Red" Holzman died at the age of 78. Holzman, named the NBA Coach of the Decade for the 1970's, led the New York Knicks to their only two NBA titles in 1970 and '73.

BIRTHDAYS:

Jack George, 1928; Rolly Massimino, 1934; Kevin Gamble, 1965; Ron Artest, 1979

TRIVIA:

When Tom Kelly stepped down as manager of the Minnesota Twins in 2001, Jerry Sloan became the longest tenured coach with one team in professional sports. Kelly managed the Twins for 16 years, while Sloan had been Utah's head coach since 1988.

QUIZ:

Gene Hackman plays coach Norman Dale in what 1986 movie about a small town high school basketball team?

ANSWER: *Hoosiers*

TODAY'S THOUGHT:

T"he game is too long, the season is too long, and the players are too long." *–Jack Dolph*, former ABA commissioner, on the NBA

HISTORY:

On this date in 1997 an NBA game went to four overtimes for the first time in a decade. Phoenix outlasted Portland, 140-139, despite 34 points and 17 rebounds from the Trail Blazers' Brian Grant. Grant played a game-high 61 minutes.

BIRTHDAYS:

Jack Sikma, 1955; Lionel Simmons, 1968; David Wesley, 1970

TRIVIA:

Former Trail Blazers' marketing guru Jon Spoelstra helped the team sell out every home game in his 11 years with Portland. Spoelstra was so good, in fact, that he was "traded" to Indiana in 1983. The Pacers gave up guard Don Buse in return for one week of Spoelstra's time as a management consultant.

QUIZ:

Before coaching Portland and two other Western Conference teams between 1989 and 2006, I played three seasons with the Trail Blazers from 1970-73. Who am I?

Sacramento (1999-2006)
ANSWER: *Rick Adelman, who coached Portland (1989-94), Golden State (1995-97) and*

TODAY'S THOUGHT:

"**M**y biggest thrill came the night Elgin Baylor and I combined for 73 points at Madison Square Garden. Elgin had 71 of them." *–Hot Rod Hundley*

HISTORY:

On this date in 1960 Lakers forward Elgin Baylor broke his own NBA scoring record, tallying 71 points in a 123-108 win over the Knicks in New York. Baylor had set the mark the previous season when he put up 64 points against the Boston Celtics.

BIRTHDAYS:

Bob Dandridge, 1947; Aleksandar Pavlovic, 1983

TRIVIA:

Baylor's record-breaking game overshadowed a fine performance that night by Cincinnati rookie Oscar Robertson. Robertson outscored Wilt Chamberlain, 44 to 36, as the Royals beat the Warriors, 124-115, ending a 13-game losing streak to Philadelphia.

QUIZ:

Wilt Chamberlain won all seven of his NBA scoring titles in consecutive years. What player ended the string in 1966-67?

ANSWER: *Rick Barry, with 35.6 points per game – Chamberlain finished behind Barry and Oscar Robertson.*

TODAY'S THOUGHT:

"**R**ussell told me I better bring salt and pepper to the next game. He told me I was going to eat basketballs." *–Bill Bridges*, St. Louis Hawks, on Bill Russell

HISTORY:

On this date in 1957 Boston's Bill Russell pulled down 49 rebounds in a 111-89 win over the Philadelphia Warriors. Russell's total included an NBA-record 32 boards in the first half alone, a mark that has yet to be surpassed.

BIRTHDAYS:

Jo Jo White, 1946; Wayne Cooper, 1956; Amare Stoudemire, 1982

TRIVIA:

In 1972, Russell insisted his uniform number 6 be raised to the Boston Garden rafters in a private ceremony with no fans present. Then, in 1999, he had a change of heart, and allowed his number to be re-raised at the Fleet Center in front of thousands of cheering spectators.

QUIZ:

Who is the shortest player in NBA history to win a rebounding title?

ANSWER: *6'5". Charles Barkley, who averaged 14.6 rebounds per game in the 1986-87 season*

TODAY'S THOUGHT:

"**I**t wouldn't have happened if I started." *–Rony Seikaly*, on hurting his back while getting off the bench to enter a game

HISTORY:

On this date in 1959 the Syracuse Nationals' Connie Dierking became the first player in NBA history to foul out of a game in the first quarter. His services, however, were not needed as Syracuse went on to beat the Cincinnati Royals, 121-116.

BIRTHDAYS:

Jim Boeheim, 1944; Elvin Hayes, 1945; Steve Stipanovich, 1960; Jerome James, 1975

TRIVIA:

In the 1975-76 season, the ABA's last, the league instituted a "no foul-out rule." When a player committed his sixth personal foul, he could stay in the game. However, subsequent fouls by that same player resulted in two free throws plus possession of the ball for the opposing team.

QUIZ:

Two players have won the NBA's Sixth Man of the Year Award in consecutive years. Can you name them?

ANSWER: *Kevin McHale (1984, '85) and Detlef Schrempf (1991, '92)*

TODAY'S THOUGHT:

"**T**he Atlanta Hawks are a bunch of guys who would prefer to pass kidney stones than pass a basketball." *–Bob Weiss*, former Hawks coach

HISTORY:

On this date in 1989 two players from the Soviet Union met on the basketball court for the first time in NBA history. Atlanta's Alexander Volkov faced off against Golden State's Sarunas Marciulionis. Volkov and the Hawks came out on top, 112-96.

BIRTHDAYS:

Forrest "Phog" Allen, 1885; Len Bias, 1963; Sam Cassell, 1969; Jason Williams, 1975

TRIVIA:

Marciulionis and Volkov were teammates on the Soviet squad that won gold at the 1988 Olympics in South Korea. The Soviet Union, which also won in 1972, became the first team other than the United States to win multiple gold medals in basketball.

QUIZ:

What nation's basketball team won the gold medal at the 1980 Summer Olympics in Moscow?

ANSWER: *Yugoslavia – The United States boycotted the Olympics that year.*

TODAY'S THOUGHT:

 or, $58,000 I'd have liked to have hit him more than once." *–Michael Jordan*, on being fined that much after a fight with Reggie Miller

HISTORY:

On this date in 2004 The Palace of Auburn Hills was the site of the infamous Pacers-Pistons brawl. The incident involved Indiana's Ron Artest and several others charging into the stands after Artest was hit with a drinking cup by a fan while shamelessly lying on the scorer's table. Of the numerous suspensions, Artest's was the worst- the final 73 games of the year.

BIRTHDAYS:

Eric Musselman, 1964; Vladimir Radmanovic, 1980; Marcus Banks, 1981

TRIVIA:

As a rookie with the Bulls, Artest applied for a part-time job at a Circuit City in Chicago so he could get the employee discount. Said Artest, "I thought it would be fun. And I had a friend who worked there." The team made sure he didn't get a job interview.

QUIZ:

True or false? Reggie Miller was the first Indiana Pacer to start in an NBA All-Star Game.

ANSWER: *True - in 1995*

TODAY'S THOUGHT:

"**W**e took a vote as to what he might have said, whether it was 'golly' or 'gosh'." –Lakers coach *Randy Pfund*, on the deeply religious A.C. Green getting tossed out of a game

HISTORY:

On this date in 1997 the Dallas Mavericks' A.C. Green made NBA history by playing in his 907th consecutive game, a loss to the Warriors. Green, who broke Randy Smith's record, would go on to play a total of 1,192 games in a row through 2001.

BIRTHDAYS:

Jerry Colangelo, 1939; Louie Dampier, 1944; Chris Childs, 1967; Ryan Bowen, 1975; Carlos Boozer, 1981

TRIVIA:

Green was known for a conservative lifestyle and his firm stance against pre-marital sex. Playing off that, *Sports Illustrated* once dubbed Green, "The Only NBA Player Who Has Never Scored."

QUIZ:

Who was the first basketball player to win the "Sportsman of the Year" award from *Sports Illustrated*? (Hint: The year was 1961.)

ANSWER: *Jerry Lucas*

TODAY'S THOUGHT:

"I don't have an ulcer. I'm a carrier. I give them to other people."
—Bill Fitch

HISTORY:

On this date in 1996 Bill Fitch became the first head coach in NBA history to lose 1,000 games when his Los Angeles Clippers fell to the Dallas Mavericks, 105-94. That same year, Fitch, with 944 career wins, was named one of the NBA's Top Ten Coaches of all-time.

BIRTHDAYS:

Terry Dischinger, 1940; Earl Monroe, 1944; Cedric Maxwell, 1955; Olden Polynice, 1964; Reggie Lewis, 1965; Stromile Swift, 1979; Josh Boone, 1984

TRIVIA:

Dolph Schayes was the first head coach of the Buffalo Braves, the Clippers' predecessors. In the team's inaugural campaign, Schayes led the Braves to a mark of 22-60 and was retained for the following season. After losing the season opener however, he was fired. Without Schayes, the Braves again finished 22-60.

QUIZ:

This man began his NBA head coaching career with 17 straight losses with the expansion Miami Heat in 1988. Can you name him?

ANSWER: *Ron Rothstein*

TODAY'S THOUGHT:

"**A**nybody who doesn't know who George Mikan is, is not a basketball fan." *–Kevin Garnett*

HISTORY:

On this date in 1950 the Fort Wayne Pistons defeated the Minneapolis Lakers, 19-18, in the lowest-scoring game in NBA history. Without a shot clock, the Pistons "froze" the ball to keep it away from Lakers star George Mikan. But the big man still managed a game-high 15 points, scoring all of Minneapolis' four baskets.

BIRTHDAYS:

Mel Hutchins, 1928; James Edwards, 1955; Benoit Benjamin, 1964

TRIVIA:

Mikan's 15 of the Lakers' 18 total points remains the highest percentage (83.3%) of a team's offense in an NBA game. He also owns the second highest mark (67%) after scoring 61 of Minneapolis' 91 points in a 1952 contest.

QUIZ:

Who led the NBA in scoring average its first two years, in 1946-47 and '47-48?

ANSWER: *Joe Fulks, Philadelphia Warriors, with 23.2 points per game in 1947 and 22.1 in '48*

TODAY'S THOUGHT:

I have a new philosophy. I only dread one day at a time."
–Jerry Reynolds, former Kings head coach, during Sacramento's leaner years

HISTORY:

On this date in 1991 the Sacramento Kings finally won a game away from home, ending their NBA-record 43-game streak on the road. The 95-93 win in Orlando was the team's first victory as a visitor since November 20, 1990.

BIRTHDAYS:

Andrew Toney, 1957; Steve Alford, 1964; Vin Baker, 1971; Malik Rose, 1974; Hilton Armstrong, 1984

TRIVIA:

During the 1990-91 season, the Kings' Lionel Simmons was sidelined two games due to tendonitis in his wrists caused by playing his Game Boy too much. The following season, Seattle's Derrick McKey suffered a similar fate, missing seven games.

QUIZ:

What Pro Football Hall of Fame quarterback played on the Rochester Royals (precursor of the Kings) when they won the 1945-46 National Basketball League championship?

ANSWER: *Otto Graham*

TODAY'S THOUGHT:

"**I** never thought I'd lead the NBA in rebounding, but I got a lot of help from my teammates - they did a lot of missing."
—Moses Malone

HISTORY:

On this date in 1960 the Philadelphia Warriors' Wilt Chamberlain pulled down an NBA-record 55 rebounds in a 132-129 loss to the Celtics. Wilt went on to collect a record 2,149 boards that season, averaging 27.2 per game, another NBA mark.

BIRTHDAYS:

Oscar Robertson, 1938; Dave Bing, 1943; Rudy Tomjanovich, 1948; Henry Bibby, 1949; Ledell Eackles, 1966

TRIVIA:

Moses Malone is the only player in NBA history to win an MVP Award while averaging less than two assists per game for the regular season. He did it not once, but all three times he won the award – in 1979 (1.8), '82 (1.8) and '83 (1.3).

QUIZ:

Can you name the only player to win the NBA's MVP Award and the Sixth Man Award in his career?

ANSWER: Bill Walton - He won the MVP in 1978 with Portland and the Sixth Man Award with Boston in 1986.

TODAY'S THOUGHT:

 e'll see how the game goes. If they're scoring, keep feeding them. If they're missing, then I'll do me. That's talent. I'm multitalented. Like Bo Jackson!" *—Gilbert Arenas*, explaining whether he would be a distributor or a scorer

HISTORY:

On this date in 1961 Boston's Bob Cousy became just the second player in NBA history to score 15,000 career points, as the Celtics defeated the New York Knicks, 116-96. Dolph Schayes had already reached the mark in 1960.

BIRTHDAYS:

Terry Stotts, 1957; Anthony Peeler, 1969; Jared Jeffries, 1981

TRIVIA:

While few players have led the league in scoring three times, Neil Johnston managed to do it three consecutive seasons with a losing team. From 1953-'55, the Philadelphia Warriors never won more than 33 games in a season. Then, when Johnston finished third in scoring in 1956, the Warriors won the championship!

QUIZ:

The man who became the third player to score 15,000 points played just ten seasons in the NBA, but scored over 1,500 points in all but two of them. Name him.

ANSWER: *Paul Arizin*

TODAY'S THOUGHT:

As long as his joints hold up." *–Peter Vecsey*, columnist, on how long Robert Parish might keep playing in the NBA

HISTORY:

On this date in 2000 John Stockton conducted business as usual, distributing 15 assists in a win over Detroit. The unusual was that the Utah guard set a record for longevity, appearing in his 1,271st NBA game, all of them with the Jazz. Stockton passed John Havlicek of Boston for the most career games played for one team.

BIRTHDAYS:

Mario Elie, 1963; Shawn Kemp, 1969; Luther Head, 1982

TRIVIA:

Officially, Robert Parish owns the NBA record for most career games played overall, with 1,611. However, if playoffs are factored into the equation, it's Kareem Abdul-Jabbar who holds the title. Abdul-Jabbar played in 51 fewer regular season contests, but 53 more playoff games, therefore edging out Parish, 1,797 games to 1,795.

QUIZ:

Known as "The Big E," I played exactly 50,000 minutes in my NBA career. Who am I?

ANSWER: *Elvin Hayes*

TODAY'S THOUGHT:

 "**M**aybe he really is the next Jordan." *–Tom Fitzgerald* of the *San Francisco Chronicle*, after LeBron James took batting practice before a major league game and whiffed on the first nine pitches

HISTORY:

On this date in 2004 Cleveland's LeBron James became the youngest player in NBA history with 2,000 career points, scoring 26 in a 96-74 win over Chicago. James did it at the age of 19 years and 272 days, surpassing Kobe Bryant.

BIRTHDAYS:

Chick Hearn, 1916; Manny Leaks, 1945; Jim Price, 1949; Nick Van Exel, 1971; Donta Smith, 1983

TRIVIA:

According to *Forbes* magazine, the value of the Cleveland franchise went up by over $35 million after the arrival of King James. The Cavaliers' home attendance jumped nearly 60% in James' rookie year, and Cleveland went from 27th in road attendance to second, behind only the Lakers.

QUIZ:

Who is the Cleveland Cavaliers' all-time leading scorer?

ANSWER: *Brad Daugherty, with 10,389 points from 1986-94*

TODAY'S THOUGHT:

"**Y**ou can't coach basketball Forrest, you play it." *–James Naismith*, to Forrest "Phog" Allen, a Hall of Fame coach at the University of Kansas

HISTORY:

On this date in 1939 Dr. James Naismith, the founder of basketball, passed away at the age of 78 after suffering a brain hemorrhage. Naismith was buried in his hometown of Lawrence, Kansas, where he was a professor and men's basketball coach at the University of Kansas.

BIRTHDAYS:

Johnny Newman, 1963; Roy Tarpley, 1964; Leandro Barbosa, 1982; Andrew Bogut, 1984

TRIVIA:

In the 1890's, Naismith developed the first helmet in American football. While playing the game at Springfield College, Naismith complained of bruised ears from rough play. He took a football, cut it lengthwise, and placed it over his head to protect his ears. Ugly, but effective.

QUIZ:

What was it that *Sports Illustrated* called "the best halftime invention since the restroom?"

ANSWER: *The first NBA Slam Dunk Contest in 1976*

TODAY'S THOUGHT:

 xcept for offense, defense, rebounding, and turnovers, we had a good game." *–Bob Weiss*, Clippers head coach, after a bad loss to Houston

HISTORY:

On this date in 1989 the University of Oklahoma erupted with an NCAA-record 97 first-half points against U.S. International. The Sooners didn't let up in the second half either, adding 76 points in the 173-101 blowout victory.

BIRTHDAYS:

George Thompson, 1947; Dee Brown, 1968; Jamal Mashburn, 1972; Shannon Brown, 1985

TRIVIA:

Chris Steinmetz, "The Father of Wisconsin Basketball," was the first big-time scorer in the college game. In the 1904-05 season, the 5'9", 137-pound Steinmetz scored 462 of Wisconsin's 681 total points. More stunning was the fact that he scored 23 more points than all opponents tallied against the Badgers.

QUIZ:

I was the first three-time First Team All-American to never play in the NCAA Tournament. Do you know me?

ANSWER: *Pete Maravich, of LSU*

TODAY'S THOUGHT:

"Larry Bird just throws the ball in the air and God moves the basket underneath it."** *–Howie Chizek*, Cleveland public address announcer, after Bird scored 60 points against the Cavaliers

HISTORY:

On this date in 1990 and 1996 two of the game's greatest, Larry Bird and Michael Jordan, reached scoring milestones. In 1990, Bird joined the 20,000-point club in a Celtics win over the Bullets. Six years later to the day, Jordan reached 25,000 points as his Bulls defeated San Antonio.

BIRTHDAYS:

Richie Regan, 1930; Jim Chones, 1949; Paul Westphal, 1950; Mark Blount, 1975; Andres Nocioni, 1979; Jordan Farmar, 1986

TRIVIA:

In 1985, Michael Jordan had hoped to sign an endorsement deal with the shoe company, Converse. But since their roster already included Larry Bird and Magic Johnson, Converse didn't want Jordan. Nike, a minor player in the NBA endorsement wars at the time, signed Jordan for $500,000. In M.J.'s first year with the company, his Air Jordan line generated $153 million in revenue.

QUIZ:

Two of the NBA's top ten all-time scorers never played on a championship team. Name them.

ANSWER: *Karl Malone (36,928 points) and Dominique Wilkins (26,668 points)*

TODAY'S THOUGHT:

"**B**ill Russell helped make my dream a better dream because when you play with the best, you know you have to play your best." *–Wilt Chamberlain*

HISTORY:

On this date in 1956 the United States basketball team, led by Bill Russell and K.C. Jones, downed the Soviet Union, 89-55, to win the gold medal at the Summer Olympics in Melbourne, Australia. The Russians' finish would be their second of four consecutive Olympic silver medals.

BIRTHDAY:

Walter Simon, 1939

TRIVIA:

Bill Russell delayed his NBA debut with the Celtics so he could compete in the Olympics. He still managed to play in 48 games in the 1956-57 season, leading Boston to its first NBA title. In his career, Russell won a remarkable eleven championships in thirteen years with the Celtics.

QUIZ:

When this player made his pro debut in 1991, he became the first Australian to play in the NBA. Can you name him?

ANSWER: Luc Longley, who began his career with the Minnesota Timberwolves

The Basketball Almanac

TODAY'S THOUGHT:

"**W**ar is the only game in which it doesn't pay to have the home-court advantage." *–Dick Motta*

HISTORY:

On this date in 1986 the Washington Bullets beat Boston, 117-109, to end the Celtics' impressive 38-game winning streak at home. Even though the game was played at the Hartford Civic Center rather than the Boston Garden, it still counted as a home contest for the Celtics.

BIRTHDAYS:

Alan Henderson, 1972; Jarron and Jason Collins, 1978; Dorell Wright, 1985

TRIVIA:

With Los Angeles leading the Celtics in Game 7 of the 1984 NBA Finals in Boston, die-hard Lakers fan Jack Nicholson began taunting the crowd with the choke sign from his private box. But Nicholson soon became disgusted when the Lakers dropped the lead, so he, in turn, dropped his pants, mooning the entire crowd. Los Angeles lost.

QUIZ:

Three NBA arenas have parquet floors. Boston's TD Banknorth Garden is one. Can you name the other two?

ANSWER: *The TD Waterhouse Centre in Orlando and the Target Center in Minneapolis*

TODAY'S THOUGHT:

"**T**he 76ers need a center in the worst way. And Dana Lewis is the worst way." *–Jack Kiser*, sportswriter, on the 76ers' draft choice in 1971

HISTORY:

On this date in 1966 sophomore center Lew Alcindor (later Kareem Abdul-Jabbar) played in his first varsity game with UCLA. He gave Bruins fans more than something to cheer about, pouring in a school-record 56 points in a 105-90 win over USC.

BIRTHDAYS:

Mike Bantom, 1951; Lindsey Hunter, 1970; Robert Swift, 1985; Marcus Williams, 1985

TRIVIA:

Exactly ten years earlier, another future NBA Hall of Fame big man, Wilt Chamberlain, made his collegiate debut for Kansas. And just like Alcindor, Chamberlain set a school record, tallying 52 points in the Jayhawks' 87-69 victory over Northwestern.

QUIZ:

What high school did Kareem Abdul-Jabbar attend?

ANSWER: *Manhattan's Power Memorial Academy*

TODAY'S THOUGHT:

"**I**t's unfortunate that I can't function as a normal person in today's society." *—Derrick Coleman*, former NBA bad boy

HISTORY:

On this date in 1997 Golden State's Latrell Sprewell was suspended for one year without pay for choking coach P.J. Carlesimo during a Warriors practice. Sprewell's suspension would be reduced to 68 games, but he would not play again until 1999, after Golden State traded him to New York.

BIRTHDAYS:

Dick Ricketts, 1933; Bernard King, 1956; Howard Eisley, 1972; Brian Cook, 1980; Corliss Williamson, 1973; Martell Webster, 1986

TRIVIA:

Early in his NBA career, Shaquille O'Neal was constantly late for practice and often a source of frustration for Orlando coach Chuck Daly. One day Shaq hurried up to not be tardy yet another time. He appeared on the court wearing his shoes… and his birthday suit.

QUIZ:

In 1996, what Denver Nuggets guard was suspended by the league for refusing to stand for the national anthem?

ANSWER: *Mahmoud Abdul-Rauf (formerly Chris Jackson)*

TODAY'S THOUGHT:

I look at a golf course as a great waste of pastureland."
–*Karl Malone*, on his former job as a cattle farmer

HISTORY:

On this date in 2000 a finger roll in the lane moved Karl Malone past Wilt Chamberlain and into second place on the NBA's all-time scoring list. Malone tallied 31 points in Utah's 98-84 win over the Raptors, giving him 31,443 for his career, 24 more than Chamberlain.

BIRTHDAYS:

Eddy Curry, 1982; Josh Smith, 1985

TRIVIA:

Exactly nine years earlier, another Malone, Moses, reached a scoring milestone of his own. In a 109-101 loss to the Nets, Moses scored 12 points for Milwaukee, making him just the sixth player in NBA history to record 26,000 points. He finished his career with 27,409.

QUIZ:

Karl Malone has played in the most career playoff games without winning an NBA championship. How many?
a.127 b. 193 c. 219 d. 260

ANSWER: *b. 193*

TODAY'S THOUGHT:

"**I** had an awful first quarter, but I picked it up. To all you single guys out there, it's not how you start the date, it's how you finish it." –*Shaquille O'Neal*, after a big-scoring second half

HISTORY:

On this date in 2000 the Warriors' Antawn Jamison and the Lakers' Kobe Bryant each scored 51 points in Golden State's 125-122 overtime win. It was just the third time in NBA history, and the first since 1962, that opposing players scored 50 points in the same game.

BIRTHDAYS:

Bill Hanzlik, 1957; Matt Maloney, 1971; Jelani McCoy, 1977

TRIVIA:

That night, Jamison also became just the sixth NBA player to score 50 points in consecutive games. Three days earlier, he pumped in 51 points in a loss to the Seattle Supersonics.

QUIZ:

Antawn Jamison is the brother-in-law of what former North Carolina teammate and current NBA star?

ANSWER: *Vince Carter- He and Jamison married sisters.*

TODAY'S THOUGHT:

 "**T**he ball is round, the ground is flat; it will come back to you when you bounce it." *—Red Auerbach*, on basketball's simplicity

HISTORY:

On this date in 1948 the Indianapolis Jets defeated Red Auerbach's Capitols, 94-78, snapping Washington's NBA record 15-game winning streak to begin the season. That record stood for 45 years, until the Houston Rockets matched the mark at the start of the 1993-94 season.

BIRTHDAYS:

Max Zaslofsky, 1925; Larry Bird, 1956

TRIVIA:

When the Rockets moved from San Diego to Houston in 1971, their attendance was so poor that the team couldn't meet operating expenses. The Rockets tried everything that season, including playing their home games in seven different venues in Houston, San Antonio, El Paso, Waco, and, even San Diego.

QUIZ:

Can you name the only NBA team other than the Rockets that Rudy Tomjanovich has coached?

ANSWER: *Rudy T. coached the Lakers for 43 games in the 2004-05 season.*

TODAY'S THOUGHT:

"**I**'m like the Pythagorean Theorem. Not too many people know the answer to my game." *–Shaquille O'Neal*

HISTORY:

On this date in 1961 Philadelphia's Wilt Chamberlain scored a record 78 points and grabbed 43 rebounds as the Warriors lost to Los Angeles, 151-147, in triple overtime. The Lakers' Elgin Baylor, who set the record of 71 points a year earlier, led the winners with 63 points.

BIRTHDAYS:

Johnny Green, 1933; Bob Love, 1942; George Johnson, 1956; Teresa Weatherspoon, 1965; Dwight Howard, 1985

TRIVIA:

In his 14-year career with the Lakers, Elgin Baylor played in eight NBA Finals without winning a championship. Baylor even scored a record 284 points in the 1962 Finals, but Los Angeles lost to the Celtics in seven games. The day after Baylor retired in 1971, the Lakers began their historic 33-game win streak and went on to win the NBA title.

QUIZ:

What Hall of Famer played in ten Game 7's in his NBA playoff career, winning all of them?

ANSWER: Bill Russell - Five of the ten came in the NBA Finals.

TODAY'S THOUGHT:

"**A**n old friend told me never to get into a fight with a pig. You both get dirty and the pig likes it." *–Jon Barry*

HISTORY:

On this date in 1977 the Lakers' Kermit Washington sucker-punched Houston's Rudy Tomjanovich during a game, hospitalizing him with a fractured jaw and concussion, among other things. The disturbing incident resulted in a 26-game suspension for Washington, but it ended the season for Tomjanovich.

BIRTHDAYS:

Cliff Hagan, 1931; World B. Free, 1953; Otis Birdsong, 1955

TRIVIA:

Tempers flared in a 1983 playoff game when Atlanta's Tree Rollins elbowed Boston's Danny Ainge. As the two wrestled on the floor, Rollins sank his teeth into one of Ainge's fingers, resulting in stitches for the Celtics' guard. The headline in a Boston newspaper the next day read: "Tree Bites Man."

QUIZ:

Who said it? "They better not put me in the All-Star Game… I'll be playing hard defense. I'll be fouling. I'll be flagrant fouling. Everyone will be like, 'What are you doing?'"

ANSWER: *Ron Artest*

TODAY'S THOUGHT:

"**I** hope they give me a parking pass for it." –*Adolph Rupp*, on Kentucky's Rupp Arena

HISTORY:

On this date in 1977 Kentucky coaching legend Adolph Rupp died at the age of 76. Rupp won 876 games and four NCAA championships in a career that spanned 42 years at the university. He died on the same day Kentucky beat his alma mater, Kansas.

BIRTHDAYS:

Ray Felix, 1930; Lloyd Neal, 1950; Mark Aguirre, 1959; Bryant Stith, 1970

TRIVIA:

In 1951, Alex Groza and Ralph Beard, two members of Kentucky's "Fabulous Five" that won back-to-back NCAA titles, were found guilty of point-shaving in an NIT game. The men, then NBA teammates, were banned from the league. In addition, the NCAA suspended the Kentucky men's basketball program for the 1952-53 season.

QUIZ:

Can you name the only men's basketball coach to post a losing record with the University of Kansas?

ANSWER: *James Naismith (55-60)*

TODAY'S THOUGHT:

 "Sport is the only profession I know of that when you retire, you have to go to work." *—Earl Monroe*

HISTORY:

On this date in 1971 the NBA's Silver Anniversary team was announced, commemorating the league's first 25 seasons. It consisted of the ten best retired players at the time, including Bob Cousy, George Mikan, and Bill Russell. Red Auerbach was named the coach.

BIRTHDAY:

Shareef Abdur-Rahim, 1976

TRIVIA:

Silver team member Dolph Schayes, who could battle under the boards with the best of them, took the fight to a mascot later in his life. Attending a 1997 playoff game in Miami, Schayes was sprayed with a squirt gun by Heat mascot, "Burnie." The displeased 69-year old got out of his seat and clocked "Burnie" with a right hook.

QUIZ:

What Silver Anniversary team member, who retired in 1961, led the NBA in free-throw percentage a record seven seasons?

ANSWER: *Bill Sharman of the Boston Celtics*

TODAY'S THOUGHT:

 "We got no shot to beat the Lakers." *–Doug Moe*, Nuggets coach, on his team's chances in the 1987 playoffs (They were swept.)

HISTORY:

On this date in 1971 the Los Angeles Lakers defeated the Atlanta Hawks, 104-95, for their 21st straight win, breaking the NBA record of 20, shared by the Washington Capitols and Milwaukee Bucks. The Lakers would add another 12 wins to their streak before it finally came to an end at 33.

BIRTHDAYS:

Bob Pettit, 1932; Randy Smith, 1948; John Salmons, 1979

TRIVIA:

At the beginning of the 1979-80 season, new Lakers head coach Jack McKinney suffered a serious head injury from a bicycle accident while on his way to play tennis with assistant Paul Westhead. Westhead took over the team, and guided Los Angeles to the championship. The next season, McKinney found work with the Pacers, becoming the 1981 Coach of the Year.

QUIZ:

True or false? In their franchise history, the Lakers have never lost 50 or more games in a single season.

ANSWER: *False - They had three 50-plus loss seasons.*

TODAY'S THOUGHT:

To win, you've got to put the ball in the macramé."
–Terry McGuire

HISTORY:

On this date in 1983 the highest scoring game in NBA history took place as the Pistons defeated the Nuggets, 186-184, in triple overtime. Among the contributors to the 370 combined points were Detroit's Isiah Thomas (47) and Denver's Kiki Vandeweghe (51) and Alex English (47).

BIRTHDAYS:

Gus Johnson, 1935; Larry Kenon, 1952; Phil Hubbard, 1956

TRIVIA:

Better foul shooting by Detroit would have taken the NBA into uncharted territory. The Pistons shot just 61.7% from the foul line that night, making 37 of 60. Had they made 85% of their foul shots, they would have scored 200 points in the game.

QUIZ:

In 1983, Denver's Alex English (28.4 points per game) and Kiki Vandeweghe (26.7) finished 1-2 in the NBA scoring race. What Piston was third?

ANSWER: *Kelly Tripucka (26.5 points per game)*

TODAY'S THOUGHT:

I'm scared. I think I'm the best player here." –*Scott Hastings*, on the expansion Miami Heat

HISTORY:

On this date in 1988 the expansion Miami Heat enjoyed the thrill of victory for the first time, beating the Los Angeles Clippers, 89-88. Miami had dropped its first 17 games of the year, setting an NBA record for consecutive losses to start a season. The mark would be matched by the woeful Clippers in 1999.

BIRTHDAYS:

John Brown, 1951; Carl Herrera, 1966; Anthony Mason, 1966; Pat Burke, 1973

TRIVIA:

The expansion Charlotte Bobcats made a "rookie mistake" in their inaugural ticket sales campaign in 2004. Because of a mix-up in the local telephone book, fans who dialed what they thought was the number to order tickets, were, instead, directed to a sex chat line!

QUIZ:

In the 2005 NBA Draft, the Bobcats selected two North Carolina Tarheels with their two first round picks. Name them.

ANSWER: *Raymond Felton, with the fifth pick, and Sean May, at number thirteen*

TODAY'S THOUGHT:

"I don't want to shoot my mouth in my foot, but those are games we can win." *–Sherman Douglas*

HISTORY:

On this date in 1973 Tennessee defeated Temple, 11-6, in the lowest-scoring NCAA game since 1938. Temple's stalling tactics prevented the Volunteers from taking a single shot in the second half, but it wasn't enough. Tennessee's Len Kosmalski was the high scorer with five points.

BIRTHDAY:

Charlie Scott, 1948

TRIVIA:

In a 2005 contest between the Pistons and Grizzlies, Detroit's Richard Hamilton became the first player in NBA history to lead his team in scoring without making a field goal. Hamilton went 0-10 from the field, but hit all 14 of his free throws. Not surprisingly, Detroit lost to Memphis, 101-79.

QUIZ:

How many seconds is an NBA player given to shoot a free throw after the referee has handed him the ball?

ANSWER: *Ten*

TODAY'S THOUGHT:

"A man has to know his limitations and I don't have any.**"**
–Edgar Jones, former Cavaliers center

HISTORY:

On this date in 1961 the Philadelphia Warriors' Wilt Chamberlain scored 50 points in a win over the Chicago Packers, beginning an NBA-record seven-game stretch in which he tallied 50 or more. Wilt would reach the half-century mark an astounding 118 times in his Hall of Fame career.

BIRTHDAYS:

Jan Van Breda Kolff, 1951; Jeff Ruland, 1958; Orlando Woolridge, 1959; Clifford Robinson, 1966

TRIVIA:

The Big Dipper's 50-point game came two days after he had a consecutive streak of scoring at least 50 stopped at five games. Chamberlain put up "just" 43 points in a win over the Nationals. If not for that night, he would have reached the big five-oh in 13 straight games.

QUIZ:

Which one of these NBA players has *never* scored 50 points in a game?
a. Tony Delk b. Sam Cassell c. Damon Stoudamire d. Jamal Crawford

ANSWER: *b. Sam Cassell*

TODAY'S THOUGHT:

"I knew it was time to retire when I was driving the lane and got called for a three-second violation." *–Johnny "Red" Kerr*

HISTORY:

On this date in 1976 the Philadelphia 76ers retired Billy Cunningham's uniform number 32. One of the NBA's 50 Greatest Players, Cunningham scored 13,626 points in nine NBA seasons with the 76ers. He captured an NBA championship as both a player (1967) and head coach ('83) in Philadelphia.

BIRTHDAYS:

Brad Davis, 1955; Albert King, 1959

TRIVIA:

Forced into retirement because of bad knees, Jeff Ruland decided to make his NBA comeback with the 76ers in 1991 after a five-year layoff. But Ruland's season was cut short after just thirteen games when a luggage cart slammed into his leg while he waited for the team bus, leaving him with a torn Achilles tendon.

QUIZ:

In 2003, the Heat retired their first uniform number, but it wasn't for a Miami player. Who was it?

ANSWER: *The #23 was raised into the American Airlines Arena rafters for Michael Jordan before his final game in Miami.*

TODAY'S THOUGHT:

"Just how good was Oscar Robertson? He is so great-he scares me." *–Red Auerbach*

HISTORY:

On this date in 1964 Cincinnati's Oscar Robertson scored a career-high 56 points as the Royals defeated the Los Angeles Lakers, 111-107. The versatile Robertson would average a double-double for the season, finishing with 30.4 points and 11.5 assists per game.

BIRTHDAYS:

Gene Shue, 1931; Jim Davis, 1941; George Johnson, 1948; Bobby Jones, 1951; Charles Oakley, 1963; Lucious Harris, 1970

TRIVIA:

In 1970-71, the Milwaukee Bucks ended the regular season farther ahead of the competition than any other team in NBA history. Led by Oscar Robertson and Kareem Abdul-Jabbar, the Bucks finished at 66-16, 14 games better than the 52-30 Knicks, who held the league's second-best mark. Milwaukee went on to win the championship.

QUIZ:

In NBA history, only four men have recorded over 13 assists per game in one season. How many can you name?

ANSWER: *John Stockton (five times), Magic Johnson, Isiah Thomas, and Kevin Porter*

TODAY'S THOUGHT:

"**T**he taste of defeat has a richness of experience all its own."
  –Bill Bradley

HISTORY:

On this day in 1968 New York traded Walt Bellamy and Howard Komives to the Pistons for Dave DeBusschere. The day after the trade, the Knicks crushed Detroit, 135-87, in the franchise's most lopsided win ever. The Knicks would win 54 games in the 1968-69 campaign, and their first NBA title the following season.

BIRTHDAYS:

Leonard Gray, 1951; Kevin McHale, 1957; Arvydas Sabonis, 1964; Tom Gugliotta, 1969; Maurice Williams, 1982

TRIVIA:

In 1991, the Cleveland Cavaliers set the NBA record for the largest margin of victory, beating Miami by 68 points, 148-80. Leading by 20 at halftime, the Cavaliers outscored the Heat, 75-27, in the second half. Despite all the offense, no Cleveland player scored 20 points in the game.

QUIZ:

The most lopsided NBA Finals game in history took place in 1998. The score: 96-54. Supply the two teams.

ANSWER: *The Chicago Bulls defeated the Utah Jazz in Game 3, and won the series in six.*

TODAY'S THOUGHT:

"**I** put Phil Jackson's name (on the board), along with Kobe Bryant and Shaquille O'Neal. I told them, 'You guys probably want Phil Jackson. I probably want these guys. What we have is each other.'" –Cleveland coach *John Lucas*, on his team speech

HISTORY:

On this date in 2005 Kobe Bryant scored a career-high 62 points - in three quarters! Bryant outscored the entire Dallas Mavericks team, 62-61, before the fourth period. Since the Lakers had a 34-point lead at that point, Bryant sat out the final quarter of the game. L.A. wound up winning 112-90.

BIRTHDAYS:

Dave Stallworth, 1941; Trent Tucker, 1959; Bobby Phills, 1969; Royal Ivey, 1981

TRIVIA:

Bryant's unique first name comes from a type of Japanese steak, as "Kobe beef" is produced from cattle in the city of Kobe, Japan. His parents originally saw the name on a menu while eating at a restaurant prior to his birth.

QUIZ:

What high-scoring Maverick became the first Latin American NBA player to have his number retired by a team?

ANSWER: *Rolando Blackman, who was born in Panama, had his #22 retired in 2000 by Dallas.*

TODAY'S THOUGHT:

"**W**hen they're all dunks, you should make the most of them."
–7'4" *Mark Eaton*, on hitting ten shots in a row

HISTORY:

On this date in 1984 Georgeann Wells, a 6'7" center for West Virginia University, became the first woman to dunk a basketball during a college game. The historic slam dunk came with 11:58 remaining in the Mountaineers' 110-82 win over Charleston.

BIRTHDAYS:

Ervin Johnson, 1967; Terry Mills, 1967

TRIVIA:

Track and field star Jackie Joyner-Kersee also made a name for herself in basketball, earning All-America honors at UCLA. Joyner-Kersee even played briefly for the Richmond Rage of the American Basketball League when she was 34 years old.

QUIZ:

In the Basketball Hall of Fame, what female player comes first alphabetically?

ANSWER: *Carol Blazejowski - "The Blaze" tallied 3,199 points during her college career at Montclair (NJ) State College from 1974-78.*

TODAY'S THOUGHT:

 "**Y**ou can say something to popes, kings and presidents, but you can't talk to officials. In the next war they ought to give everyone a whistle." *–Abe Lemons*, college basketball coach

HISTORY:

On this date in 1969 Louisiana State's Pete Maravich set an NCAA record by sinking 30 of 31 free throws against Oregon State. That's the main reason why Pistol Pete finished with 46 points, because he hit only 8 of 23 shots from the field. The Tigers defeated the Beavers, 76-68.

BIRTHDAYS:

Tom Hawkins, 1936; Dave Robisch, 1949; Marcus Haislip, 1980

TRIVIA:

Maravich's 31 free throw attempts resulted from Oregon State's decision to foul him hard each time he attempted a shot. The result was a flurry of technical fouls and fights. Pistol Pete was charged with three technicals, and LSU coach Press Maravich (Pete's father) was given two.

QUIZ:

Playing by the Rules: On a jump ball in college basketball, when does the ball become live – when it leaves the official's hand or when it is tapped legally by one of the players in the jump circle?

ANSWER: When it leaves the official's hand

TODAY'S THOUGHT:

 "**N**o, but they gave me one anyway." *–Elden Campbell*, when asked if he earned his college degree while at Clemson

HISTORY:

On this date in 1982 in one of college basketball's biggest upsets, Chaminade University, an 800-student NAIA school from Honolulu, beat Ralph Sampson and number-one ranked Virginia, 77-72. The Silverswords' Tony Randolph, giving up nine inches to the 7'4" Sampson, outscored the All-American, 19 to 12.

BIRTHDAY:

Jerry Reynolds, 1962

TRIVIA:

Virginia agreed to play Chaminade only after failing to secure a game against the University of Hawaii. Before the contest, the little known school was set to be renamed the University of Honolulu, but after the monumental upset, administrators decided against the change.

QUIZ:

What current NBA coach was a teammate of Ralph Sampson at Virginia in 1983?

ANSWER: *Rick Carlisle*

TODAY'S THOUGHT:

 "The strong take from the weak and the smart take from the strong." –*Pete Carril*, former Princeton basketball coach

HISTORY:

On this date in 1967 UCLA won its 39th consecutive game, a 114-63 victory over Notre Dame. Center Lew Alcindor led the way with 21 points, as the Bruins matched college basketball's second-longest winning streak.

BIRTHDAY:

Paul Pressey, 1958

TRIVIA:

Kareem Abdul-Jabbar (the former Lew Alcindor) has appeared twice on *Celebrity Jeopardy!*, winning handily both times. In 1994, he defeated Larry King and Alexandra Paul. Four years later, he beat Martina Navratilova and Reggie Jackson in a special "athletes" edition.

QUIZ:

This Princeton grad made two All-Star teams in the '70s with Portland and has been named the NBA's Executive of the Year with Sacramento. Do you know him?

ANSWER: *Geoff Petrie*

TODAY'S THOUGHT:

"**I**t was the best Christmas present I ever had." *–Dick Motta*, on Christmas Eve, 1991, after being fired as the coach of the Kings while in the midst of a third-straight losing season

HISTORY:

On this date in 1984 New York's Bernard King electrified the Madison Square Garden crowd by scoring a franchise-record 60 points. It wasn't enough, though, as the Knicks fell to the New Jersey Nets, 120-114, in the fourth consecutive Christmas Day meeting between the two clubs.

BIRTHDAY:

Bernie Fryer, 1949

TRIVIA:

In 1982, Bernard King was traded by Golden State to New York for Micheal Ray Richardson in a deal involving players with substance abuse issues. While King overcame his problems to be a success with the Knicks, Richardson lasted only 33 games with the Warriors. He was eventually banned from the league after several failed drug tests.

QUIZ:

Since the turn of the century, only one team has played every year on Christmas Day. Can you name the club?

ANSWER: *Los Angeles Lakers*

The Basketball Almanac

TODAY'S THOUGHT:

 ony Campbell might be the NBA's Defensive Player of the Year - if everybody else dies." *–Chick Hearn*

HISTORY:

On this date in 1976 the Spurs' Larry Kenon set a new NBA record for steals in a game, with 11, as San Antonio defeated the Kansas City Kings, 110-105. Just three weeks earlier, Seattle's Fred Brown joined Jerry West and Larry Steele as the only players to get ten steals in a game.

BIRTHDAYS:

Bill Wennington, 1963; Tim Legler, 1966; Bernard Robinson, 1980

TRIVIA:

The NBA did not record blocks or steals as official statistics until the 1973-74 season. That year, the league leader in steals was, appropriately, Portland's Larry Steele. The Trail Blazers' guard had 217 swipes, 2.68 per game. The leader in blocks was the Lakers' Elmore Smith, with 4.85 a game.

QUIZ:

In 1987, what former NBA point guard set an NCAA Division I record with 13 steals in a game, and then tied his own mark the following season?

ANSWER: Oklahoma's Mookie Blaylock

TODAY'S THOUGHT:

"It's beyond explanation. There are some things you can't understand- the Kennedy assassination, where the aliens are hiding, and our ups and downs. Oh, and Stonehenge." *–Troy Murphy*, on his Golden State Warriors

HISTORY:

On this date in 1991 Golden State's Tim Hardaway had a bad day at the office, missing all 17 of his field goal attempts. The NBA's new record-holder did score two points on free throws and dished out 13 assists in the Warriors' 106-102 win over Minnesota.

BIRTHDAYS:

Dike Eddleman, 1922; Rich Jones, 1946; Kent Benson, 1954; Kevin Ollie, 1972; Dahntay Jones, 1980

TRIVIA:

In the early 1990's, the Golden State Warriors talented trio of Tim Hardaway, Mitch Richmond, and Chris Mullin was nicknamed "Run-TMC," a take-off on the famous three-member rap group, Run-DMC. The rap trio, not the hoops trio, is credited with breaking hip hop into mainstream music.

QUIZ:

What musical group is Basketball Hall of Famer Bill Walton a die-hard fan of?

ANSWER: *The Grateful Dead*

TODAY'S THOUGHT:

"**I**'ve been doing a little bit too much music, just needed the rest...After the album comes out I'm going to make sure all of my time is focused on winning a championship." –*Ron Artest*, on taking time off from the NBA to record his rap album

HISTORY:

On this date in 1991 nine people were crushed to death in a gymnasium stairwell prior to a celebrity basketball game at the City College of New York. The mismanaged event, held by rap mogul Puff Daddy, was over before it even began, as impatient fans pushed down the gym doors and broke into a stampede.

BIRTHDAYS:

Frank Card, 1944; Melvin Turpin, 1960

TRIVIA:

Rap artist Master P (aka Percy Miller) earned a basketball scholarship to the University of Houston, but his career there was quickly cut short due to an injury. He later had stints on several NBA summer league squads, but was unable to stick with a club once the regular season began.

QUIZ:

What famous rapper is a part-owner of the New Jersey Nets?

Jay-Z (aka Shawn Carter)

TODAY'S THOUGHT:

"**W**e lost some mighty good boys from last year because of paroles, but, crime being what it is, we've picked up some good ones since then, too." *–Joe Kirkpatrick*, on coaching the Oklahoma State Penitentiary basketball team

HISTORY:

On this date in 1934 the first college basketball doubleheader was held at Madison Square Garden in New York. A crowd of over 16,000 watched New York University defeat Notre Dame in the opener, 25-18, and Westminster (PA) upset St. John's, 37-33, in the nightcap.

BIRTHDAY:

Ron Perry, 1943

TRIVIA:

In December, 2003, the largest crowd ever to attend a basketball game, 78,129, packed Ford Field in Detroit to watch Kentucky defeat Michigan State, 79–74. Two years earlier, Michigan State also set an all-time attendance record in hockey, when an outdoor contest against rival Michigan drew 74,554 fans to Spartan Stadium.

QUIZ:

The basketball floor at Duke University's Cameron Indoor Stadium is currently referred to as what?

ANSWER: *Coach K Court, in honor of head coach Mike Krzyzewski*

TODAY'S THOUGHT:

"**I** know the guys are out there somewhere; I just don't know where."
—*Buck Williams*, on his career average of two assists per game

HISTORY:

On this date in 1990 Magic guard Scott Skiles took ball distribution to another level, dishing out an NBA record 30 assists in Orlando's 155-116 win over the Denver Nuggets. Skiles, who broke Kevin Porter's mark of 29, did not get his last assist until 20 seconds were left in the game.

BIRTHDAYS:

Steve Mix, 1947; Don Reid, 1973; Kenyon Martin, 1977; Devin Brown, 1978; LeBron James, 1984

TRIVIA:

A former first-round pick of the Nets in 1994, center Yinka Dare set an NBA mark for futility by playing in 77 games and 770 minutes of action before getting his first career assist in 1997. He ended his four-year career with four assists, and more turnovers (96) than field goals (86).

QUIZ:

John Stockton has the most career assists in NBA history, with 15,806. What player, with 10,334, is a distant second?

ANSWER: Mark Jackson

TODAY'S THOUGHT:

 "Not to kill myself." *–Darrell Walker*, head coach of the 4-26 Toronto Raptors in 1997, on his New Year's resolution

HISTORY:

On this date in 1935 an official scoring error left Notre Dame and Northwestern locked in a 20-20 tie, a first in NCAA college basketball history. A notable participant in the New Year's Eve contest was the Irish's Ray Meyer, a future Hall of Fame coach at DePaul.

BIRTHDAYS:

Tyrone Corbin, 1962; Bryon Russell, 1970; Brent Barry, 1971; Shandon Anderson, 1973; Francisco Garcia, 1981; Luke Schenscher, 1982

TRIVIA:

In 1986, an NBA first, and probably last, occurred when a Suns-Supersonics game was called due to rain. A heavy downpour and a leaky roof on the Seattle Center Coliseum forced officials to stop action in the second quarter. The contest was finished the following day, with Phoenix winning, 114-97.

QUIZ:

This Notre Dame grad played ten seasons with Seattle and Denver, but may best be remembered as the man who lost 71 games with the Nuggets in his lone season as an NBA coach. Who is he?

ANSWER: *Bill Hanzlik, in 1997-98*

"SPORTS CUT ACROSS RACIAL,
LANGUAGE, CULTURAL, AND
NATIONAL BOUNDARIES. IT IS
WHAT COUNTRIES SHOULD USE
TO COMPETE INSTEAD OF WAR."

—Hakeem Olajuwon